Conservatism and the Conservative Party in Nineteenth-Century Britain

Conservatism and the Conservative Party in Nineteenth-Century Britain

Bruce Coleman

*Senior Lecturer, Department of History and Archaeology,
University of Exeter*

Edward Arnold

A division of Hodder & Stoughton

LONDON   BALTIMORE   MELBOURNE   AUCKLAND

to
David and Roger
fraternally

© 1988 Bruce Coleman

First published in Great Britain 1988

British Library Cataloguing Publication Data

Coleman, Bruce
  Conservatism and the Conservative Party
  in nineteenth-century Britain.
  1. Great Britain. Political parties :
  Conservative party, 1800–1900
  I. Title
  324.24104′09

  ISBN 0–7131–6496–4

Typeset in Linotron Baskerville
by Wearside Tradespools, Fulwell, Sunderland
Printed and bound in Great Britain for Edward Arnold, the educational academic and medical publishing division of Hodder & Stoughton Limited, 41 Bedford Square, London WC1B 3DQ by Richard Clay plc, Bungay, Suffolk

Contents

Preface

This work is intended to meet the lack of a convenient textbook treatment of Conservative or Tory politics across the whole of the nineteenth century. Too many of the most helpful and familiar works have started around 1832, which, despite the Reform Act and the almost simultaneous emergence of the name 'Conservative', was certainly not the start either of specifically Tory politics or of a less narrow but still self-conscious conservatism. The reaction of the 1790s against French Jacobinism and domestic agitation stood out as a more natural and revealing beginning of the story and, as a starting-point, would also provide a coverage more suited to the chronological span of many courses offered in higher education.

The work was never conceived as one of sheer originality and innovation. Indeed much of its content amounts to a personal synthesis of quality research and writing on aspects of nineteenth-century British politics over some two decades. The subject is now much better served for both breadth and depth than in the author's own student days. The expansion of historical studies in universities and elsewhere over a generation, though now in reverse, has transformed the understanding of the period substantially. But the danger of greater output and sophistication, as the monographs and articles flood from the presses, is that both the serious student and that publishers' hero, the intelligent general reader, will be overwhelmed. Survey works which synthesize new ideas and approaches, dispose of redundant myths and assumptions and indicate the sorts of questions historians are now asking have a clear justification. Any novelty I have provided beyond that is a bonus.

My main debts, therefore, are acknowledged in the Select Bibliography. I would also like to thank colleagues, students and friends in this University and elsewhere for their help and encouragement, particularly Dr Michael Duffy, Mr John McKenzie, Mr Robert Bedward and Mr David Gardner. Perhaps above all I should thank my publisher. The idea of a work on Conservative politics spanning the whole century was originally his and I have kept faith with it over an unduly prolonged period since. In this one respect, though perhaps no other, I have not tested his tolerance.

Bruce Coleman
University of Exeter
December, 1987

Introduction

The writing of any book requires some sense of purpose. Apart from the considerations mentioned in the Preface, this work was inspired initially by the author's doubts about an approach that pervaded much of the literature on the nineteenth-century Conservative party. The party's most familiar figures were being elevated not just to the Pantheon of the Good (always a hazard for dead politicians) but also to the Pantheon of the Progressive. One could hardly see the Tories for Liberal Conservatives. Peel and Disraeli were among the conspicuous beneficiaries of this tendency, each being celebrated for contributions to progressive causes well beyond the call of duty for a Conservative leader. It was really very strange. One might presume that most Conservatives wished to prevent major change, yet, despite their party's evident distaste for much the nineteenth century had brought them, here were its great names apparently seeking to usher in the twentieth century before its time. This historiographical slant seems to have stemmed from the liberal progressivism prevalent among post-war academics, who apparently found it hard to celebrate anything in the past unless it too could be depicted as progressive. There was also an element of in-house history. Many studies of the party were written by sympathizers who, perhaps unconsciously, were concerned to present a sanitized version of the party's past which conformed to mid-twentieth century assumptions about the purposes of politics. The recent collapse of the post-war consensus in British politics may now have liberated us to ask rather different questions about the modern party's precursors. Even before the writing of this book had begun the historiography of the period was beginning to display new freedoms and a new realism. The recent and numerous studies of Salisbury (it is significant too that Salisbury has attracted the attention) seem to have experienced few problems in depicting his essential conservatism.

It is sensible to assume that people who called themselves Tories or Conservatives (this work treats the two terms as almost interchangeable) were concerned primarily to stem change, not to encourage it. We should, first, try to identify what they did not wish to change and why not. Even when legislative or other changes were the outcome of events, we should establish the real motives of the people concerned and not lose sight of the often equally important matters which they did not change. The essential conservatism of most Conservatives is no mere presumption. The columns of the Parliamentary Debates, the articles in the thinking periodicals, the press leaders and the correspondence and diaries of political activists all put flesh on its bones. It soon becomes clear that most of the people we are studying did not welcome radical change, that they often disliked the signs of the times (the jeremiad was an art form among Tories) and resented much that was happening around them and that they distrusted the future. They opposed democracy resolutely, until, suddenly, they found themselves landed with something which had to be called 'democracy' and, even then, they did not relish it or want to extend it. They were, on the whole, illiberal in matters of religion and they did not like Protestant Nonconformists and Roman Catholics (or, for that matter, Jews and free-thinkers). They tended to respond with repression when confronted with lower-class agitation of any radical character. Coercion in Ireland was a regular favourite. And they were strongly committed to the rights, security and influence of property – by which they meant substantial property. 'Property against numbers' (later 'the classes versus the masses') was a recurrent idea. It is hard to believe that these people wanted measures the post-1945 generation would regard as progressive as their monuments. If we accepted them at their own valuation, we would identify them with other sorts of achievements – such as having preserved the Irish church establishment until 1869 and having safeguarded much of its property even then, or having confined serious legislative interference with the rights of landownership to the detested Irish Land Act of 1881, or having restricted fiscal exactions on property inheritance to the modest succession duties introduced in the 1880s and 1890s. Perceptions of this kind might help us to understand why the overwhelmingly Conservative House of Lords would veto the Liberal budget of 1909.

The Conservatives who wrote, spoke and thought in these ways were not only the Famous Names. One of the purposes of studying in depth is to move beyond the celebrated and their more familiar utterances to read what the less prominent were telling each other – to gauge, in other words, the *mentalité* of Toryism. Most of this opinion was not only hostile to many of the 'reforms' commended by textbook piety; they were often highly critical of their party leaders for what they viewed as betrayals of their own cause and for needless concessions to opponents. Partisan opinion at large tended to be more conservative than the requirements of government and Parliament made its leaders. The examination of this larger gamut of Conservatism thus provides a context and a standard for the assessment of the major figures. It suggests that they should be measured not against our own anachronistic conceptions of what 'statesmen' should have been doing but against their own motives and purposes and against those of their supporters, against the possibilities of the circumstances they faced and against the choices of tactics and strategy available to them. The need for this broadening of the coverage and the context of party history is all too apparent. Though studies of Peel and Disraeli have always abounded, there have, for example, been only one biographical treatment of a Tory whip in the century and only one serious study of a leading party manager. Even as central a figure as the 14th Earl of Derby, who led the party for longer than any one else in the period, has received scant attention until recently, perhaps because he was not considered a candidate for the Pantheon. Another reason for the comparative neglect of Derby was that he had spent most of his time in opposition and this suggests a further limitation of the old kind of party history. It assumed that governments were what really mattered and that party history was much the same thing as the history of the ministries formed by its frontbench luminaries. This assumption, one clearly fed by the belief that Tory politicians were supposed to make things happen, rather than prevent them, not only encouraged a skimpy and dismissive treatment of periods of opposition but also ignored the rather obvious fact that a party is not at all identical with a government. Nineteenth-century parties and governments were certainly rather different entities, even if they influenced each other in various ways. The present study does not seek to tell the party's story with government left out – that would be neither possible nor desirable – but it does try to suggest that the realities of Tory government were not always as natural and straightforward as older studies suggested and that the party and its governments often posed problems for each other. The front bench, the back benches and the more amorphous Conservatism outside Parliament were never one and the same.

If one argument here is the essential conservatism of Conservatism, another is that the party needs to be considered in relation to other kinds of conservatism existing outside its own confines. Almost by definition party history is the story of small numbers of partisans trying to enlist the support of much larger numbers of the less partisan. People who assumed the designation Tory or Conservative clearly had no monopoly of conservatism in its broad utilitarian sense of a material interest in and preference for stability and order. Most of the Whigs saw themselves as essentially conservative on crucial questions of social and political order; arguably Palmerston was the most successful conservative premier of the century. The political balance was often held by types of opinion – whether centrist, third party, floating or, particularly early in the century, 'independent' – which stood outside the two main political groupings. Both main parties experienced periodic disintegration of major or minor kinds, the most dramatic cases on the Tory side occurring in 1827-30 and 1845-46. Often the party's fortunes depended on the appeal it could make to basically conservative opinion outside its own partisan ranks. Though the initial base of Toryism had been considerable, it still needed to develop a wider appeal – the appeals of patriotism, of social order, of political stability, of 'Protestantism' and of the security of property. Positions of this kind were so commonplace for Conservative politicians during the century that they came to seem integral to the Tory canon, yet they were broader in their conception than the entrenched and sometimes dogmatic 'Church and King' Toryism which Eldon personified and they always appealed to many people who did not care to call themselves Tories or Conservatives.

This interaction of a self-conscious partisanship with a more generalized conservatism had existed from the start. The Toryism emerging under Pitt and his heirs had been shaped by its origins in a coalition with former Foxite Whigs. The recovery under Peel from 1834 owed much to Whig schisms and the incorporation of ex-Reformers into the Conservative ranks. From 1886 Conservative governments survived by grace of Liberal Unionists. Each situation required a narrowly conceived Toryism to compromise with other forms of conservatism. Even Derby and his colleagues made a bid or two to wrest the command of consensus politics from the Whigs. Most thinking politicians recognized that their prospects of prolonged office depended on their appeal to a larger segment of the political nation than their own most committed partisans. This feature of nineteenth-century politics adds to the difficulties of writing anything like a one-party history, for the party – or at least its general staff – had so often to look beyond itself and to behave in ways which it might not have chosen if left to its own devices. Usually it was the parliamentary leaders and managers, particularly those in the Commons, who manoeuvred the party towards the centre-ground and the deals, concessions and compromises which it involved. The tensions inevitable between party leaders and followers were intensified by the differences between the approaches natural to party tacticians and strategists and to partisans without those responsibilities, between the perspectives of the cerebral and the more atavistic.

The understanding of the party's development is complicated by the absence of any firm evidence of its size and limits. Party membership is an elusive concept for the historian of this period. Beyond a relatively small élite, mostly associated with the party's parliamentary and electoral activities, it is hard to be certain just who the Conservatives were. There was no clear criterion of personal affiliation (that took time to develop even for MPs and candidates) and, once the historian looks beyond London Society and the leading activists of the constituencies, it can be difficult to identify Conservative support. The pollbooks provide some assistance down to 1872, but clearly there was a considerable difference between simply voting for a Tory candidate and having a more formal and permanent party tie. Some of the gap was filled by the numerous associations and clubs which developed around and in support of parties in this period, but party membership as such is probably best regarded as an idea alien to most contemporaries. They understood their politics well enough without it and no doubt assumed that partisan Conservatism shaded almost imperceptibly into other kinds of conservative opinion.

Many aspects of both Conservatism and conservatism were doubtless as uncertain for contemporaries as they are for the wondering scholar now. Many thinking men knew that the economy and society were changing around them and they suspected that this process would, in time, jeopardize many entrenched interests and put the inherited structures of the constitution under pressure. Some were determined to resist change, particularly those changes that threatened their own interests, others came to believe that certain adjustments were inevitable. The former, however, were not always certain how best to buttress the status quo and the latter did not always see how to manage and control the process of necessary adaptation. Nor was the line between inevitable modification and resistible change entirely clear. The tactical aspects of conservatism were always debatable. Were unwelcome changes best resisted by timely concessions on minor matters or by unyielding resistance in the last ditch? Was inevitable change best administered by cautious conservatives (even by committed Conservatives) or by men of more radical inclinations? Should Conservatives always seek to hold office or were the arts of resistance sometimes better practised in opposition? Questions of this kind and the different answers men gave to them were often at the heart of Tory politics. Men of property and position who felt their interests threatened were often perplexed about the best means of resistance. In practice their choices were usually confined by the concrete realities of Westminster politics which would decide both the nature of government and the course of legislation. The parliamentary game had to be played. Sometimes it developed in ways Tory politicians could not control, unpalatable measures had to be accepted and so conservatism itself was forced to evolve. Conservatives in the mid-1830s had to think and behave in different ways from their Tory equivalents of the mid-1820s. The societal aspects of politics changed much less and more slowly – doubtless there were English parishes where squire and parson constituted the Tory presence in 1900 much as their predecessors had done in 1800 – but, though conservative interests and attitudes were always influential within British society and culture, Conservatism was almost by definition focused on the party game at Westminster and on matters of government and legislation. The party's politics were thus shaped to a considerable extent by the activities and strategies of its parliamentarians and particularly those of its small cadre of leading figures. It is right to give them a prominent position in any account of the party, so long as one does not ignore the context within which they operated and the demands and limitations which the nature of their following placed upon them. The variations in the sensitive relationship between the parliamentary élite and the forces which supported them in and out of Parliament are central to the party's history.

The study of nineteenth-century Conservatism has suffered, ironically, from a 'Whig interpretation of history' which takes too much of the direction of events for granted and so fails to ask enough questions about the motives and intentions of those involved. Much that happened in the period was not inevitable – certainly not pre-determined as to when and how it happened – and many contemporaries were not prepared to accept it as inevitable. The Tories who form the subject of the present work believed that they had a legitimate and defensible case and that the interests they represented were entitled to their stake in and the protection of the constitution. They did not always accept it easily when they found themselves on the losing side and the strength of their resistance ensured that often they were not on that side anyway. Conservatives had to make the best of a political order which they often found far from ideal. Consequently much of the political practice of Conservatism was tentative and problematical, a matter of controversy and tension within the party itself, not straightforward and self-evident. Problems arose about the nature of the party itself. For all the early recognition of the need for a 'party of order', there were widespread doubts whether a party distinct from the Treasury was compatible with traditional values of loyalty to the Crown, of personal 'independence' and of government above 'faction'. Difficulties also arose in the late-Victorian period when the party had to come to terms with a mass electorate of which its traditionalists remained nervous and distrustful. The enlistment of new forms of electoral support by means very different from traditional forms of influence created tension and unease within a party now extended far outside its old base in Parliament, London Society and the great houses of the counties. Tories of the old school, unwilling to rest authority and legitimacy upon 'democratic' majorities, remained unsure whether they wanted the populism of 'Tory Democracy' at all.

Inevitably the more of these complexities that emerge from the story, the more of them have to be left with less than adequate exploration. Time and space limit everything. The concentration of the present treatment is upon the Westminster party, its politics and fortunes and its leading figures, while the societal base of Toryism is left largely as background to the main story. Nor are the ideological components of Conservatism explored in depth, interesting as they are; the present author regards them as having been more derivatives than determinants of the main lines of the party's character and development. This omission does not constitute a denial that certain kinds of ideas figured prominently in Tory argument, propaganda and self-justification throughout the century, only an argument that hard theory was much less important than a range of less intellectual attitudes, 'principles', loyalties and preferences. As the more dogmatic Tories, the young Gladstone among them, found with the question of church establishment, nice theory usually had to give way to real politics. Much of the focus of what follows is upon the 'high politics' of the parliamentary party, but without any intention of replicating the narrowing and trivialization of understanding which that label has sometimes denoted. Parliamentary politics are considered in relation to the interests which Conservatives represented and the purposes which they pursued. Westminster politicians, whether frontbench or backbench, were normally well aware of the interests and sentiments which a much greater number of people, including many of their own class, looked to them to protect and express. They were also aware of the dangers which the world around them posed to those interests and attitudes. Even the most eminent practitioners of 'high politics' knew that they did not practise in a vacuum.

1

The Conservative Interest

During the late eighteenth and early nineteenth centuries there evolved within British politics, which had not formerly sustained a clear division between what we would call right and left, a coalition of forces for the defence of the established order in state and society. This conservative interest may have been emerging even before the French Revolution, for the American troubles had generated domestic tensions, but, if so, the events of the early 1790s accelerated and intensified the process. Among the fundamental characteristics of the social order which sustained this reaction were some which were almost timeless. It was, as it had always been, a society of great inequalities of wealth and income, of status and influence, of power and authority. The overriding concern of most beneficiaries of the distribution was to maintain it intact. This conservative inclination became more self-conscious and explicit in this period because the threats to the existing order had become more prominent and more troubling. What became known in the 1830s as the Conservative party was the most significant political form of this defensive reaction of rank, property and privilege. However complex certain passages of its history were to be, however much individuals, issues of the moment and tactical considerations might distract the party from its underlying purpose, that purpose was never totally obscured and never in doubt for long.

Like its beginnings the development's point of maturity was far from clear. Though the Great Reform Bill of 1832 used to be depicted as the start of the modern Conservative party, it was in fact only one important stage in the evolution of the political right. There was substantial continuity in the ethos, aims and strategies of conservative politicians before and after 1832. The continuity becomes more apparent if one examines the wider social and political dimensions of conservatism and not simply the tactical shifts among leading parliamentary figures. Even at Westminster there was much more than the exalted few on the front benches. The followers in both Lords and Commons, the whips and managers, the backbench spokesmen for various standpoints and interests, all have to be reckoned in calculations of party character and behaviour. To ignore the supporting cast is to distort the party's nature and history.

The Conservative party was, however, only one of the forms of self-defence by the privileged and propertied. Even a perspective confined to parliamentary politics reveals a wider spread of fundamentally conservative inclinations than a single party could ever contain and command. There was always a quantum of centrist or independent opinion which had not overcome the old distaste for 'faction' or which distrusted the partisanship that political parties came to demand of their adherents. At times there were also distinct centrist groups like the Grenvilles and the Canningites – later the 'Derby Dilly', the Peelites and the Liberal Unionists – which, though not archetypally Tory, were predominantly conservative on the major questions of the moment and played crucial rôles on the Westminster stage and beyond. Even the Whigs, a vital component in the future Liberal party, were hardly radically reformist outside a narrow range of constitutional issues. Whatever their differences with the Tories, they were usually firm in respecting property rights, in upholding the distribution of wealth and privilege and in protecting a dominant political rôle for an educated and propertied minority. Few of them intended to strengthen the popular element in the constitution enough to threaten the aristocratic settlement which enshrined and secured the leading rôle of their own class. To anti-aristocratic radicals, Whigs and Tories could look depressingly alike. In Tory eyes, ironically, the Whigs were transforming the political system in ways which would ultimately devastate the interests on which both patrician parties depended. This suspicion of traitors within the gates was an element in Tory psychology from the 1790s onwards. Hindsight shows us, however, that much of nineteenth-century politics concerned shades of difference – perhaps dispute about means rather than ends – within a relatively cohesive and predominantly conservative élite.

Some of the strongest defences of the existing order lay outside the political parties. Among these bulwarks were the Crown, the House of Lords, the system of law and law enforcement (which included the magistracy, the judiciary and, in time, professional police forces), the Church of England and the Scottish Kirk and the military establishments. Here were central institutions of the state, all of them deployable in support of political stability and established authority. Their weight was felt in British society during a period which witnessed an increase of direct repression of popular discontent and disorder. Less formal but at least as enduring in their impact were a range of religious and moral influences directed at those classes believed to pose a threat to constitutional and social order. Movements for a conservative moralization of society had been under way since the 1780s, the causes including Sunday schools for the poor and a 'reformation of manners', and the political tension of the following years only encouraged them. How far the 'lower orders' warranted this sort of attention is far from clear. They seem to have been less radical than the more alarmist politicians believed and there were times during the French wars when conservative governments could exploit a strain of popular loyalism and patriotism. When grievance welled up in areas of British society, it was usually a matter of economic depression and dislocation, often temporary in nature, rather than a more permanent and irreconcilable antipathy to government and constitution. But these reassurances are retrospective. At the time many of the powerful and propertied felt genuine worries for law and order, political stability and the secure enjoyment of their own.

Thus, however strong the social defences of the existing order might be, politics seemed to matter. Parliament and government were central pre-occupations of the political classes. In constitutional theory the leading office-holders of central government were the appointees and servants of the Crown, but in practice and convention the ministry was also responsible to the House of Commons. The House's confidence was necessary to the survival of an administration, even one that possessed royal favour, and in this period the monarch was increasingly limited in what he could do to sway opinion in the Commons. Nor did that opinion operate in a vacuum. It was influenced by a wider opinion – that of magnates and patrons, of landowners and employers, of various economic and social interests, even of electors in those constituencies where they had some independence – and it was to organize and influence such opinion as well as that within Parliament that parties came to be seen as necessary. Sensitive as it was to 'respectable' and 'rational' opinion 'out of doors', the Commons possessed an influence over government that could never be ignored and which became more crucial in troubled times. Though the powers were ones of dismissal, veto and persuasion, rather than of positive and direct control, they were such that a ministry could not afford their hostile exercise while it faced a war abroad and problems at home. The ministry itself controlled the military, appointed Lords Lieutenants, magistrates and judges, set much of the tone for the administration of justice, distributed a vast range of patronage both central and local, sustained and shaped the established church which preached social order to its flocks in England, and touched in its various transactions upon many major economic interests. It also controlled the conduct of war, a matter important in itself but also influential upon the course of domestic politics. Government was thus a mighty engine of social and political power. Influence upon its working had always been sought eagerly by factions, families and individuals among the patriciate. But now the heightening of political tension meant that the personnel and policy of the ministry were of even greater importance. People with much to lose wanted an administration that would protect and reassure them. The powers of the executive could not be allowed to fall into dangerous hands.

Apart from its influence upon the executive, Parliament had functions of its own. The legislative rôle, though less developed than it became subsequently, had an importance both actual and potential. The very constitutional settlement was based on statute and so was the Union with Ireland which came into being in 1801. Though the rule of law as most lawyers understood it rested partly on common law, which was tender towards property rights, statute law had no clear limits assigned to it and nobody was more vulnerable to legislative interference than men of property and influence. One highly sensitive topic, for example, was taxation. The contribution of the land tax during the eighteenth century had shown the willingness of the dominant class to shoulder the burdens of a régime with which they identified, but they were not willing to surrender responsibility for fiscal policy into other hands. Influence in the Commons, the House that determined matters of supply, was only prudent for classes which otherwise would find themselves subject to legislation they could not control. Legislation could also put burdens upon the local rates and the sensitivity of the squirearchy to poor-law questions in the opening decades of the nineteenth century showed the concern generated whenever the rates tended to rise. Other interests vulnerable to legislative interference were tithe-holders, the holders of official places and pensions and, not least, the owners of stock in the National Debt. The fundholders waxed larger as an interest during the French wars, which extensive borrowing helped to finance, and any threat to political stability was a threat to them. The state's creditors had a vested interest in its security. The great trading companies whose privileged positions rested on statute or charter also identified themselves with the security of the régime and with resistance to change in political influence and public policy. For these interests and others besides the nature of government and of parliamentary influence was inevitably a matter of overwhelming concern.

The political imperatives did not, however, necessarily dictate a formal party organization. Indeed at first a very different assumption was more appropriate. Edmund Burke and other conservative rhetoricians of the 1790s exhorted the political nation to rally around the Crown, the constitution and social order. The solidarity of landed property in particular was to overawe and overwhelm radical subversion. One of the shibboleths of this strident constitutionalism was loyalty to the Crown and, by extension, to the king's ministers. Government was to be supported not only as the king's choice, however, but also as the essential underpinning of social order and political stability. Politics had become too important to be left to mere politicians. 'Faction' had become a threat to the constitution itself from its tendency to destabilize government and to divide the forces of conservatism. (Here Burke gainsaid his earlier argument for party as an agent of constitutional government.) Something like this did occur during the 1790s, which witnessed not just the collapse of cohesion among the Whigs around Fox but also a conscious rejection by some men of the legitimacy of party and connexion. As yet the conservative reaction took the form of a denial of party, not its assertion. It was to take the subsequent failure of the Burkean ideal of patrician solidarity before the alternative approach of party organization could emerge.

Inevitably people who had most to lose from radical change were foremost in the conservative reaction. In 1794 the future Whig politician Jeffrey noted that among the contending parties of Edinburgh

> the loudest, and ... the most powerful, is that of the fierce aristocrats – men of war, with their swords and their rank – men of property, with their hands on their pockets, and their eyes staring wildly with alarm and detestation – men of indolence ... and, withal, men of place and expectation.

Perhaps no class had more stake in the régime than the landowning aristocracy and gentry which had been installed as the effective ruling class under the Crown in the seventeenth century. Numerically this patriciate was a tiny proportion of British society. Out of a population of some nine millions in England and Wales at the turn of the century there were some 9450 armigerous families, with another 400 among the 1.6 million inhabitants of Scotland. At the head of this class in rank if not always in acres and rentals were 257 English and British peers. There were 159 Irish and 72

Scottish peers without British titles. But the bare numbers were not the full measure of this class. With their relations, tenants and other dependants the aristocracy and gentry constituted a considerable interest and even more so in terms of social status and parliamentary influence. Nor were the landed a closed caste. Men of wealth, whatever its origin, could buy their way into land. (A free market was limited but not prevented by legal devices like entail and strict settlement employed to protect the family holdings of the established patriciate.) The attraction of landownership was not only a life-style but also social status and privilege and political influence and opportunity. The Peels, with money from cotton-spinning, and the Gladstones, Liverpool merchants, were among the more conspicuous of *parvenu* families who bought landed estates to promote political ambitions. Even if historians argue about how many 'new' families rose to magnate status, there is no doubting the substantial numbers who joined the landed classes at more modest levels through purchase or marriage. The professions (the law, military and naval service, the Church), banking and commerce all generated upward mobility into the patrician ranks, as did political and governmental service, though for the moment manufacturing did so on a more modest scale. A degree of movement in the opposite direction came from daughters' marriages and from younger sons seeking employment in the professions, though only rarely in trade and manufacture. Not only did this process recruit new wealth and talent for the patrician élite; it also blurred the dividing line between the landed and the upper reaches of what were coming to be called the middle or middling classes. The relatively open nature of the aristocracy and gentry affected the attitudes of those classes themselves and of those below them, so that the patrician and middle classes of nineteenth-century Britain were never to be mutually hostile entities locked in class struggle, despite the efforts of bourgeois ideologues like James Mill and Richard Cobden. In their political sympathies the more prosperous of the business and professional classes, unless they were committed Nonconformists in religion, moved much as landed opinion did and responded to the leadership of the patriciate.

Land was expected to carry more political influence than other forms of property. Nonetheless the wealthy of all descriptions had a common interest when the security of property itself seemed to be threatened. Despite the concentration of social and political privilege in the landed élite and despite the sense of civil disability felt by certain sections of society, religious Dissenters in particular, most men of property rallied to the cause of firm government under the aristocratic constitution whenever trouble was threatened below. Then small property might stand shoulder to shoulder with great property. In the troubled year of 1817 the Whig Fitzwilliam, Lord Lieutenant of the West Riding, assured Sidmouth that no-one 'above the rank of a very inferior mechanic or shopkeeper' had supported the small insurrectionary groups that had alarmed the Home Secretary.

> Here it is considered as the war of No Property against Property, and on this ground all of the latter description show themselves eager and anxious to resist their assailants.

Similar responses were usually elicited by prospects of Jacobinism, levelling, anarchy, socialism, atheism, republicanism and constitutional upheaval. A great unorganized party of order always constituted a significant part of British society and an even larger part of the active political nation. It was a source of support to be tapped by politicians. On Palmerston's death in 1865 the *Economist* commented that he had appealed to 'fair, calm, sensible persons who have something to lose, who have no intentions of losing it, who hate change, who love improvements, who will be ruled in a manner they understand'. Much the same might have been said of the opinion to which Pitt, Liverpool, Peel, Derby, Disraeli and Salisbury addressed themselves, even if the calmness and the enthusiasm for 'improvements' varied with the times. For many people outside the patrician ranks, even people otherwise critical of particular aspects of government, the aristocratic constitution provided a symbol of stability and a guarantee of their own, more modest pretensions and position.

Thus the conservative reaction so strong among the aristocracy from the 1790s drew in other forces in society. The business and professional plutocracies, some of them making their own ways into landownership, provided conspicuous examples of loyalty to Crown and Constitution. As the Peels and the Gladstones demonstrated, business origins were no bar to conservative, indeed Tory, politics. Older merchant families and those professionals profitably integrated with the established hierarchies tended to be the most conservatively inclined. Men with new money but less status were more inclined to question the merits of a régime which seemed disinclined to recognize their merits. Lord Liverpool's judgement that merchants but not manufacturers might be appointed to the magistracy was not the best way to integrate the latter into the constitution alongside *arrivistes* of other kinds. But even manufacturing wealth might choose to work with a system that offered such reassurance and, for the lucky, so many rich pickings. Certainly not all industrialists were radicals and Dissenters. In Oldham, one of the new textile towns, half the first generation of factory builders were Anglican, constitutionally inclined and active in officering the local Volunteers in the 1790s.

The long hold of Pitt and his heirs on office helped to cement the loyalty of sections of the business community – and not only of those that obtained or sought government contracts. A government which defended and extended British territorial and commercial interests abroad during the French wars appealed to many mercantile interests. The East India and West India companies were particularly close to government and they became conspicuous among the borough-mongering connections of Tory ministries. There were domestic considerations too. A ministry which suppressed disorder and encouraged social discipline for the lower orders appealed to many large employers and, if Fitzwilliam was right, to many smaller employers and petty capitalists too. The passage of the Combination Acts at the turn of the century and the unflinching deployment of legal and military force against the Luddites later showed the régime's stance towards the wage-labour force. A government which borrowed heavily to finance long wars was not going to be disowned by its creditors either. The social distribution of government stock remains obscure and many of its holders must have had other motives for loyalism, but the very scale – a total National Debt of £840 million by 1820 with interest payments during the 1820s running above £30 million per annum and absorbing over half of central government revenue, about one-twelfth of gross national product –

indicated the stake that fundholders had in constitutional stability. William Cobbett was not the only radical to see this. Many more modest stockholders must have shared the sympathies of the long-serving judge Lord Stowell, Eldon's brother and a Tory Ultra, who left nearly £¼ million in the funds at his death.

More identifiable among the interests that had a stake in political stability and largely associated themselves with the conservative reaction were the clergy of the established churches of the three countries. Some were scions of the landed classes, many more were their clients. The established churches were part of the constitution which was threatened by Jacobinism in the 1790s; radicalism, whether popular or intellectual, tended to be anti-clerical and sometimes free-thinking; and ecclesiastical property, which was secured by the constitutional settlement, was less popular and politically more vulnerable than lay property. Add the predicament of the Church of Ireland, a minority establishment in a country with a Catholic majority, and the fervent constitutionalism among so many of the clergy was hardly surprising. In rallying to a state that secured their privilege, they were also asserting their peculiar rôle and importance within that state. The polarization of opinion and the tilting of its balance gave the establishment clergy an opportunity many of them relished. The weight of clerical tracts, sermons and charges amongst the literature of political reaction bears testimony to that. The 'Church and King' flavour of much of the polemic and the emergence of a distinctive Toryism out of Pittite conservatism owed much to the clerical contribution, even though there remained numbers of Whigs and reformers among the clergy. But the reaction among the clergy was only one aspect of the larger movement of opinion. The clergy were not a caste. They were linked to the landowning and professional classes who were themselves becoming more appreciative of churches that felt a mission to preach subordination and contentment to the lower orders in order to buttress the constitution and social order.

Another factor in the political stability of the war years was the quiescence of the agricultural interest. Despite the pressure from a rapidly growing population, agrarian society was little disposed to political unrest. Like the clergy and gentry, the freeholders and tenant farmers flourished on price levels undreamt of in peacetime. Aristocratic influence helped to keep the counties loyal, but even traditionally independent elements like the smaller gentry and freeholders mostly supported the patriotic war and domestic stability. The prosperity down to 1815 helped them to identify with the prevailing tone of government and it was only with peace that their mood was to be tested. The protectionist Corn Law of 1815 had expressed the uneasy expectations of peace among the agricultural interest and in government itself. By the 1820s the collapse of prices and the problems left by wartime over-investment were shaking the loyalty of freeholders and tenants, even of some of the gentry, to Tory governments and Cobbett was agitating the politics of the southern counties. But the politicization of the farmers fluctuated inversely with price levels and many of the local leaders of agricultural opinion were gentleman farmers and professional men whose grievances rarely stretched further than the cause of agricultural prosperity, though there were counties where the spread of Nonconformity or the influence of Whig landlords produced a different picture. The maintenance of the Corn Laws at least helped to stabilize agrarian society and to ensure that government and the agricultural interest never fell out completely.

Despite the particular concerns of interest groups, the conservative cause in Parliament and society was consolidated by patriotic feeling. During the French wars the government could claim to represent national interest and even national survival, but even before hostilities began in 1793 a strong current of anti-French xenophobia had made itself felt. In the Priestley Riots of 1791 the Birmingham mob had risen for Church and King and against sympathizers with French ideas. When war came popular patriotism, encouraged by government, lent itself to a crusade against Jacobinism at home and abroad. Criticism of the constitution and even traditional kinds of opposition politics were easily identified with disloyalty to national interests. 'England expects . . .' was an injunction that appealed to more than just Nelson's seamen and a government committed to a narrowly based constitution was able to command support across much of British society. Until peace in 1815 made it a diminishing asset, patriotism underpinned Tory fortunes and left the lesson that a national identity could be a telling reinforcement for political conservatism.

Factions and Parties

One of the patriciate's strengths, for all its openness to new money, was its social cohesion. A degree of class solidarity was derived from family relationships and intermarriage, from common values and shared experience of education, religion and culture and, not least, from self-confidence as the legitimate ruling class under the Crown. But political unity was more elusive. Government, mighty engine as it was, lacked the resources to satisfy all the seekers after place, profit and honour and so the high politics of the eighteenth century had fed on determined competition for royal favour, office, patronage and other good things of life. Court and Parliament constituted the arena for a game of adversarial politics that largely dictated the distribution of the spoils in the public domain. There were also, however, elements of ideological division ('principle' was the accepted term) to shape and intensify the rivalries between factions, families and individuals. Historically the landed élite had faced two ways: towards the Crown above and towards the mass of the population below. In the late seventeenth century the argument had concerned which of the two was the greater threat to the established order. Men who rallied to the Crown and its acolyte Church rather than risk weakening controls over the population at large had been labelled Tories. The Whigs were those who feared and resented royal autocracy more and were willing to enlist 'the People', at least in the safe form of a largely aristocratic Parliament, to clip the wings of Crown and Church. Although these positions bent to circumstances in the decades after the Glorious Revolution, there remained scope for disagreement over the relationship between Crown and Parliament and, beyond that, over the degree of political activity and influence permissible for various kinds of extra-parliamentary opinion. The argument was not, for the most part, about 'democracy', a concept of little appeal and relevance, but about the nature of representation and influence within a central state constructed around Crown and aristocracy.

The size and nature of the 'political nation' had never been defined satisfactorily but the rapid changes within late eighteenth-century society meant that even an established definition would have become outdated. As differences of approach to these questions intensified, the old nomenclature of Whig and Tory took on a new lease of life. For the first thirty years of George III's reign political controversy had focused on the influence of the Crown, but from the 1790s the more pressing question was the degree of popular influence within the constitution that was legitimate and prudent. Sovereigns and Court still helped to shape the politics of ministries and parliaments, sometimes controversially, but the greater threat to the aristocratic constitution now came from outside and below the ranks of the landed. Now the Tory identity was refurbished to denote a stance of constitutional defence and opposition to popular influence and radical change, while Fox and his supporters in opposition appropriated the name of Whig and asserted their commitment to constitutional liberty. The Tory label was accepted only slowly by most politicians and not at all by some. Neither side of the argument was a monolithic bloc. There were differences and shades of opinion among professed Tories as among self-conscious Whigs. Individuals and groups changed sides as the political balance shifted, as ministries formed or distintegrated and as the two identities evolved. The coalition Pitt formed in 1794 had a colouring of conservative and patriotic Whiggery, but over the next two decades Whiggery and Toryism were to become recognized as definable moods and standpoints which served as frames of reference among parliamentary politicians and among the wider political public who shaped their own politics with reference to the patrician connexions at Westminster. Here was the matrix of the Victorian political parties.

The turn taken by the French Revolution, which many politicians had welcomed initially, helped to polarize opinion and to heighten political tension within Britain. Prolonged war compounded that effect. But British society itself was undergoing strain from population growth, economic adaptation, commercial instability and a run of bad harvests during the 1790s. All this intensified the nervousness of the dominant classes. The broadening of Pitt's administration in 1793–94 brought in many of its erstwhile opponents and unscrambled established political alignments. It took time before this unnaturally large governing coalition fragmented and a more normal balance of opinion asserted itself. Pitt's own departure from office in 1801 hastened the disintegration, but much of the support he had put together survived in its personnel, character and purpose. The spectre of Jacobin revolution, the ideological dimension of the war, disaffection at home, growing religious tensions, the impact of the Crown's influence and the problems of Irish government, which the Union had reshaped rather than solved, all helped to confirm the conservative mood among the patrician classes and to provide a pressing agenda for the governments they formed. Though the formal structures of a distinct Tory party took longer to emerge, the necessary political identity had already emerged. Pitt had never called himself a Tory, but, as the more Whiggish components of his broad-based coalition returned to opposition, what remained had a distinctive character – one rather different from Pitt's own original standpoint. By 1812 Grenville, formerly his close collaborator and Foreign Secretary, could write with distaste of the surviving Pitties as 'the party of the Tories, & the old Court, & high Church'.[1]

Inevitably the conservative reaction had had an ideological dimension, one influenced both by proceedings in France and by the counter-theory of radical ideologues. In November 1790 Edmund Burke's *Reflections on the Revolution in France* had warned against inclinations to admire proceedings across the Channel and the injunction was more significant for coming from a figure with Rockinghamite Whig credentials. He condemned the humiliation of the French monarchy, the hostility to the aristocracy and the interference with property rights. Crown, aristocracy and Church were being overthrown by an alliance between bourgeois interests and rootless theorists. The English way was – and should be – different. Here, Burke asserted, men followed precedent and convention, a course which not only ensured stability and continuity but safeguarded both constitutional liberty and security for property, ideals which he saw as inseparable. Inheritance, as represented by Crown, aristocracy and especially landed property, was a mode of social regulation in conformity with nature itself and so with the divine plan. But now 'the property of France does not govern it' and that country's established institutions had been abandoned for abstract theorizing about liberty, equality and fraternity. Here was a struggle between 'the fixed forms of a constitution' (in Britain) and 'the rights of man' (in France). For protection from the contagion Burke looked to 'the spirit of a gentleman and the spirit of religion', in other words to a dominant landed class and an established Church.

The *Reflections*, which had sold 300,000 copies by 1797, did not disown Whiggery but it marked a shift away from the opposition rhetoric of recent years. The mood was conservative and negative, the argument a distillation of the verities of one side of the constitutional tradition. The emphasis on property rights and the leading rôle of landownership was compatible with Whiggery, but the sentimental loyalty to the Crown as the symbol of constitutional order and to the established Church as representing the highest ideal of national life had scarcely been Rockinghamite characteristics. The lauding of 'subordination' as the appropriate condition for most of the population denoted a sharper edge to concern for social order, while the attack on theory as a guide to political action and the hostility towards non-patrician interests suggested less open-mindedness towards contemporary developments in intellectual and economic life than many Whigs had shown. By now disowned by the Foxites as a traitor, Burke later explained that he represented an old style of Whiggery, that of the Glorious Revolution, against the 'New Whigs' around Fox who were keeping their options open on constitutional reform. Burke's moral categories had become sharper (the Revolution was 'a foul, impious, monstrous thing, wholly out of the course of moral nature') and the attacks on concepts of covenant, contract, rights of man, 'the people' and majority rule were less detached than in the Reflections. Above all the *Appeal from the*

---

[1] William, Lord Grenville (1759–1834), served in office from 1782 to 1801, latterly as Foreign Secretary, but declined to serve under Addington. Strong for war but liberal on Catholic claims, he moved towards the opposition and headed a coalition government with Fox in 1806–7. He became more hardline on domestic order during the post-1815 troubles. For the Grenvilles' deal with Liverpool, see below.

New to the Old Whigs signalled unease at the activities of a section of opinion within Britain itself, those men whose reformist ambitions had survived the awful warnings from France.

Huskisson had been shocked by Burke's 'strange romantic notions' and Pitt had declared his distrust of such 'rhapsodies', but the continuing polarization of opinion as the Revolution unfolded soon forced government to take matters more seriously. Foremost among the many hostile replies to Burke was Thomas Paine's *Rights of Man*, a bestseller itself which soon attracted prosecution for seditious libel. The attacks on the nature of government in Britain by Paine and other radicals added to the unease of men who saw in arguments tending towards political egalitarianism the prospect of what the veteran reformer Christopher Wyvill called a 'lawless and furious mob' sweeping away constitution and property. By late 1792 Grenville noted that the landed gentlemen were 'thoroughly frightened' and the distintegration of opposition solidarity was under way. A year later his brother Thomas warned Fox of the dangers which conservative Whigs like himself perceived at home and abroad. He differed from Fox not only over war with France but also in

> an apprehension which I entertain of there being principles & designs in this country adverse to the constitution of it, which makes me feel it to be my duty to resist whatever can give such designs either strength, opportunity or countenance. . . .

The turning-point had been the winter of 1792–93. The spread of Loyalist Associations throughout the country starting in November 1792, though not all conservative and repressive in tone at first, marked the start of the organization of national opinion against Jacobinism.[2] Encouraged by government and by the Windham Whigs, the Association movement hardened its line when war with France came early in 1793 and, against a background of popular violence against reformers, put its hand to the political and legal repression of the 'disloyal'. The spread and organization of the Volunteer movement in the following year showed the same widespread commitment to patriotism and constitutional defence through most of the country. Alongside its military aspects, it had the clear quasi-political purpose of mobilizing opinion behind government, defending the established order and isolating and harassing their enemies.[3]

From the start the war had ideological overtones. Burke, who saw it as a 'moral war' and campaigned against a 'regicide peace' in 1796–97, hammered away at two themes. One was the danger of subversion within Britain itself where bad harvests, rising prices and disruption of trade had given a new edge, as the French example had given new ambition, to popular radicalism. By 1796 he was asserting that one-fifth of 'the British public' was Jacobin in sympathy. The second theme was the necessary identity of property and political power. He had emerged as a self-

---

[2] They are sometimes known as Reeves societies after John Reeves, the founder of the Crown and Anchor association of London businessmen and an energetic promoter of societies elsewhere. See D. E. Ginter, 'The Loyalist Association Movement of 1792–93 and British public opinion', *Historical Journal*, IX, 1966.

[3] See J. R. Western, 'The Volunteer Movement as an Anti-Revolutionary Force 1793–1801', *English Historical Review*, LXXXI, 1956.

conscious theoretician of the right of property, above all landed property, to rule. He lectured the Commons:

> ... the first principle of [government] ... must necessarily be security to property, because, for the protection of property, all governments were instituted.... it was property alone on which government was formed. If the formation of government was committed to the no-property people, the first thing they would do obviously would be to plunder those who had property ... the object of liberty was property; and when the no-property got the power into their hands, they would soon begin to rob and murder.

This almost obsessive theme ran through much of the anti-revolutionary polemic of the decade. Arthur Young, clergyman's son and the leading agricultural writer, warned that if the poor were granted the vote,

> then all the property of the society is at the mercy of those who possess nothing; and ... attack and plunder would ... follow power in such hands.... The leading conclusion deducible from the French experiment ... is this, IF PERSONS ARE REPRESENTED, PROPERTY IS DESTROYED. We know then what to think of the proposals for reform hitherto made in this kingdom.[4]

Always implicit, the concept of the rightful rule of a propertied élite was now at the forefront of conservative argument. Rank and property, affronted and threatened, now articulated their legitimacy and authority more strenuously and self-consciously than before. For many men, as for Burke, Crown and Church appeared as pillars of a constitutional settlement that embodied the interests and authority of property. Eighteenth-century conservatism had begun to wear the garb of nineteenth-century Toryism. By 1796 Burke, his inhibitions over names gone, described his warnings as 'the cackling of us poor Tory geese to alarm the garrison of the Capitol'.

By 1800 most of the attitudes that were to characterize early nineteenth-century Toryism had crystallized, though the religious dimension awaited further development from the prominence of the Catholic Emancipation issue and from the mounting difficulties faced by the Church of England itself. Whatever Pitt's own opinions, the *bêtes noires* of his conservative supporters were radical reform of the constitution, the widening of political participation and the weakening of the authority of the propertied élite. Government in both Britain and Ireland stood for property against numbers and the landed classes were both expected and entitled to play the leading rôle. Loyalty was due to the Crown and to the other institutions of the state, but above all to 'established authority' in both its political and its social forms, authority which controversialists now endowed with something of the divinity that kings alone had once enjoyed. The dividing line between sedition and mere criticism of constitutional forms or of a ministry was narrowed and blurred. If the blessedness of the British constitution was an article of faith, another was the inherent danger of major institutional change which might easily run out of control and destabilize the whole political and social order. Popular agitation of a radical kind should

---

[4] Quoted by H. T. Dickinson, *Liberty and Property. Political Ideology in Eighteenth-Century Britain* (1977), p. 290. Dickinson's chapter on 'The Conservative Defence of the Constitution' is a helpful summary of the contemporary argument.

go unrewarded with concession. If necessary, it should be repressed. Politicians who played to the radical gallery by encouraging 'clamour' against government and constitution, who raised popular expectations or appointed themselves spokesmen of grievances, who kept alive issues of reform, found themselves beyond the political pale and branded as unfit for office. The Whig aristocracy were above the attentions of a Braxfield, but the polarization of parliamentary politics ensured that the Foxites' resistance to the tide of reaction condemned them to something approaching permanent opposition.

The social composition of the 'party of order' across the nation defies precise historical analysis. But in a hierarchic society the cause of hierarchy was inevitably led *de haut en bas*. In 1827 Wellington had no doubt:

> Our Party consists of the Bishops & Clergy, the Great Aristocracy, the landed Interest, the Magistracy of the Country, the great Merchants and Bankers, in short the *parti conservateur* of the Country.

None of these elements was wholly committed to Wellington and his friends, for Whigs and even radicals could be found among most sorts and conditions of men, but the part Wellington's categories had played in the consolidation of conservatism was beyond argument. Above all the aristocracy and gentry had provided the core of leadership in parliament and in the localities, even though more obscure professional men like Reeves could sometimes exceed their betters in zeal. Two other elements, though, helped to shape the mentality and practice of the emerging Toryism. One was the Crown itself. Suddenly the object of effusive loyalty in the 1790s, the Crown had good reason to share the reaction against the French example and to seek to prevent similar proceedings in Britain. The monarchy in the persons of George III and the Prince of Wales, despite the latter's sometime preferences for Whig politicians, became even more resolutely conservative than its ministries. Royal obstruction and influence was clearest on Catholic grievances, but the Court's more general nervousness about radicalism and unrest contributed to the near-monopoly of office by ministries of constitutional defence. Only one ministry until 1827 included significant Whig participation of anything like Whig terms and even that one, Grenville's 'Ministry of All the Talents' in 1806-7, was committed to continuation of the war and to domestic order. The ministerial and parliamentary alignments of the next two decades were influenced by the Crown's evident preference for a government of conservative complexion. Indeed at one point, during the Queen Caroline affair in 1820, George IV was inclined to seek a more hardline ministry than Liverpool's. George's main ministerial confidants were Sidmouth and Wellington on the Tory right, though he never wholly succumbed to the influence of his stridently illiberal brother, the Duke of Cumberland. Wellington's later reflection that 'with . . . shades of difference [over means] I believe that all Sovereigns are Conservative' was a view based on experience and a tribute to the benefit his *'parti conservateur'* had derived from royal support.

The second element was the Church of England. We have seen how the clergy of the established churches had rallied in the 1790s to the constitution of which the churches were part and to the social order which secured their position. The Anglican tradition of preaching on the duty and wisdom of political submission had reasserted itself (Archdeacon William Paley's sermon *Reasons for Contentment*, first preached in 1793 and 'addressed to the Labouring Part of the British Public', was only the best known example), while the strengthened emphasis on the rights and defence of property suited a Church so closely associated with the landowning classes and itself, in its corporate capacity, the greatest property-owner in the country. But the Church had special problems too. It was threatened by the now rapid growth of Dissent within English society, it faced an intellectual challenge from free-thinking rationalism and the new prominence of the Catholic Emancipation question threatened to subvert a crucial component of its constitutional privilege. Even if the State survived substantially intact, the Church's position within it might suffer. Even with constitutional reform blocked, the clergy might feel themselves to be challenged in public debate and in their own parishes. The clergy not only helped laymen like Burke to give an odour of sanctity to the conservative reaction but also used the anti-Jacobin cause to promote the Church's own interests. The 1807 general election, in which Catholic claims were a major issue, seems to have been the first in which the Anglican clergy as a distinct interest figured prominently. Indeed the emergence of a distinctive Toryism out of Pittite conservatism owed a good deal to the Church of England and to the prominence of religious issues. Grenville by 1812 could identify 'high Church' with 'the party of the Tories' and Wellington later was able to take 'the Bishops & Clergy' for granted in his *'parti conservateur'*. Government reciprocated the support it received from the Church. Sidmouth and Liverpool, not always of one mind, shared a concern for strengthening the established Church by equipping it to play its social rôle more effectively. Parliamentary money was granted for the supplementary endowment of poor livings and, in 1818 and 1824, for building additional churches in populous districts. Voluntary efforts worked to the same ends. Clergy, gentry, merchants and professional men were among those who established the National Society for Educating the Poor in the Principles of the Established Church in 1811 – it was to be one of the most important social institutions of the century to follow – and founded the Church Building Society in 1818.

The sharp edge of the alliance between ecclesiastical and political Toryism owed more perhaps to the Catholic question than any other issue. The Union with Ireland had pushed the question of Catholic Emancipation to the front of the political stage and, at the same time, helped to divide Tory from more liberal or pragmatic conservatives. For the first three decades of the century resistance to Emancipation served as a major component of the Tory identity, even though some of the leading ministerialists professed themselves ready to honour the commitment to the repeal of Catholic disabilities which Pitt and Castlereagh had made in 1800. The outcome of the 1807 general election showed that most of their supporters in Britain thought otherwise. Emancipation, a major constitutional change, was an alarming prospect to embattled conservatives who declined to represent the constitution as negotiable; it would also be a great step towards that ideal of 'religious liberty to its utmost extent' to which Fox had committed the Whigs. That too terrified most of the establishment clergy and the zealous laity. The Emancipation issue also, however, raised large questions of political dominance and social control, just as the Irish rebellion of 1798 had done. Many Irish landlords, of whom the Union had brought larger numbers to Westminster, and their British counterparts felt concern about the threat to aristocratic dominance from the Catholic majority in Ireland. Here was a test case not only for the constitution and the privilege of established churches but also for the nature of social authority and class relations. Should the government of Ireland surrender – could it afford to surrender – to the agitation which O'Connell was leading during the 1820s? But for most British opinion the response was more one of emotion. The issue enlisted the conscience of the Crown on the Tory side (both Georges felt that the coronation oath committed them to uphold Protestant supremacy) while among the less exalted it appealed to traditional anti-Irish and anti-Catholic chauvinism. Resistance to Catholic claims had much the appeal of patriotism itself. It swayed even sections of Protestant Nonconformity, notably Wesleyan Methodists, and even areas like Lancashire where Tory sentiment was otherwise weak. Frontbenchers close to the problems of governing Ireland might see matters more pragmatically, but resistance to Catholic claims generated intense commitment outside as well as among the landed classes and the clergy. The cry of Crown, Church and Constitution had outlived its origin in resistance to Jacobinism. There had developed too a significant Orange interest on the Ultra wing of the government's support under the patronage of a number of Tory peers, the Duke of Cumberland prominent among them.

Government and Party

The stages by which something that could be called a Tory party emerged from the conservative alliance of the 1790s were inevitably uncertain and sometimes equivocal. There was no one point when such a party came into being, no moment when a 'modern' party replaced the very different alignments familiar in eighteenth-century politics. There was evolution, not genesis. Perhaps the historian's concern with party is in itself distorting. When conservatives had called for a rallying of the patriciate around Crown and Constitution, they had not perceived their resistance to Jacobinism, disorder and radical change as factional or partisan. Loyalty was due to legitimate government and authority and to the King's ministers as the parliamentary and executive extension of the Crown itself. Loyalty to individuals who embodied the qualities required by the occasion might play a part, as the rôle of Pitt in life and of the cult of Pitt in death showed, but hardly loyalty to a party as such. That was precisely the factionalism many Tories condemned in the Whig coterie.[5] This attitude helped to perpetuate uncertainty over the nature and legitimacy of party for decades and it retarded its development in both institutional and psychological terms. Only with opposition and electoral defeat after 1830 did more distinct concepts and organization of party develop. Until

---

[5] Reality never wholly matched the ideal, as the prominence of connexions like the Grenvilles and the Addingtonians showed. There were other old-style family connexions, though increasingly they assumed Whig or Tory labels. The ideal of government above party had a special appeal to the almost permanent ministerialists, the surviving placemen of the old Court party and the larger numbers of independent backbench gentry – people, that is, who either took office for granted or did not expect it at all.

then many Tories had preferred to identify with government, social authority and political legitimacy rather than with a party interest.

The long hold on office was crucial to this attitude. From the early 1790s until Wellington's resignation in late 1830 there was substantial continuity in the personnel of government and only two brief ministries not dominated by the professed friends of constitution and order. For many men there was little need or opportunity to ask where loyalty to the Crown and its ministers ended and loyalty to a party began. While this situation lasted, the irreconcilable Whigs could be written off as not only a discreditable faction but also a permanent opposition. The idea of Toryism in opposition was almost a contradiction in terms and the phenomenon, when it occurred, had to be seen as a temporary disturbance of the natural order.

For figures like Pitt, Perceval, Liverpool and Castlereagh who bore the main responsibilities for government, matters were often less straightforward. Ministries rarely seemed wholly secure. Danger might come from the King or Regent himself, as in 1801, 1807, 1812 and 1820 when royal preferences dictated or nearly dictated changes; from the House of Commons where majorities were often precarious and where the decay of the old Court party and the restiveness, indifference or complacency of backbench support threatened governments; and from doubts, demoralizing to supporters, about the quality and performance of the Commons frontbench, a problem for some years after 1815 when the ministry was unduly dependent in the Lower House upon Castlereagh's sterling qualities. There was also the problem of opinion outside Parliament. 'Public opinion' – the phrase was familiar by the 1820s – was the opinion of a larger political nation than the aristocracy, even than the 'gentry, clergy and freeholders' of the counties. It was provincial as well as metropolitan, urban and commercial as well as agrarian. Increasingly articulated and orchestrated by a press that government could never satisfactorily control, this opinion, though predominantly loyal during the war and always friendly to constitutional order, was sensitive to styles of government, prickly on certain aspects of policy and protective of its interests in matters of taxation, trade and prosperity. The controversy over the Orders-in-Council was a case in point.[6] Governments knew that they had to pay some heed to the more 'rational' and respectable kinds of opinion and a ministry which visibly lost the confidence of 'the country' was likely to find its support in the Commons disintegrating. It was, however, both the problem and the advantage of government that public opinion of this kind was far from homogeneous.[7]

Initially there had been few problems of ministerial stability. The rallying of the propertied to Crown and Constitution had brought a substantial body of the opposition over into Pitt's camp. In 1794 some of the leading figures of the opposition under the lead of the Duke of Portland entered office and even the successive ministerial crises of 1801, 1804 and 1806 did not return all of them to old allegiances. Though Fitzwilliam and Spencer drifted back to the Foxites and Windham allied

---

[6] The Orders-in-Council (1807–12) were trade embargoes designed to aid the prosecution of war against France. Inevitably they were unpopular with the business interests most affected.
[7] On the interaction of government and public opinion, see J. A. Cookson, *Lord Liverpool's Administration. The Crucial Years 1815–22* (1975).

himself with Grenville in opposition, Portland remained to head a virtually Tory administration in 1807–9. Pitt's resignation in 1801 over the issues of Catholic Emancipation and royal confidence marked the end of the great coalition he had constructed. The new ministry headed by Henry Addington, the former Speaker, drew strength from the King's personal backing, from the making of the Peace of Amiens, from an image of financial responsibility and competence and from its good standing among many of the gentry and clergy. It was resented, however, by many personal followers of Pitt and among parliamentarians factionalism was once again rife, with personal rivalries and ambitions compounding disagreements over the peace, disarmament and Catholic claims. Pitt's return to office in 1804 after the resumption of hostilities failed to restore stability and his ministry was tottering even before his death in 1806. For some time the personal and connexional in-fighting, the influence of George III and the Prince Regent and the strength of policy differences created a sense of politics in flux. At the level where ministries were constructed the new conservatism was not a united and impressive force. But the substantial continuity of approach which governments of these years showed over the prosecution of the war and over resistance to disorder and radicalism at home was at least as significant as factional strife and ministerial instability. The body of support in Parliament and in the country for firm government was solid enough to permit the periodic shifts of ministerial combinations.

Even the 'Ministry of All the Talents' in 1806–7 confirmed rather than broke the pattern. It remained committed both to the war and to domestic order. Fox had moderated his views and behaviour by now and Grenville himself was not notably more liberal or reformist than the heirs of Pitt except on the Catholic question. Significantly it was on this issue that Sidmouth's machinations and a royal putsch brought him down after Fox's death. Here the Talents had been at odds with dominant opinion. The Crown, the country gentlemen, the Orange factions, the clergy, all needed more reassurance than a ministry tinged with religious liberalism could provide, despite Grenville's personal and social prestige. The spectacle of Whigs in office had anyway restored resolve and solidarity among former Pittites. George Canning, busy organizing opposition, noted after one gathering of the like-minded that there had been 'nothing factious, but everything so provokingly and pointedly loyal as to amount precisely to the same thing'. Fortified by the 1807 general election's strongly Protestant mood, the ministries of Portland and Perceval provided both the partisanship and the reassurance which the loyal required. The stance was now more distinctively Tory. The prominence of the Catholic question, the severity of the threats to domestic order and the conservative Evangelicalism of Perceval himself helped to establish this identity, despite the continuing factionalism of ambitious rivals.[8] By the time of his assassination in 1812 Perceval had done much to re-establish a solid conservative grouping, though one with a more partisan edge than Pitt's coalition of 1794–1801. The Pittite men of business like Liverpool and Castlereagh had

---

[8] Spencer Perceval (1762–1812), prime minister 1809–12 and a son of the 2nd Earl of Egmont, had been Solicitor, then Attorney General under Addington and in Pitt's second ministry and had served as Chancellor of the Exchequer and Leader of the Commons under Portland.

been firmly ensconced in office, the Addingtonians had been brought in and bought off, the Crown had been satisfied and the country gentlemen and clergy had been reassured and attached. The difficulties following Perceval's death owed more to the Prince Regent's personal predilections and to the lack of a dominant personality for first minister than to any divisions among the surviving ministers or to any restiveness among parliamentary or public opinion. Indeed the old Cabinet held together during the weeks of crisis in unexampled fashion, showed a clear sense of its own identity and helped to secure the succession to the premiership of Charles Jenkinson, second Earl of Liverpool. The survival of Liverpool's ministry for fifteen years was helped by the improving fortunes of war, which rallied patriotic opinion behind the promise of victory, and by the changing mood of the Prince Regent, now more influenced by his brother Cumberland and less inclined to make a bolt for the Whigs. It was also based, however, on the predominantly conservative sentiments of the main political interests in the nation.

The fifteen-year ministry looked less secure at the time than it does in retrospect. Liverpool's strained personal relations with George IV became a liability and, though final victory over Napoleon brought acclaim and prestige to the administration, the process of peacetime readjustment after 1815 brought new problems for government when the force of patriotic solidarity in and out of Parliament was inevitably diminishing. But the long hold on office, the continuity of much of the ministry's personnel and of its basic approach to major questions, all showed the degree of support which a government of social order, constitutional defence and responsible administration could command. It was a government of centre-right conservative consensus, in contrast to the Whigs who were gathering assorted radical and Irish causes around them in opposition. The years of office helped to establish habits of allegiance and support, to consolidate voting patterns among backbench MPs and in many of the constituencies, to tie patrons and interest groups to a cadre of parliamentary leaders and to provide a focus for the forces of deference and conservatism in British society. A political leadership was rivalling the Crown as the focus of loyalism. On the other side the long exclusion of Fox's heirs from office reinforced their own party identity and loyalty and made the dividing line between ministerialists and Whig opposition into one of the fundamentals of politics. Though independent and floating elements had certainly not been eliminated, by the 1820s there was a prevailing sense in parliamentary and national politics of a great and established divide between two sides. Much of the press had already shaped itself to this polarization and the recently founded reviews, the Whig *Edinburgh Review* (established 1802) and its Tory rival, the *Quarterly Review* (1809), represented the confrontation's intellectual dimension. Two London clubs, Brooks's and White's, though less narrowly partisan (particularly the latter) than the creations of the 1830s, carried the parliamentary division into metropolitan high society.

The process of consolidation under Liverpool culminated in the early 1820s when the ministry, still shaken by the Queen Caroline episode, was looking to reinforce its parliamentary position. The Addingtonians had long subsumed their identity and ambitions within the administration – indeed Addington, now Lord Sidmouth, had as Home Secretary pursued a

hard line on law and order to match his Anglican and anti-Catholic zeal –
but the Grenvilles, in increasingly uneasy alliance with the Whigs, had
fought shy of Liverpool's embrace, perhaps because of their pro-Catholic
sympathies, perhaps because of the minimal ambition of the ageing
Grenville. But now the family head, the Marquis of Buckingham, was
sniffing the wind for patronage and indeed a family connexion so well
entrenched in what radical critics were depicting as Old Corruption was
likely to look to Tory government as a bulwark of the spoils system. The
Grenvilles had anyway always been tough on domestic disorder and the
troubles of 1817–20 had placed severe strains on their co-operation with
the Whigs. The ministry, seeing the advantages of what Castlereagh called
'taking this connection out of that central position in the House of
Commons which invites intrigue, and might facilitate an intermediate
arrangement', seized the opportunity. The deal of 1821–22, which brought
the Stowe Grenvilles and eleven Commons votes over to the ministry in
return for a dukedom for the Marquis and sundry places and favours,
entailed the elimination of the last distinct family connexion. Henceforth
even the more maverick Grenvilles would have to operate within the
framework of national political alignments.

Even the disintegration of the government after Liverpool's departure in
1827 was a matter of shifts at the centre of the political spectrum under the
pressure of issues and personalities – a recurrent phenomenon of
nineteenth-century politics – rather than a reversion to the eighteenth-
century pattern. Two characteristic features of the old system had all but
gone. One was the Court party, the permanent support of eighteenth-
century administrations. The 'King's friends' had been withering on the
bough of 'economical reform' since the 1780s and measures like Curwen's
Act of 1809 had made it impossible to replenish the diminishing number of
placemen in the Commons.[9] The shrinking corps of professional administrators surviving in the House had itself slowly taken on a party colouring
and identified with the long Tory administration. The coming of Whig
government in 1830 heralded its elimination. Even in the 1820s there had
been a shortage of the old kind of permanent, non-partisan support for the
King's ministers. Wellington's question – 'How would the king's government be carried on?' – would have to be answered with a very different
kind of support in future. As for the other great force in the eighteenth-
century Commons, the large body of independent backbenchers, mostly
gentry, its members had become gradually more identified with the rival
leadership groups. The enduring division at the heart of parliamentary
politics had forced most of the independents, even the majority of the
county members who were usually drawn from the well established and
substantial gentry families, to hoist party colours. 'Independence' retained
prestige on the backbenches but more as nostalgia for old values, as an
assertion of the social standing of members and as a legitimation of
occasional rebellion than as a permanent and decisive rejection of party
allegiance. Even the House of Lords, though not directly subject to
electoral exigencies, featured a growth of party alignment. This absorption

---

[9] On 'economical reform' and the decline of the Court interest, see A. S. Foord, 'The Waning
of the Influence of the Crown', *English Historical Review*, 62, 1947.

of the independents was to proceed further in the 1830s, but the Commons and the constituencies had gone much of the way even by 1827.[10]

Uncertainties about the nature of party and some resistance to its implications and dictates remained. The distaste for 'faction' was still a force and the gulf between the rival leaderships remained bridgeable by centrist elements of the kind that figured in the reconstructions of 1827–37. Nonetheless a new pattern of politics had emerged by the late 1820s based on something different from the eighteenth-century structure of connexions, Court party and independents. Alignments were now largely national in scope, not based simply on family or personal connexion; recognized party leaderships drew regular support from large numbers of parliamentarians and used whips and managers as intermediaries with their followers; parties had an enhanced dimension of ideology or at least 'principle' relating to opposed positions of reformism and conservatism and organized and encouraged relations between the metropolitan centre and the constituencies. The two main groupings were not identical either in their structure or in their understanding of party. The long identification of Toryism with government meant that the Treasury still figured largely in its management and loyalty to the King's ministers in its state of mind. But a conservative party different from anything in the first half of George III's reign had established itself in national politics. Though the schisms and cross-alliances of 1827–28 showed the weaknesses of the new structure, there was no doubting either the pedigree or the general character of the party which came together again under Wellington early in 1828. Though the Duke, who was to remain acknowledged overall leader until 1834, believed as much as anyone still could that duty to the Crown was the highest political principle, his stance was unmistakably partisan in its hostility to radical reform and Whig compromise.

---

[10] See D. E. D. Beales, 'Parliamentary Parties and the "Independent" Member, 1810–1860', in *Ideas and Institutions of Victorian Britain*, ed. R. Robson (1967). On the party alignments of the period see also F. O'Gorman, *The Emergence of the British Two-Party System 1760–1832* (1982).

2

Problems of Defence, Problems of Change: 1793–1830

One of the problems of party history lies in the definition of what constituted the party at any particular time. In this period there were no clearly defined party institutions or membership. Instead we find an amorphous grouping of interests and shades of opinion around an administrative élite confirmed in leadership largely by its long hold on ministerial office. The process of evolution into something people could call a party revealed the uncertainties and diversity of an often-shifting coalition. Toryism was never monolithic; even less so was the broader conservatism of which self-conscious Toryism was a part. The centrality and prestige of Crown and Parliament ensured, however, that the leadership provided by ministers and other parliamentarians was widely and readily accepted by British society. Many men supported the ministries of Pitt, Portland, Perceval and Liverpool because they were the King's ministers and because ministerial instability during difficult times might endanger social order, national survival and even government itself. The figures familiar from successive cabinets came to appear the natural administration in terms of experience and principled consistency.[1] The crucial element in the Commons, the backbench gentry from the shires, concurred. Despite their periodic displays of 'independence', only a minority showed an active preference for the opposition Whigs.

All this did not, however, produce an agreed policy or philosophy for a Tory party. Men who asserted that 'principle' determined their behaviour still found that not all principles pointed in the same direction. Not all the interests among the 'friends of order' were easily reconciled. Cabinets often found themselves caught between opposing pressures and competing demands. Even the central concern of ministerialists for social and political order was qualified by an insistence upon the importance of constitutional liberties and by a careful distancing from the autocracies manifest over much of Europe. Even the gentry mixed their support with a traditional distrust of the executive, just as the localities continued to resent central

[1] Except for a period of little more than a year Liverpool served in office from 1793 to 1827.

direction. Tensions of this kind explain why the near-permanent occupation of office by the former Pittites was combined with a near-permanent
state of anxiety about its continuation. Though a partisan cohesion was
developing among ministerial supporters, the legitimacy of the concept
and practice of party (still often seen as 'faction') at the expense of loyalty to
the Crown, to the constitution, to constituency interests and to the
solidarity of the patriciate remained open to question. One recalls Burke's
warnings about the difficulty of defining the ideological content of British
politics with any precision.

Nonetheless one cannot mistake certain attitudes and purposes in the
behaviour, speeches and writings of governments and their partisans. The
men who rallied to the constitution had their reasons. They sought political
and social stability and the maintenance in much its existing form of the
'aristocratic settlement' of Crown and Parliament. They sought to buttress
a hierarchic society and its distribution of privilege, property and their
associated rights. Constitutional authority and constitutional liberty were
the two sides of this coin. The emphasis on property perhaps warrants
more stress than many historians have given it. The identification of
Toryism with the determined defence of property – that of fund-holders,
of merchants and industrialists, of corporations like the East and West
India companies and the established churches, as well as of the landed
classes – gave it considerable force in a society where great property
enjoyed so much influence and where middling property was so widely
spread. Toryism never attracted the totality of these interests, though its
publicists sometimes argued as though it did. Within the landed classes
themselves there were families who, for reason or idiosyncrasy, trod other
paths. The enthusiastic loyalty to the Crown and Church which shaped the
Tory identity was not universal even among people of broadly conservative
sentiment. But the Toryism which emerged in the opening decades of the
nineteenth century held, initially at least, the commanding heights of
conservative opinion in a society where conservative interests were strong.

But that society was not static. Many of the tensions of the time sprang
from an accelerating rate of social and economic change within both
Britain and Ireland. The stability which governments sought was not the
condition of much of the population beneath them. The French Revolution itself was an interruption of a longer process of strain, conflict and
adjustment on this side of the Channel. It was not self-evident how best to
stabilize institutions in these circumstances. Men of conservative purpose
had available to them a choice of strategies ranging from a diehard defence
of established interests and obstruction of institutional change to a sensitive
management of opinion and a careful adjustment to what was perceived as
inevitable change. It had become clear by the late 1820s how divided
conservative opinion – even Tory opinion – had become among these
options.

The Challenge of Ideas

Ideological confrontation had not been entirely a French import. Hanoverian Britain had possessed its own uncertainties and disagreements about
the nature of government, the relationship between Crown and Parliament
and the relationship between those institutions and society at large.

Any major shock to the credibility of government generated criticism within and without Parliament that challenged not merely the current ministry but even the nature of government itself. John Wilkes's campaigns, Wyvill's Yorkshire Movement and the anti-Court Whiggery of the Rockinghamites all illustrated the possibilities. After the crisis of confidence at the end of the American war, the ministry which Fox and North had imposed on the King required the full force of royal influence to overthrow it. Subsequently George and his minister, the younger Pitt, had restabilized government, but even Pitt displayed an urge to purify and rationalize the régime. Constitution, administration and economic regulation were to be adapted to social change. The polity had shown enough potential for constructive evolution not to warrant the *'ancien régime'* label which some historians would pin upon it.

The French Revolution, however, subjected British politics to a turbulence and polarization that checked the tendency to gradualist reform. By assaulting monarchy, aristocracy and established religion it promoted ideas that legitimized breaks with tradition and that could be applied destructively almost as well to Hanoverian Britain as to Bourbon France. The most influential exponent of radical theory in Britain was Thomas Paine whose *Rights of Man* (1790–92) and *The Age of Reason* (1793) pulled together the implications of the American and French revolutions in a gospel that was to influence populist radicalism in Britain until the Chartist period. The more conventional and genteel critics of government, their enthusiasm rekindled when France established representative government in 1789, the centenary of England's Glorious Revolution, had seen themselves as restoring an inherited constitution to health and virtue, perhaps adjusting its balance, but not substituting a novel system. But Paine's stress on 'natural rights' shared by all men had egalitarian implications which threatened the existing constitution and perhaps the social order too. His rejection of traditional forms of religion also challenged conventional moral teaching and alarmed those powerful institutions, the established churches. Indeed all interests with a stake in the constitution had reason to take alarm. Even many radicals, fearful of the ignorant and unpropertied, failed to share Paine's enthusiasm for full male suffrage. Though less subversive of the distribution of property Paine, by encouraging a climate of radical idealism, opened the way for yet more visionary and sectarian ideas, among them Thomas Spence's call for the confiscation and socialization of landed property. Respectable politics could not easily accommodate aspirations of this kind. Activity which represented government as corrupt, exploitative and illegitimate and which preached the political equality of republican citizenship invited retaliation from established authority.

The combination of the French example and the spread of radical ideas and activity in Britain produced both an ideological polarization and a mood of alarm and suspicion among people of position. The reassurance about popular attitudes provided by Birmingham's Church and King riots in 1791[2] and by Burke's argument that sedition was unBritish began to

---

[2] See R. B. Rose, 'The Priestley Riots of 1791', *Past & Present*, 18, 1960, Local magistrates, gentry and clergy connived at the attacks on Dissenters and reformers, but central government was unhappy with the mob violence. Dundas suspected a 'levelling principle' behind the riot and plunder.

wear thin. Burke himself became convinced that some 80,000 people, one-fifth of the political nation, were 'pure Jacobins' engaged in 'restless agitating activity' which, if left unchecked, would produce political upheaval and 'violation of property'. This image of subversion and particularly a fear of the spread of political literature and organization among the unpropertied masses became staples of Tory thinking. Reaction was being intensified by terror.

The Challenge from Below

The masses could now be perceived as both a problem and a danger. Whig theory from Locke onwards had sometimes conceded a marginal and rather theoretical rôle to 'the People' in legitimate resistance to tyranny. Late eighteenth-century reformers had looked to a wider political participation through parliamentary reform as a counterweight to Court influence, Old Corruption and overmighty government. The triumph of the Parisian mob, however, represented something quite different – the overwhelming of rank and property by the combined force of the masses. In Britain, despite the initial popularity of war in February 1793, the lack of military success, disruption of trade, increased taxation and higher food prices after poor harvests soon generated discontents among sections of the populace. The balance between patriotic loyalism and discontent was to shift often during the war years. There is no consensus among historians on the extent of popular sympathy for Jacobinism and other forms of radicalism, but there were times when government feared that it was facing a sizeable part of the lower orders dissatisfied with their lot and actually or potentially hostile to government and constitution. Confidence in social harmony founded on hierarchy, patronage and deference gave way to an obsessive fear of confrontation between property and unpropertied numbers. Repression of popular agitation and of 'unconstitutional' activity was an almost inevitable response. Though the weight of repression fluctuated with the intensity of discontent, Burke's conviction of sedition and insecurity had echoes in every moment of social tension. In 1830, for example, the High Tory *Blackwood's Magazine* was alarmed by events on the continent and by reform stirrings at home:

> Even against British property in various modes, there exists an organized conspiracy – against the property of the West Indians – against the property of the fundholders, and, finally, against the property of the Church. But above all the great and paramount conspiracy lies against the guardians of all our property and rights – the aristocracy of our land . . .

What it called 'plebeian insolence and profligacy' were not to be tolerated. Even the Whig Francis Jeffrey responded similarly to that year's agrarian disorders in England:

> The real battle is not between Whigs and Tories, Liberals and Illiberals and such gentleman-like denominations, but between property and no-property – Swing and the law.

This queasy but aggressive nervousness about present and future became a hallmark of the attitudes of many professed Tories towards the lower classes. An almost timeless presumption was now being made explicit.

Society was necessarily ruled by a propertied élite, the landed patriciate at their head, while the great majority of the population with little or no property beyond their labour could be only the governed. The constitution was being interpreted more clearly than before in terms of social and economic relationships.

Men who felt this way were often disturbed and perplexed by the tensions they felt in their society. Through this period recurrent trade depressions and dislocations, surges of unemployment and destitution, high food prices in wartime and then their peacetime collapse, rapid population increase and economic transition, all generated unrest and helped to convince thinking men of the instability and uncertain direction of their times. Even if discontents often evaporated with economic recovery, their political manifestations were sometimes such as the governing élite could neither ignore nor forget. An experience of domestic troubles that included the Gordon Riots, the Corresponding Societies, attempts at insurrection, the crisis of Burdett's imprisonment in the Tower in 1810, Luddism and the post-Waterloo difficulties warranted a degree of unease. Liverpool seems to have served his fifteen-year premiership convinced that London, the seat of government, was itself fundamentally ungovernable and would one day explode in revolutionary upheaval.[3] The very constituency in which were Court, Parliament and Whitehall was dominated from 1807 by radical artisans and shopkeepers whom the loyalist press designated 'Jacobins'. Though the wartime administrations enjoyed substantial support across the nation and tapped the vein of popular patriotism, the Tory consciousness distrusted mass opinion and remained antipopular in its rhetoric and purpose. The idea of a substantial measure of electoral reform to broaden the base of the constitution was anathema even to Tories like Castlereagh, Canning and Palmerston who were willing to concede Catholic Emancipation.

The Challenge of Politics

Even parliamentary politics posed a threat. One factor helping to establish the Tory identity and cohesion was a Whig opposition ready to take office when opportunity offered. Sometimes diminished and disorganized, notably when Fox withdrew melodramatically from Parliament in 1797, this opposition never disappeared. The new term 'His Majesty's Opposition', first used ironically during the Regency, was to be a tribute to its endurance in adversity. Here in Tory eyes were traitors within the gates of the constitution, capable by design or fecklessness of conceding it to its enemies. Admittedly not every Whig was quite beyond the pale. Spencer had served under Pitt and shown his patriotism and responsibility; in the 1820s Lansdowne was a beacon by which centrist Tories navigated. Some Whigs were related to Tory families and the gulf between the sides was never completely unbridgeable in either London or county society. Some ministerialists still saw themselves as heirs to Whig traditions of constitutionalism and the reluctance of most ministers to call themselves Tories

---

[3] Robert Southey, Poet Laureate and regular reviewer for the *Quarterly*, shared this distrust of London and extended it to include the growing industrial districts: 'Governments who found their prosperity upon manufactures sleep upon gunpowder'.

even in the 1820s signalled a willingness to cultivate conservative Whig opinion. Former Pittites like Grenville and Canning, both 'Catholics', were able to negotiate coalitions with Whig elements when circumstances required. Nonetheless the persistence of a body of Whigs in opposition, so ensuring the failure of the Burkean ideal of patrician solidarity against radicalism, was troubling and provoking to ministerialists, particularly when the Whigs not only exploited government's temporary difficulties but developed a counter-programme of their own. Fox's vision at the turn of the century –

> Religious liberty to its utmost extent, Reform in Parliament, liberty of the press and indemnity to others (radicals), not only peace but a good understanding with Bonaparte.[4]

– was almost the reverse image of the Pittite position. Inevitably accused of disloyalty during the patriotic war, the Whig coterie had continued to sympathize with French developments too long for their political futures. Their apparent hostility to the Crown and its prerogative offended many who still viewed government as the King's own, an attitude confirmed by the symbolic rôle accorded the Crown in the years of war and social tension. There was also the religious character – rather the lack of it – of leading Whig circles. The lifestyle of the Foxite coterie offended the pious, many Whigs scarcely disguised their anti-clericalism, rationalism and heterodoxy, and the causes of Catholic Emancipation and fuller religious equality threatened the established churches. The bishops, clergy and zealous laity of the Church of England came to dread the prospect of a Whig ministry from which, it was believed, Dissenters, Catholics and radicals would all demand reward for their support. Catholic Emancipation itself was more than a narrowly ecclesiastical issue and the commitment of the Whigs to it spread distrust of them widely through British society.

Whigs might argue that they had no itch to radicalize the constitution, only to update it and restore its balance. They often claimed that they were more intelligent conservatives than the Tories. Tories countered that the effects of Whig government might differ from their intentions. Girondins had been swept away by Jacobins. Behind a conservative Whig like Lansdowne stood the more radical Grey, Fox's lieutenant in the campaign for parliamentary reform, and behind Grey more menacing figures like his brother-in-law Whitbread, the radical brewer, Burdett, the baronet fond of playing to the London mob and member for radical Westminster, Hume, the retrenchment fanatic, and Brougham, the restless lawyer and Queen Caroline's counsel in 1820. Behind the parliamentarians, 'out of doors', stood disturbing, demotic figures like Benbow, Hone and Thelwall. Many Tories felt that the Whig opposition sheltered such 'revolutionists' from the appropriate rigour of the law and provided a respectable front for sedition. The *Quarterly Review* was convinced that Whigs who attacked 'the crown, the legislature, the church, and laws' gave 'all the latitude to the revolutionary ones which they desire, and in truth are revolutionary themselves in everything but motive'. Only when they 'expel from their ranks all the

---

[4] Quoted by F. O'Gorman, *The Emergence of the British Two-Party System 1760–1832* (1982), p. 27.

friends of revolution, and dissolve all connexion with radicalism' would the Whigs find favour with 'the wealth, intelligence and wisdom of the nation' who 'in chusing a ministry ... chuse the guardians of their lives and fortunes'.[5] The appearances of the Whigs in office in 1806–7 and 1827–28 galvanized their critics into the vigorous opposition which contributed to the more decidedly Tory tone of the successor ministries of Portland and Wellington and it was the Whig challenge in Parliament, together with the grumblings of the country gentlemen, that shaped much of the policy of Liverpool's administration. One of the most compelling and widespread motives of government supporters was simply keeping the Whigs out of office.

The Habit of Authoritarianism

One way to defend the established order, at least in the short run, was to stamp on any opposition that could be characterized as subversive or unconstitutional. The 'habit of authority' which has been attributed to the ruling classes of nineteenth-century Britain turned to authoritarianism when challenged at the start of the century. Some of the means of repression employed were informal – like social pressure and harassment, the diversion of custom by the wealthy, the encouragement of or connivance at the violence of loyalist mobs – while others were more formal and legalistic, like the tightening of statutory prohibitions and controls, campaigns of prosecutions, the increase of military establishments to overawe or put down the disaffected. Sometimes these responses were considered and calculated, sometimes they were inspired by something close to panic.

Even by 1792–93 there had been growing queasiness about the spread of radical propaganda and the exent of lower-class disaffection. The sales and circulation of Paine's *Rights of Man* were alarming, while the Corresponding Societies, sympathetic to Jacobinism, were claiming to speak for 'the People' against government which they characterized as corrupt, tyrannical and illegitimate. The Societies were composed largely of tradesmen, shopkeepers and artisans, men outside the political nation as the patriciate interpreted it and without the ballast of substantial property. Here, worryingly concentrated in the cities, were Britain's equivalent of the Jacobins. Meanwhile less plebeian bodies like the Society of the Friends of the People, an association of aristocratic and largely youthful parliamentarians, and the Society for Constitutional Information were cultivating and organizing reformist opinion among the respectable. But the weight of propertied opinion, alarmed by revolutionary excesses and French victories abroad and by radical stirrings at home, was in no mood for concession. In May 1793 Grey's motion for parliamentary reform was crushed in the Commons 282–41. Already, a year earlier, Royal Proclamations had signalled a drive against seditious publications and meetings, the circulation of Paine's works being a main target. Dykes were being erected against what Portland, now drifting away from Fox, called 'an inundation of Levelling Doctrines'. As the campaign of prosecutions of radical literature dented reformist enthusiasm, Scotland's Lord Justice Clerk, the vituperative Braxfield, set an example of severity in sentencing. In the autumn

---

[5] *Quarterly Review*, 28, 1822, article 'The Opposition', pp. 197–219.

more French victories and the Convention's Fraternal Decrees ('calculated everywhere to sow the seeds of rebellion and civil contention', according to Pitt) triggered a new wave of prosecutions of radical publications, the embodiment of part of the militia to supplement regular troops at home and the passage of an Aliens Act to strengthen government control over foreigners within the country. Paine was tried and found guilty in his absence and military garrisons in and around London were increased. Now came the first nationwide organization of loyalist opinion in the form of the Reeves societies, the title of the London prototype, 'The Association for Preserving Liberty and Property against Republicans and Levellers', underlining its political character. Ministers, notably Grenville, were well aware of this development and gave every encouragement to the associations, many of which applied intimidatory pressure against people in the localities active in agitation or suspected of radical sympathies. Here, in the pre-emptive strikes of counter-revolution, was the emergence of a hardline constitutionalism fiercely hostile to any radicalization of the political system.

The coming of war early in 1793 gave the campaign a further twist. Despite some parliamentary criticism, the passage of the Treasonable Correspondence Act restricted traffic with the enemy and extended the definition of treason. It was an example of how the pressure of war fed into the domestic situation, polarizing opinion and heightening suspicion and intolerance. Again repression met with short-term success, though a revival of radical activity in the autumn, including a National Convention in Edinburgh, necessitated a further wave of prosecutions. Now even Pitt, initially cool about repression, was in a frenzy of nervousness. The most determined repression so far began in May 1794 with the arrest of the leaders of the London societies and the seizure of their papers. A Secret Committee of the Commons established to examine them alleged seditious conspiracy, *Habeas Corpus* was suspended despite Foxite opposition and remained so for fourteen months, and twelve radical leaders faced charges of high treason. The truculence of London juries turned the trials into fiascos for the Crown, but their independence and the popular celebrations of the verdicts only confirmed suspicions being voiced in high places about the loyalty of London and other cities. The lower classes inspired the real alarm and bore the brunt of official pressure. Radical opinions among the literati and their patrons were an irritant; among the masses they were an intolerable danger.[6]

The raising of the Volunteer corps in 1793–94, though a response to fears of invasion and to doubts about the loyalty of regular troops, was also, like the Reeves societies earlier, an attempt to organize respectable opinion behind Crown and Constitution and to isolate and overawe critics of the régime. From the start the Volunteers were instruments of repression, undertaking police work and acting as the executive arms of unofficial local committees of loyalists. At the same time the militia was augmented and a programme of barracks-building undertaken in order to reduce popular discontent at the quartering of troops and to isolate the military from civilian influences.

---

[6] Apparently Pitt himself decided against the prosecution of William Godwin's *Inquiry Concerning Political Justice* when it was published at the safely high price of three guineas.

The level of repression continued to fluctuate. Circumstances were not always as tense as in 1793–94. A pattern of response, however, had emerged. Though concern for constitutional liberty survived even among ministerialists, its force had been weakened by fears of political destabilization. A perceived emergency now warranted the heavy hand of authority. The pattern was repeated in 1795 when high food prices increased popular discontent. A mobbing of the King's carriage in London led to a Proclamation against seditious meetings and the passage of two measures that made it a treasonable offence to incite hatred against King, government or constitution and restricted the size of and gave magistrates wider powers over public meetings.

The 'English Terror' has received a kindlier handling from historians lately and they have emphasized the influence of war on the restriction of constitutional liberties.[7] Certainly war added to the pressures on government and to the general sense of insecurity and instability. The force of wartime patriotism also helped government to push measures through Parliament which would have failed in other circumstances. But the war of 1793 was, from the start, different from most wars. It had clear ideological and political implications within Britain itself and the debate on war and peace interacted with argument about the appropriate relationship between a well-established but now nervous ruling élite and the mass of the population which they governed. The question of war involved the confrontation between conservatism and radicalism. This dimension of politics and ideology had been pushed to the fore by Burke and other critics of French developments well before war broke out and such people were insistent that it should not be concluded by a 'regicide peace'. Domestic politics were dictating attitudes to war as much as the reverse. The dominance of conservative and repressive attitudes continued for some years after Waterloo and only abated when relative domestic stability arrived in the 1820s. It would be sensible to accept the domestic concerns underlying government's authoritarianism and to recognize that the policy, though patchy and never wholly effective, may have contributed to the stability of the régime over this period, though clearly it could be only one of the reasons for that outcome. To treat repression as an accident of war would be to underestimate an important aspect of the practice of government and a significant element in the psychology of emergent Toryism. It would also risk a failure to understand the bitterness of the reaction of many of their opponents.

The circumstances of the new century continued the patterns of repression established in the 1790s. Ireland, where Emmet's rising of 1803 followed the more serious rebellion of 1798, added to the sense of confrontation between official power and popular disaffection. In England the provision disturbances of 1799–1801 added to the distrust of the popular mood felt by government and the Combination Acts illegalizing trades unions were passed. The Despard affair of 1802–3, part of a revolutionary plot with Irish and French connexions, hardly added to the sense of security. In fact the peace of Amiens in 1801 was generally popular and lessened the sense of confrontation between government and sections of public opinion. Addington's government could afford to be

---

[7] Notably C. Emsley, *British Society and the French Wars 1793–1815* (1979), p. 48 ff.

more hesitant about infringing constitutional liberties and this approach was assisted by the absence from office of hawks like Grenville and Windham. Even when war resumed, the invasion threat of 1804–6 helped to keep opinion overwhelmingly loyal and patriotic, much as a similar threat had done in 1798. Prosecutions of anti-war and radical publicists ran at modest levels and the authorities relied more on propaganda of kinds exemplified by Hannah More's pamphlet exhortations to the lower orders and the artist Gillray's 'Little Boney' prints. But from 1808 a revival of anti-war feeling in conditions of economic dislocation attributable partly to the Orders-in-Council of 1807 pushed government back towards cruder means of controlling opinion. With sections of the press intensely hostile to Perceval's ministry, Parliament and London radical opinion played out a major confrontation in 1810 centred on Sir Francis Burdett, radical MP for Westminster. Barricades were seen in the capital's streets for the first time, but the mobs were confronted with large forces of police and military and the crisis passed. In 1811 a wave of Luddism (machinery-breaking) pressed hard the resources of the magistrates in many of the textile districts and by the second half of 1812 12,000 troops were deployed in the disturbed areas. It was hardly the most reassuring background for a ministry disrupted by the assassination of Perceval. But Parliament passed five bills for 'public safety' with Luddism its target, military preparations to which Perceval had given personal attention had their effect, Sidmouth (the former Addington) proved to be both tough and efficient at the Home Office, and the sense of insecurity rallied the propertied classes around the constitution, social order and the reshuffled administration headed by Liverpool.[8] The repeal of the Orders-in-Council, a decision in which prudential calculation by a worried government played a part, and Wellington's successes in the Peninsula contributed to the relative stability of the last years of the war.

Peace in 1815 ushered in another phase of tension heightened by the economic readjustments after prolonged war. The passage of the Corn Law that year necessitated the deployment of troops in the capital again. 1816, a difficult year for the ministry in Parliament, ended with the Spa Fields riots in the capital which the Spencean radicals tried to turn into insurrection. (Their leaders were acquitted of high treason by London juries.) Sidmouth at the Home Office was all for an early recall of Parliament and stringent security measures. Though Liverpool hesitated, the government response was decided by an apparent attempt on the Regent's life in January 1817. Another bout of orchestrated panic saw Secret Committees of both Houses investigating evidence of sedition, the suspension of *Habeas Corpus*, the passage of measures against secret or seditious societies and a spate of prosecutions of the radical press on charges of seditious and blasphemous libel, though again London juries thumbed their noses at government.[9] In March Sidmouth circularized

---

[8] The fullest account of this phase remains F. O. Darvall, *Popular Disturbances and Public Order in Regency England* (1934).

[9] Fox's Libel Act of 1792, which had made juries the judge of what constituted libellous intent, became one of the main obstacles to successful prosecution and a shield for the radical press. Without it official action against the press would have been more effective and probably more extensive throughout these decades.

magistrates lecturing them on their powers over publications considered seditious, an invitation to an open season of harassment of the disaffected and an attempt to extend the normal area of magistrates' discretion. Even Liverpool was now fully convinced by the evidence produced by the Secret Committees and the Grenville connexion, now edging away from the Whigs, gave his ministry strong backing for its maintenance of order.

During 1817 the disturbed state of the country and tactical concessions over financial retrenchment by the government had firmed up its support in the Commons. Castlereagh, leader in the Commons, could claim at the session's end that 'We separated the questions of economy from that of seditious reform, and we became masters of both'. The ministry held its own in the general election of 1818, though the widespread criticism of government among respectable opinion disturbed ministerialists used to wartime loyalism. In Sussex Huskisson found 'our yeomanry . . . no longer what they were ten years ago in their attachment to old Tory interests and principles which are prevalent in the Nobility & Gentry' and he held the 'low periodical press' mainly responsible for the decline. The tightening grip of agricultural depression and the ebbing of wartime patriotism were also contributing to the revival of the traditional distrust of government among the gentry and freeholders. Yet the ministry could still rally its support when the régime was perceived to be under threat. In 1819 a heightened feeling for parliamentary reform in the manufacturing districts collided with the truculence of the local magistracy. The 'Manchester Massacre' or 'Peterloo' in mid-August was not planned by government, but ministers had no hesitation in backing the magistrates who had precipitated the violence. The opportunity to make capital out of Whig criticisms of magistrates and ministers was too tempting. Parliament was recalled early (itself a way of mobilizing opinion among the propertied), the Six Acts of future legend were hurried into law and the Whig Fitzwilliam, a public critic of the episode, was dismissed as Lord Lieutenant of the West Riding. Though Sidmouth, ever preoccupied with the 'struggle between those who have property and those who have none', complained of the lukewarmness of colleagues towards his measures, most ministerial and parliamentary opinion was solid. Once again a crisis of order had rallied the country gentlemen, many of them magistrates themselves, and there was little objection, despite previous calls for retrenchment, to a temporary increase in the military establishment. The Commons had taken its lead from the warnings in the Speech from the Throne that 'a spirit is now fully manifested, utterly hostile to the Constitution of this Kingdom', and government had found itself strengthened. Whatever posterity was to make of Peterloo, that was the real lesson of 1819.

The Toryism of Normalcy

A transformation of the tone and practice of government in the early 1820s used to be assumed by the textbooks. The aftermath of the Queen Caroline affair in 1820, when government found itself out of touch with prevailing opinion, was supposed to have seen the transformation of the policies of Castlereagh and Sidmouth into the 'liberal Toryism' of coming men like Canning, Robinson, Peel and Huskisson. Certainly 1820 was traumatic for the ministry. Its early months uncovered the Cato Street conspiracy, a stark confirmation of fears about plot and sedition, while the year's end saw the metropolis controlled by the military and the ministry on the defensive even in the House of Lords. The problems of George IV and his consort had become a reminder of government's need to respect the 'rational' opinion that made itself felt in Parliament. Certain ministers were willing to seize the lesson. There was also a significant reconstruction of the ministry in 1821–23. Sidmouth's retirement and Castlereagh's suicide brought Peel and Canning into the leading positions in the Commons and they were soon joined in the Cabinet by Robinson and Huskisson. The buying-in of the Grenvilles, conservative Whig in stance, gave the government a more liberal slant in religious matters and Wellesley, appointed to Ireland in 1822, was the first 'Catholic' Lord Lieutenant since Grenville's ministry of 1806–7.

But the liberalization of the ministry was on a restricted front. Two of the fastest rising figures, Wellington and Peel, were 'Protestants' and stood towards the tough and distinctively Tory end of the spectrum of opinion that supported Liverpool. Peel, MP for Oxford University from 1817, was the Church's most prestigious champion in the Commons; Wellington emerged as a trenchant critic of what he saw as a disturbingly liberal trend in Canning's conduct of foreign policy. Neither the ministry as a whole nor its wider support renounced the credentials established in the years before 1820. Though a more tranquil Britain gave little cause for further repression, Ireland tested the resolve of government to deal with disorder and agitation. Until 1828 O'Connell and his Catholic Association felt the hard edge of Tory government which still stood for toughness in dealing with threats to the constitution and social order. Whigs were still accused of weakness and equivocation in these matters. Indeed something of the Tory attitudes towards the post-Waterloo troubles survived down into the period of Chartism.

Nor were the perceptions of ministerialists by their opponents transformed rapidly during the 1820s. Whigs still distrusted them as custodians of constitutional liberties and found little that was liberal in their continuing defence of the constitution in Church and State. Radical opinion, particularly its lower-class component, shared this view with an added bitterness after the experience of repression and prosecution. Exaggerated though Shelley's picture of bloodstained power in *The Masque of Anarchy* (1819) was, it represented the currency of radical opinion. Nor, despite government's concessions to demands for retrenchment of expenditure and the efforts of certain ministers, including Liverpool, to purify the practices of government in matters of place and patronage, did the ministry shed the image of Old Corruption. The impact of the radical John Wade's *Black Book*, a compendium of places and pensions first published in 1820 and reissued in 1831, suggested that reformist opinion still doubted the disinterestedness of the nation's rulers.[10] The determination of the Whigs and their allies to press a substantial measure of parliamentary reform in 1831–32 was fuelled by a conviction that there were better ways of governing than those practised by their opponents over the preceding decades. Whatever 'liberalism' Liverpool's last years provided had not

---

[10] W. D. Rubinstein, 'The End of "Old Corruption" in Britain 1780–1860', *Past & Present*, 101, 1983, suggests that doubts about Tory distinterestedness were justified.

transformed the older images of Tory rule. By corollary the fierce resistance of most Tories to reform reflected their continuing distrust of popular opinion and their fear of the antagonism which they had stored up for themselves.

The early 1820s thus witnessed a change of style and presentation rather than of fundamental purpose. Nearly all those prominent in the reshuffled ministry had held office earlier; there was no sharp break in the continuity of personnel. Liverpool, who had insisted on Canning's succession to Castlereagh and who encouraged the 'liberal' trend in economic policy, was himself an arch-survivor of administrations stretching back to the 1790s. There was no sharp change in his view of the purposes of government, though he had a keen appreciation of changing tactical possibilities. The real change was in the circumstances as more settled and expansionary economic conditions arrived in the early 1820s. Discontent and agitation ebbed and pressures on government eased. In Britain at least repression was no longer required and government to this extent appeared to be more liberal. The need now was to maintain and consolidate support within the recognized political nation, above all within Parliament itself, rather than to resist external pressures. Though it was scarcely the normalcy understood before 1789, it was nonetheless, except in Ireland, a return to a style of rational, responsive government after years of desperate survival. A reactive conservatism was replacing that of reaction. The cultivation of respectable opinion had never been neglected, but now opinion could no longer be swayed so easily by appeals to patriotism or by the manipulation of crises of order. After the shock of 1820 when the ministry, acting at George IV's behest, had found itself not only at odds with radical opinion but also out of touch with the greater part of the propertied and respectable, ministers began to believe that that 'public opinion' which could not be ignored required a modicum of common-sense modernity from government. Canning in foreign policy and Peel by criminal law reform advertised their adaptive qualities to a wider audience than their own party faithful. Furthermore instincts for constructive amendment which had been overlaid for years by crisis management began to reassert themselves and the pragmatic, improving administrators within the government began to influence its actions.

The overriding purpose in constitutional and social matters, however, remained conservative. Though Liverpool and his colleagues had agreed to leave Catholic Emancipation an 'open question', even 'Catholic' ministerialists remained resolutely hostile to any substantial parliamentary reform. Even when they disagreed on some of its essentials, the constitution remained the framework within which they operated and the cause which they defended. An element of 'liberalism' was not incompatible with this stance. Though never disowning their record in suppressing disorder and sedition, ministers preferred a more conventional style of constitutional government. Most of them understood that some flexibility was necessary in handling the diverse problems of the three countries and they preferred the maintenance of political order by natural means – the practical and moral influence of landowners and others of property and position in their own localities while central government provided example and exhortation – rather than by the direct operation of a centralized bureaucracy and military. The difficulties with the backbench gentry in the post-Waterloo

Commons was a reminder of the tether on which a parliamentary constitution kept the executive. Government could not take the tolerance of even its regular supporters for granted. Ministers understood the limitations of their position. For all his authoritarian image, Castlereagh in his dealings with continental autocracies recognized, as the Leader of the Commons was bound to do, the political and constitutional restrictions on Britain's executive. Sidmouth's complaints about the coolness of colleagues towards repression and the indifference of the magistracy at large to his circular were revealing comments upon prevailing attitudes even in the difficult days of 1817. Liverpool was clear that government could not develop in a 'continental' direction.[11] Indeed constitutional tradition could be bent to the government's purposes. The ministry found advantage in presenting itself as a non-partisan and high-minded executive serving King and country in a disinterested and conciliatory fashion. Such was the pitch of the pamphlet *The State of the Nation* issued in 1822 when ministers were irritated by press criticism and worried about the mood of the gentry. Described by *The Times* as 'a sort of manifesto ... well understood to emanate from authority', the work asserted the government's integrity and sincerity in pursuing the 'public good' and called for

> such a spirit of concurrent effort between the people and their governors, as to give manners the effect and authority of laws, and ... bring into disuse any statutes, if such there be, required in more turbulent times to repress public disorders.

Significantly the term 'party' was not used except in the derogatory sense of faction. Nor was the ministry labelled Tory. The omission may have been partly deference to the newly recruited Grenvilles but it also suggested that an appropriation of national consensus might serve the government's purposes and leave their Whig opponents tarred with the brush of a crude and self-interested partisanship. A decent and responsible conservatism without too strong an admixture of divisive Toryism might be the best way to keep the Whigs firmly in opposition.[12]

The cultivation of opinion inevitably involved the press. Tories railed often against the evils of the radical press and sometimes they anathematized the press as a whole, but in practice ministerialists sought to harness the medium's potential. Relations with sections of the metropolitan press had been normal for eighteenth-century governments and ministries from the 1790s had developed the links so far as the amenability of owners and editors and the availability of secret service money had permitted. Even without such manipulation the conservative reaction found ready representation both from newly established journals and from papers captured from the Whig opposition. The most important of the latter was the *Courier* which served as the main mouthpiece of government from 1807 to 1830. Government sought to hit its enemies in the press while encouraging its friends. Its answer was not a blanket censorship or licensing of the press

[11] He had written of Wellington in 1822 that 'he is rather *more continental* than we either are or ought to be *permanently*. I say permanently, because from circumstance we were brought into a course which was quite right at the time, but to which (with our different prejudices and form of Govt.) we never could expect to adhere indefinitely.'

[12] See the chapter on *The State of the Nation* in N. Gash, *Pillars of Government* (1986), pp. 26–42.

but a combination of campaigns of selective prosecution of the more subversive publications in times of political tension with increases in the stamp duties designed to price newspapers beyond the means of the lower classes.[13] The success of the first tactic was limited by the independence of juries, particularly in London. The second was much more effective and illustrated the distinction made between respectable opinion to be courted and lower-class opinion to be restricted. Here policy was shaped by Tory conceptions of the constitution and of legitimate influence within it. (It also illustrated government's assumption that the more prosperous were its natural supporters.) As late as the early 1820s the London press was fairly evenly divided between the ministry and its opponents. Even in 1820 the weekly *John Bull* established by the Tory polemicist Theodore Hook to counter the radical press on its own ground quickly built a circulation of 9000. This degree of support was not, however, to survive the disintegration of the conservative consensus during the rest of the decade. Perhaps an even greater problem for the future was the fast-growing provincial press, less easily courted by government and now developing a clear liberal predominance. The impact of this vehicle for the many varieties of liberal reformism produced by the commercial and industrial centres of the provinces was already becoming apparent during the 1820s.

As we have seen, newspapers were not the only element in the efforts of ministerialists to influence a wider opinion. The *Quarterly Review*, established in 1809 to counter the Whiggish progressivism of the *Edinburgh Review*, flew the Tory flag among the literati. *Blackwood's Edinburgh Magazine* articulated an even more trenchant High Toryism monthly from 1824 and reminded contemporaries of the strength of Scottish conservatism. All levels of social and intellectual opinion felt the impact of loyalist conservatism. The lower classes, however, were a special target. The nervousness felt about their loyalty and contentment directed attention to their instruction. Loyalist movements from the 1790s had promoted the distribution of tracts, pamphlets and other propaganda to 'the poor', many of the works giving a strong moral and religious flavour to their exhortations to contentment and submission. The Church of England began to organize itself for the better instruction of the lower orders. The National Society for Educating the Poor (1811) and the Church Building Society (1818) encouraged and assisted the wealthy and influential to build schools and churches in their localities. Though some Tories questioned the wisdom of any education of the lower classes, opinion was moving in favour of pre-emptive instruction of a suitably safe kind which would guard them against subornment by radicals and 'revolutionists'. To leave the field to enemies would simply enable them to 'unsettle the minds of thousands in their confidence in the grand foundation of the British Constitution'.[14] Initiatives to control mass opinion usually coincided with phases of political tension and thus threats to order helped to establish an apparatus of conservative pressure and persuasion throughout society.

---

[13] Not all the campaigns were official. During the Queen Caroline proceedings in 1820 a Constitutional Association was established with the support of 40 peers and bishops to curb the 'licentiousness' of the press by promoting prosecutions for seditious libel. For the question of the press see A. Aspinall, *Politics and the Press c. 1780–1850* (1949).
[14] The phrase of a critic of the capital's 'licentious' Sunday press in 1811.

Commons and Catholics

The opinion which mattered most to ministers was within Parliament, above all within the Commons. So long as the Crown continued its confidence, the ministry was vulnerable only in the House. A great deal of nervous energy was expended on parliamentary management. After 1801 governments were never secure from reverses in the Commons and there were times when the disintegration or lukewarmness of their support boded ill. In such moments the stature and quality of the front bench could sway minds and votes and Perceval, Castlereagh and Canning all provided leadership of a wide appeal, though the long-serving whip William Holmes established a reputation for implacable endeavour. But survival was a matter of measures as well as men, particularly in the troubled sessions after 1815 when the discontents of the economy unsettled the backbenches, when ministers no longer personified national survival during war and when Castlereagh had little effective support from his Commons colleagues. The stock of the Whig opposition revived and the gentry became more inclined to exercise their independence at the expense of ministers and their measures. Peacetime Toryism promised to present more problems of management than its wartime equivalent had done latterly. Ministers suffered a series of defeats, some disguised as tactical retreats, on issues like the income tax (abolished in 1816 despite the Treasury), the civil list, the military establishments and retrenchment of expenditure. Yet the ministry, now alert to Commons opinion, bent to its wind, avoided defeats on matters of confidence and used the opportunities afforded by crises of order in 1817 and 1819 to consolidate its position. Even in the darkest moments of 1820 the greatest threat to the government's survival came from the restlessness and irritation of a beleaguered King convinced that his ministers had failed him. Yet the lesson left by Queen Caroline was that government had over-extended itself in deference to the King's wishes and that even a ministry with royal favour could not take the opinion of Parliament and political nation for granted. Tory government needed to be more than just the King's servants.

The term 'public opinion' which gained currency in the years around 1820 referred to feeling 'out of doors' as well as within Parliament. Yet it was still the opinion of a political nation which, though constantly broadened by economic change, was predominantly propertied, educated, respectable and conservative in social and constitutional matters. Governments needed to understand and cultivate this opinion, particularly as it found expression in Parliament much more effectively than caricatures of the unreformed system used to assume. Political management was inevitably more a matter of pragmatic adjustment, of judging the prevailing mood and assessing the balance of interests, than of clarion assertions of narrowly Tory principle, important though principle remained to many of the government's supporters. In its last years Liverpool's government moved towards an administrative, even dispassionate style that played down the nervous, aggressive Toryism of its previous phase. It looked to appease centrist opinion rather than simply its own zealots. Here was the wartime sense of a non-partisan national purpose being applied to the different problems of peacetime as rival interests began to assert themselves. Inevitably leadership of this kind blurred its own image and one result of the attempts to cultivate responsible, centrist opinion through the 1820s was the growing disaffection of fundamentalists whom contemporaries labelled as 'Ultras'. As the cement provided by war and subversion weakened, the fissures widened within the broad conservative coalition that Liverpool had inherited and consolidated. Over foreign policy, over agricultural fortunes, over Ireland and ecclesiastical policy – over 'Cash, Corn and Catholics', as a biographer of Peel put it later – government found itself stumbling and its supporters divided.

Once British society reached calmer waters after 1821, the maintenance of order in Ireland was perhaps the best issue for government to rally a conservative consensus. Goulburn's Act of 1825 suppressed O'Connell's Catholic Association with the support of most sections of parliamentary opinion. But Catholic Emancipation divided ministers, as it had done since Pitt and Castlereagh promised it in 1800. Centrist opinion within Parliament was drifting towards the 'religious liberty' which the Whigs had long supported and within the ministry itself the view that the government of Ireland would benefit from the conciliation of respectable Catholic opinion was gaining ground. Burdett's Emancipation Bill of 1825 highlighted Tory divisions. Though unacceptable to the established churches and to diehard constitutionalists, the measure passed through the Commons comfortably and had to be vetoed in the Lords where the Duke of York, heir to the throne, led the resistance. In a ministerial crisis Peel, the only 'Protestant' among the Commons Cabinet ministers, offered his resignation and Liverpool himself was determined to resign at one point. But the general election of 1826 showed British opinion to be predominantly hostile to Emancipation still. Though Ireland moved the opposite way, there were some 'Protestant' gains of seats in Britain and Palmerston, the Secretary-at-War, was opposed in his Cambridge University seat for his support of Catholic claims. The issue contributed to the split in the leadership after Liverpool's stroke in 1827 and to the creation of a coalition between the Canningite Tories and a section of the Whigs. But the question survived the experiment in coalition and added to the tensions within the Tory government reunited under Wellington in 1828, his Cabinet initially containing seven 'Catholics' to six 'Protestants'. The continuing success of emancipationist candidates in by-elections was convincing some members of the Ascendency interest that a package deal which traded Emancipation for the disfranchisement of the 40s freeholders would improve an increasingly unstable Irish situation. Wellington had been of this mind, privately, since 1825. But, when O'Connell's election for County Clare brought matters to a head in 1828–29, a spate of foundations of Orange Lodges and Brunswick Clubs across Britain and Ireland showed the determination of Tory Protestantism to resist not only O'Connell but also its own government. In the heat and bitterness of the moment, as the government pushed its Emancipation measure through Parliament despite the opposition of some 200 MPs and over 100 peers and despite the presentation of over 2000 petitions against the bill, Wellington had to dismiss his Attorney-General, outface the King and his brother Cumberland, fight a duel with an Ultra peer and press a state prosecution of the ultra-Protestant *Morning Journal*, normally a friend of government, for seditious libel of ministers. Peel, Leader in the Commons and more resolutely anti-Catholic than Wellington, submitted himself for re-election for Oxford University, only to be defeated by the Church's new champion, Sir Robert Inglis.[15] The gulf between ministers, pragmatic in their responses and concerned to minimize the damage to the authority of government when change became inevitable, and their principled and passionate support in the country was never better illustrated. Zealots for the Church were not the only ones to see 1829 as a betrayal. Although the ministry lingered until late 1830, Emancipation heralded the effective end of the long Tory dominance of national politics.

The Management of Change

For some thirty years down to the early 1820s governments had been preoccupied above all with problems of defence. Their overriding purpose had been to prevent radical change or upheaval in an established order apparently beleaguered by enemies. By the mid-1820s the problem, even for a ministry fundamentally conservative, had become how best to manage and accommodate change rather than simply resist it. British society was changing rapidly and in many different ways – growing in population and in the size and number of its cities, transforming its economic base as old industries declined or modernized and new ones arose, recovering from the strains and distortions of prolonged war, suffering from the instabilities of the trade cycle, the financial system and food prices. In these circumstances political practice had to be different from what might have been feasible in a static or more stable society. Change was harder to counter, at least in the long term, when its causes were natural and unavoidable. The danger arose not from war or subversion, specific challenges which government could meet by resolute action, but from trends in society and economy which were scarcely within government's power to halt, let alone reverse. As the ground shifted beneath them, responsible and intelligent men were forced to make tactical, even strategic, decisions about what was indispensible and what was not. Even the constitution itself might have to be appraised in this way. Certain sacrifices might become necessary in order to safeguard the rest, just as Wellington decided that Catholic Emancipation had to be conceded for the sake of stable government in Ireland. Inevitably the sometime government of resistance began to seem to many of its supporters like a ministry of trimmers at best, of traitors at worst. The Toryism hardened by years of crisis did not easily understand the more flexible, tactically-minded conservatism that changed circumstances dictated. The political nation, furthermore, required a government to look in control of itself and of the problems of the moment. By the late 1820s Tory governments could hardly sustain this image. It was significant that the century's second quarter would see three governing majorities, each apparently secure for a long tenure of office, founder on the problems of the times. A series of

---

[15] The Emancipation Act disfranchised the 40s freeholders in Ireland. The drift towards religious liberalism had produced the repeal of the Test and Corporation Acts as they affected Protestant Dissenters in 1828, a relatively uncontroversial measure. The outcry of 1829, however, showed that majority opinion in Britain was less liberally inclined towards Catholics. Even most Wesleyan Methodist opinion opposed Emancipation, despite the support the leading Wesleyan Tory, Jabez Bunting, gave to the measure.

party reconstructions would bear testimony to the strains to which national development was subjecting party politics.

The Tory leadership of the 1820s was composed of highly experienced administrators imbued with the executive mentality natural to men who had spent most of their political lives in or near high office. They saw with the eyes of national government and they tended to despise the sectionalism of their own partisans.[16] Around their banners had gathered men much less inclined to sacrifice self-interest or high principle to the dictates of what ministers regarded as expediency or inevitability. Though few denied the importance of both interest and principle to the Tory connexion and to the stability of government, the question was how far they should dictate or circumscribe the practice of governments responsible for mediating the conflicts of a fast-changing society – or rather, to give Ireland its weight, of two changing societies not entirely compatible. The backwoods gentry of the old 'country party'; the agricultural lobby; the clergy of the established churches; Irish landowners fearful for their estates and social influence; the business plutocracy anxious for social stability and for the representation of their interests; and that broad swathe of middle opinion which demanded firm and effective government at home and abroad combined with rigorous retrenchment which restricted government's means to secure those ends: all made demands on government more insistently than they had done before or during the French wars. Many of the demands were irrational or illegitimate in the eyes of ministers. Some were just incompatible with others. However sensitive government wished to be to 'public opinion', it soon found that it was not monolithic but badly divided and sometimes self-contradictory. As the artificial unity imposed by war, Jacobinism and crises of order faded, even basically conservative interests began to pull in different directions. The redress of one grievance might simply create others. The agricultural lobby could hardly be placated without alarming City financiers, mercantile interests and urban food consumers. The Church of England could hardly be given what it considered to be its due without antagonizing Nonconformists, the religiously indifferent and perhaps taxpayers and ratepayers too. Catholic Emancipation became necessary to conciliate respectable Catholic opinion in Ireland and to secure the Ascendancy interest, but it triggered a backlash elsewhere. Even parliamentary reform, long the *bête noire* of virtually all Tories, was beginning to divide conservative opinion between potential gainers and potential losers.

The general line of policy under Liverpool was clear. The ministry remained committed to a firm and principled defence of the social and political order in Britain and Ireland, the maintenance of the Union, the defence of the established churches, the maintenance of the constitution against radical change and the support of the rights and influence of property. So far it was a stance suitably negative and 'Tory'. But from a combination of choice and necessity the government also pursued retrenchment of expenditure, financial stability, a reappraisal of import

---

[16] 'Catholic' Tories tended to be more scathing. Palmerston complained of 'the stupid old Tory party who bawl out the memory and praise of Pitt while they are opposing all the measures and principles which he held most important'; Canning was contemptuous of the 'bumpkins' of the agricultural interest.

duties and prohibitions, some improvement of central administration, the encouragement of trade and industry (as commercial depression so evidently fuelled political agitation) and a prudent degree of agricultural protection. In total it was an intelligent, commonsense conservatism which sought to work with the grain of the times and it was probably broadly acceptable to the majority of the political nation. In detail, though, certain issues were highly controversial. Religious and economic questions in particular did not lend themselves to consensus politics of the kind Liverpool sought. His vision of a more-or-less impartial government acting as the broker between contending interests ('It is the duty of Government and of Parliament to hold the balance between all the great interests of the country, as even as possible,' he told the Lords in 1822) entailed a constant balancing act and risked the discontent of most of the contending interests. It also entailed friction over policy which fed into the increasingly bitter personal rivalries within the ministry after Canning's assumption of the Commons leadership in 1822. The crisis of 1825 showed that Tory government was more likely to be destabilized from within than toppled by assault from without.

Matters came to a head with Liverpool's stroke in 1827 and the King's commission to Canning to form a ministry. Canning and Peel had given the ministry a powerful Commons front bench since 1822, but Canning, despite his Pittite pedigree and Liverpool's personal support, did not integrate easily into the collective leadership. His tactlessness over the Catholic question and a policy as Foreign Secretary which men like Wellington saw as reckless and unprincipled support for liberal, if not revolutionary, régimes abroad made him more Tory enemies than Whig ones. He seemed to be playing to the gallery of liberal and urban opinion which many Tories continued to fear.[17] It was also a matter of personality. Croker noted his 'character for intrigue and insincerity which will expose whatever he does to peculiar suspicion'. As early as 1824 he had been suspected of intriguing with the Whigs in anticipation of Liverpool's retirement and his egocentricity and evident ambition made colleagues resentful of the influence he enjoyed over the premier and even, in time, over his former foe, George IV. Now his advancement to the premiership was too much for Peel, Wellington and a substantial body of Tory opinion. The old ministry split down the middle and Canning recouped his losses by bringing in a group of moderate Whigs around Lansdowne, Devonshire and Tierney. The success and direction of this centrist coalition were still uncertain when Canning died. His successor Goderich (Frederick Robin-son, Liverpool's Chancellor of the Exchequer) had little stomach for the battles ahead and resigned early in 1828 to make way for a restored Tory administration headed by Wellington with Peel leading in the Commons.

Governmental stability, however, had not been restored. The coalition episode had left bitterness between the Canningites and the Tory loyalists – some of the Ultras had attempted to have the former excluded altogether from the new ministry – and personal relations between Wellington and the leading Canningites, Huskisson and Palmerston, were strained. Within

---

[17] Canning's sensitivity to mercantile interests and opinion, heightened by his experience as MP for Liverpool 1812–22, influenced his policy towards constitutional movements in Spain and Portugal and towards the post-colonial régimes in South America.

a few months most of the former coalitionists had resigned, leaving the government short of votes in the Commons and weak in the political centre ground. Early in 1828 Peel had drawn a significant distinction: the objective was 'to re-unite the old Party which was in existence when Lord Liverpool's calamity befell him' and he feared for the prospects of the government 'without more assistance than the mere Tory Party, as it is called, would afford me'. Now the ministry was in this exposed position in the Commons. No longer a broad enough coalition of conservative interests and opinion to command the political centre, it was beginning to look narrowly sectarian. The reconstruction after the Canningite defection had left it heavily packed with Wellington's former military subordinates as well as light in debating power in the Commons. The militaristic and authoritarian image which opponents sought to foist upon the government, comparing it with Polignac's in France, seemed to be confirmed by Peel's creation of the Metropolitan Police in 1829. The force, much criticized as a para-military body directly responsible to the Home Office and replacing the former civilian and locally-controlled forces, only added to the already intense unpopularity of the ministry with the larger part of metropolitan opinion.[18] The balance of opinion in the London press had swung strongly against the government and now matched that of most of the provincial cities.

Initially the administration had seemed to promise a firmness, particularly on Ireland, which conservative opinion welcomed, but it was soon to falter on three issues which presented it with difficult, perhaps intractable, choices and helped to erode its support. One was the state of agriculture and particularly the question of protection against imports. For some time a gulf had been opening on the issue between ministers and a significant part of their natural support in the Commons and in the agricultural constituencies. The 1815 Corn Law had not saved agriculture from sharp falls in prices and within a few years the discontents of the freeholders and tenant farmers were being heard in the Commons and through the Central Agricultural Association formed by the Bristol solicitor and grazier George Webb Hall.[19] In 1821–22 ministers found themselves harassed by a ginger-group of backbench gentry nicknamed the 'Boodle's Cabinet' (after a club) and a confrontation between the agricultural lobby and the official line, powerfully reinforced by the economist Ricardo, was played out in a Commons Select Committee. The sliding scale which modified the Corn Law in 1822 was a technical change that satisfied few, though in some years to follow higher prices took the edge off the discontents of the farmers and their friends. Ministers anxious for political stability and mindful of the severe disturbances the original Corn Law had provoked in London knew

---

[18] The unpopularity was increased by the additional expense of the new and wholly professional force and by the imposition of compulsory rates to finance it upon the metropolitan parishes. Radicals inevitably condemned this new taxation without representation.

[19] On Hall and his Association (full title The Legal and Constitutional Association of Agriculturists, for the Protection of the Rights and Interests of Agriculture in the United Kingdom) see T. L. Crosby, *English Farmers and the Politics of Protection 1815–1852* (Hassocks, 1977), pp. 29–43. The support for the county associations came from the small gentry, freeholders, tenant farmers and rural tradesmen rather than the larger landowners.

that the claims of depressed agriculture were not easily reconciled with the interests of urban consumers or, indeed, of manufacturing and commerce. Liverpool's assertion of the government's duty to hold the balance between 'all the great interests of the country' had come in a Lords debate on agricultural distress in 1822 and he had added, 'The agricultural is not the only interest in Great Britain. It is not even the most numerous.' Liverpool, Huskisson and Robinson were inching towards a liberalized trade policy which would enhance opportunities for industry and commerce and ensure lower and stabler food prices for consumers while maintaining some degree of agricultural protection. Both political prudence and the influential free-market economic theory represented by Ricardo encouraged this approach.

As agricultural depression continued through the 1820s and poor rates and social tension increased in rural areas, the loyalty of agrarian opinion to a Tory establishment apparently indifferent to its problems inevitably weakened. Government's financial and currency policies rankled too. Agricultural debts incurred through over-investment in marginal production during wartime years of high prices had now to be repaid or serviced in times of price deflation. Many agriculturalists, taking their lead from the Birmingham banker Thomas Attwood, criticized the ministry's return to gold payments under Peel's Act of 1819 and saw its austere deflationary policy as geared to the interests of fundholders and City financiers rather than those of agriculture. Nor were demands for relief from the burden of taxation on agriculture welcome to ministers, financiers and economists anxious for balanced budgets. Battles with the agricultural lobby scarred several ministers, Peel and Huskisson among them, and, as the bucolic radical Cobbett exploited the discontents of the agricultural constituencies, the county members in the Commons and their electorates became restive. Wellington's ministry was to feel the impact of the erosion of this crucial political base.

Ironically Wellington was one of the Tory leaders who had sympathy with the agricultural interests and there was enough division within his Cabinet to leave government policy in some uncertainty. The sliding scale was modified in 1828 but the experience was a bruising one for ministers and the ill-will generated within the Cabinet contributed to the later resignation of the Canningites, now led by Huskisson, the *bête noire* of the agriculturalists. Yet the latter were not mollified and after the 1830 general election the government found itself able to rely on only 28 of the 80 English county members. Agriculture was an issue on which government, aware of the pressures in both the counties and the cities, had faced both ways. As Melbourne's Whigs and Peel's Conservatives were to learn later, it was impossible to please both agriculturalists and urban consumers. Wellington had found that the issue had not only divided his government but also weakened the bonds of sentiment that tied the gentry and freeholders to it and so reduced its electoral base. The Whig opportunity of the early 1830s owed a good deal to the impact of agricultural depression on the counties.

The second issue was Catholic Emancipation which, as we have seen, divided the Tory leadership while the question was alive and divided their followers in the country and in Parliament even more when it was settled in 1829. Inevitably, given the ministry's initial image of firmness, the concession appeared as a surrender of a central part of the constitution to unconstitutional agitation and as a betrayal of the established churches and of Protestantism to Catholic enemies. Triumphs for O'Connell were not the purpose for which men supported Wellington and Peel in office. The ministry retained the support of Tories who recognized arguments based on necessity and on the interests of Irish government, but it had already in 1828 lost the support of the former Canningites, the convinced 'Catholics' of Liverpool's years. In the event Emancipation conciliated almost nobody and antagonized many. Though brave talk of replacing Wellington with a 'Protestant' premier such as the Duke of Cumberland came to nothing, the government had alienated many of the Tory right to whom it needed to look for solid support. The episode also convinced some Tories that a Commons which passed Catholic Emancipation against the force of British opinion warranted a reform which would give public opinion more weight and reduce the influence of the executive.[20] High Tory defectors helped to defeat Wellington in November 1830 and a small group of them, headed by the Duke of Richmond in the Cabinet, took office in Grey's largely Whig ministry committed to parliamentary reform.

Electoral reform itself had not been as prominent an issue as Catholics for most of the decade and virtually all Tories of any significance had been hostile to any major initiative on the question. The mode in which members of the Commons were selected was one of the most sensitive points of the constitution and even Tories who doubted the total sanctity of existing constitutional arrangements feared an extension of popular influence in Parliament and of the weight given to numbers against property. The opposition to reform was also backed by substantial interests with a stake in the existing system and with voices in the House – borough patrons, borough corporations, the East and West India companies. A few Tories, concerned by the increasing contrast between representation in the Commons and the distribution of wealth and property in the country, had toyed with the idea of a limited and pre-emptive reform to settle an issue which might otherwise come to damage government. Better that Tories should control and limit the process of change themselves than leave it to the less tender mercies of Whigs and radicals. Castlereagh and Liverpool had accepted the principle of the disfranchisement of grossly corrupt boroughs and the transfer of their seats in 1819. Grampound's loss of its seats to Yorkshire in 1822 began what some ministers hoped would be a gradual and piecemeal amendment of the representation. But when Penrhyn and East Retford faced a similar fate in 1828, it was clear that the approach had hit problems. Ministers and their supporters were divided over the choice of the recipients of any seats for reallocation and over the choice of franchise qualification if they went to new boroughs. The Tory majority in the Lords was more hostile to even modest reform than the Commons was and particularly to transfer of seats to large unrepresented towns like Manchester, Birmingham and Leeds. Cabinet squabbles on the issue were the occasion of the Canningite secession in the spring and contributed to the perpetuation of a Tory image as entrenched opponents of moderate change. This stance not only alienated powerful forces in the cities and industrial areas which stood to gain from reform but also alarmed the more

---

[20] The element of Tory support for reform is discussed by D. C. Moore, 'The other face of Reform', *Victorian Studies*, V, 1961–62.

pragmatic aristocratic parliamentarians who saw how much property and influence were being excluded from representation and believed that prudent conservatives should remedy the deficiency.

Another factor was the unsettlement of the country gentlemen and of opinion in their constituencies with prolonged agricultural depression and with government's unresponsiveness to their grievances. Perhaps a reformed House including, inevitably, extra seats for the counties would add to their leverage. When Grampound was being put down, Liverpool had been disconcerted by 'the idle conceit of the Country Gentlemen that a temperate Reform would put an end to grievances and distress'. Catholic Emancipation further weakened the front against electoral reform. It not only convinced a small but important group of Tories that the existing House was not worth defending but also, by settling a most divisive issue, removed a bar to co-operation between disenchanted Tories and the Whig opposition. Here now was scope for an alliance of Whigs and centrist or 'independent' Tories, of the large boroughs and the counties, against a Tory government, bolstered by Old Corruption, which had become insensitive to the opinions of too many men of property and position.

The End of Tory Rule

1830 brought the death of George IV and the accession of William IV,[21] the consequent general election and the deposition of the Bourbons in France. Wellington's ministry, unable to rely on either the former Canningites or the Ultra element smarting over Emancipation, was precariously placed. Unless it could recruit further support, it would remain vulnerable to shifts of parliamentary opinion and to any failings of its own political management. Despite the new King's professed confidence the ministry failed to strengthen itself in the elections – the first time this had happened – and the opposition even made a small net gain of seats. Neither the revolution in France (in fact an installation of a more liberal and constitutionalist monarchy) nor the 'Swing' riots among the agricultural labourers of southern England towards the year's end provoked the sharp reaction of opinion which Wellington needed and which perceived crises of order had formerly achieved. Meanwhile the personal antipathy between Wellington and the former Canningites had given little chance of Tory reunion either before or after Huskisson's death in September. As a commercial depression revived demands for parliamentary reform in the industrial regions and as centrists urged the government to signal its commitment to a moderate measure of reform, Wellington, seeing the Ultras as his most likely game and believing that revived radicalism and agitation would again rally the aristocracy and gentry around the constitution, gave free rein to his own instinct that 'Beginning reform was beginning revolution'. In any case the government could hardly turn its coat again while the wounds of Catholic Emancipation were fresh. In the

---

[21] As Duke of Clarence William had been more Whiggish than his brothers York and Cumberland and he had supported Emancipation in 1829. His accession was widely regarded as the end of any royal veto on Whig participation in government and particularly on Grey, whom George IV had detested. This change of circumstances certainly revived Grey's ambition and it also encouraged floating Tories to consider coalition with the Whigs.

Lords on 2 November Wellington opted for conviction politics reassuring to the Tory right rather than compromise with centrists and Whigs. The bravado of his declaration that the 'excellence' of the contitution was beyond improvement and possessed the 'full and entire confidence of the country' dismayed his Commons colleagues, provoked a surge of pro-reform feeling, particularly in the cities, and failed to prevent a revolt by Ultra MPs led by Sir Edward Knatchbull, a survivor from the 'Boodle's Cabinet', which brought the government's defeat on a Civil List motion in mid-November. It was the end of nearly forty years of almost continuous administration by 'the friends of good order', in Croker's phrase, and the start of more than fifty years in which Conservative governments with Commons majorities held office only twice.

The end of Tory rule was occasioned by a tactical situation which Wellington's distaste for compromise and bargaining made him ill-equipped to handle. He settled for principle when his government and party badly needed a politician. Yet the fall was also the consummation of the drift of events over the previous decade. Traditional explanations have suggested that prevailing opinion had become too liberal for a Tory style of government. But Wellington was put out by the Ultras as much as anybody and the response to Catholic Emancipation and other Irish developments from British opinion had not been particularly liberal. Over the Corn Laws and the wider question of agricultural grievances it was the division of interest and sentiment which beggared governments, not an overwhelmingly 'liberal' mood. The truth was that the broad consensus which conservative opinion had achieved during and after the 1790s had disintegrated during fifteen years of peace. No longer so frightened by 'revolutionists' at home and abroad, the propertied and powerful had resumed the cultivation of their own interests, ambitions and opinions. Major interests projected their rivalries onto the public scene and intensified the factionalism of aristocratic parliamentarians. Forces which might have produced alternative forms of cohesion, such as strong central party organization (not yet arrived) or the former scale of executive patronage and influence (atrophied after decades of 'economical reform'), were not available to compensate for the weakening of the solidarities of sentiment and interest.

The defenders of the constitution had not been overwhelmed by an enemy without – even Catholic Emancipation did not fit that analysis entirely – but rather divisions within the broad spectrum of conservative opinion had emerged as the old loyalism and constitutionalism became less relevant. It was not the radicalism of the Whigs which recommended them as an alternative government by 1830 but their restored acceptability as part of a legitimate governing élite. Centrist (and even some Tory) opinion could now accommodate Whigs where once it had seen little choice but to support a hardline constitutionalism. Nor had the failing of the ministry of 1828–30 been, except at the last gasp, its rigidity in the face of liberal demands. It had lost support on its Ultra wing as well as towards the political centre. Despite this narrowing of its base, Toryism had become both confused and blurred. What now was the nature of the conservatism which a Wellington ministry offered? Was it Catholic Emancipation or Protestantism? Was it freer trade and lower food prices or the protection of agriculture? Was it resistance and coercion in Ireland or conciliation and concession? Was it principle or expediency, the last ditch or an intelligent anticipation of the inevitable? And who were its true representatives: Wellington and Peel, or Eldon, Cumberland, Londonderry and Inglis, or Huskisson, Goderich and Palmerston, or Knatchbull and Richmond? All had claims to Tory legitimacy and the 'friends of good order' enjoyed a dangerous luxury of options.

If principle and leadership had become matters of uncertainty and contention, so had conservatism's appropriate form of political practice. The outright rejection of change, the challenge to would-be reformers which Wellington threw down in November 1830, now faced the competition of alternative approaches. Perhaps good conservatives should bend with the wind and respect opinion and prudence, as the ministry itself had done over the Corn Laws and the Test and Corporation Acts in 1828 and over Ireland and Catholics in 1829. Was it true that reform was the road to revolution or, as conservative Whigs and a growing number of Tories argued, that the failure to undertake pre-emptive reform in good time might ensure revolution? At issue were the tactics and strategies of conservatism. Peel's distinction between 'the old party' of Liverpool's time and 'the mere Tory party' showed how circumstances could alter tactical perceptions. But even intelligent conservatives did not all think the same way. Conservatism was undergoing a fragmentation widely experienced by political ideas and modes of understanding in this period. If Toryism felt its impact early and more acutely than its rivals, it was because Tories held office and bore the brunt of the problems and pressures of the day.

This was not simply the triumph of 'public opinion' over an *ancien régime* too decayed to defend itself. By 1830 the constitution was already in a process of amendment which indeed owed something to new forces within society at large but which owed some of its momentum to the dynamics of traditional politics. The basically conservative forces of property and respectability had not fused into a monolithic interest under the lead of the aristocracy, as Burke had once hoped. Instead their natural divisions and rivalries were being intensified by changing circumstances, divergent interests and differing appreciations of political strategy. Arguably what they required was sensitive brokerage from a point closer to the political centre than Wellington stationed himself in November 1830. What he offered then was only one variant of the styles of conservatism currently on offer within parliamentary politics. Even his own ministry might conceivably have offered a different approach.[22] Other survivors from among the near-professional administrators of Liverpool's ministry were ready to offer their own alternatives too. Intelligent men with much to lose were putting their minds to the means of survival in a changing and difficult world.

---

[22] Wellington had begun to suspect that Peel's instincts were not entirely his own and that the Commons leader had a taste for a more adaptive and flexible style of conservatism. In 1828 the Duke had predicted that 'whenever the RC Question is out of the way he will be very troublesome; and out-libertize the most Liberal'.

3

The Aristocratic Constitution and its Friends: The Party of Peel and Derby

The Reform Bill episode was both a disaster for the Tory or 'Conservative' opposition (the latter word was creeping into use during the months of crisis) and a springboard for recovery. Inevitably the first aspect was the one immediately apparent. The reform issue humbled the former party of government and handed the Whigs what promised to be a long lease on office.

Reform and Disaster

The events of late 1830 had seemed to leave opportunities for the new opposition. Grey's ministry was an uneasy coalition, even its Whig members being undecided on the details of parliamentary reform. It lacked a firm majority in the Commons and the anticipated reform proposals seemed likely to bring it down. But though the Reform Bill of March 1831 shocked many by its sweeping character, the King continued to support his ministers and soon the opposition's divisions and front-bench weakness in the Commons became apparent. Once out of office Peel had refused to lead his party further, insisting he would 'be his own unfettered man'. The lead against the bill was provided by Inglis, Peel's erstwhile Oxford opponent, and soon a medley of gentry were vying for influence and position. Among them Vyvyan, though opposing the Whig bill, insisted that a measure of some kind was necessary and so distanced himself from Wellington's stand on his line of the previous November. Other apostasies made Croker confide to his diary that 'when I see some of the steadiest old country gentlemen ratting over to Reform, I am alarmed'. With opinion in the country moving the ministry's way, the crucial division on 22 March went 302–301 for the bill. Reinforced by the return of most of the dissident Ultras to the colours, the Tories now looked to amendments to delay and cripple the bill, but when the government found itself beaten on a crucial division in May Grey persuaded the King to dissolve parliament less than a year from the previous general election.

This time the result effectively smashed Tory resistance in the Commons. Now only six of the 80 English county members could be relied on and the party had been pushed back upon the small boroughs. Of the 187 Tory members for England 165 sat for boroughs scheduled to lose one or both members under the Bill. On 6 July the modified bill was carried 367–231. Now the Tory opposition could only hope to tack on provisions of an apparently liberal tendency but of potential benefit to themselves. Such an amendment, intended to bolster the agricultural interest and known after one of its movers, Chandos, extended the county franchise to categories of large tenant farmers.

But soon the arena was the Upper House. Immune from elections (though not from Whig patronage) it continued to show an anti-reform majority, though a smaller one than previous occasions might have suggested. A division in early October produced a majority against the bill of 41 including 21 bishops. Though a Tory triumph of a kind, particularly for Wellington who had worked to keep his support together, the consequences were hardly reassuring. Outbreaks of mob violence in several cities, most dramatically in Nottingham and Bristol, showed the intensity of the mass support that had built up for reform. The hostility displayed towards the Church caused some bishops and leading laymen to repent of their votes, interests in the City became nervous about disruptions of trade and runs on gold, and the Tory peers began to divide between outright resisters and 'Waverers', among them the Archbishop of Canterbury, who supported a search by Harrowby and Wharncliffe for a compromise with the Whigs. Fears for social order if the crisis continued (the ministry had issued a proclamation against the arming of the reform unions in late November) persuaded Grey to press on with a third bill that made modest concessions on detail. It passed easily through the Commons where the Tories were now in disarray, many arguing that the small boroughs now had to be sacrificed, others joining Inglis, Peel and Croker in opposing to the end. In the Lords enough Tories either switched votes or abstained, the bishops being conspicuous in both respects, for the bill to pass its second reading but in early May the regular Tory majority inflicted a delaying amendment on the government. When William declined to give a promise to create enough peers to see the bill through, the ministry resigned and a disorganized attempt followed to form a Tory administration. It was now accepted that even the Tories would have to pass a measure of some kind, Wellington was adjudged unsuitable to head such a ministry, Peel declined to serve and a projected Cabinet headed by the Speaker subsided in embarrassment in the Commons even before it could declare itself. Much more was needed to instal a Tory ministry than the King's favour. The Whigs returned, armed with the King's promise, and enough Tories abstained to ensure that a mass creation of peers was unnecessary. The Reform Act became law on 7 June 1832.

Many Tories saw its provisions as sheer partisan malice. Wellington doubted whether 'the Ministers had any object in view, excepting the legitimate one to party men of keeping their rivals the Tories out of power *for ever*'. With the electorate increased by some two-thirds, about one-seventh of the adult male population now possessed the parliamentary franchise. In the boroughs the main qualification was the £10 household, a franchise which was mainly, though not uniformly middle-class, and which was expected to be less susceptible to traditional forms of influence than the previous ones. Most of the nomination boroughs from which recent Tory governments had benefited had lost one or both of their seats. Now the scope for the 'making' of a House in the old way and for the effective exercise of royal discretion in the choice of a ministry was gone. The 'party of the Crown', already attenuated by decades of 'economical reform', was no more. Henceforth government would be exposed more directly to the influence of opinion in the Commons and among the electorate. Of 73 new borough seats, 63 of them in England, most had been allocated to the large towns which Tories had so distrusted and to which they could now look for little gratitude. Parliamentary weight had been shifted sharply away from southern England to the industrial North and Midlands where feeling for reform had been so strong. London, where Tory governments had become so unpopular, gained ten seats. No-one doubted that urban and industrial interests would be better represented in the new Commons. For trading interests the impact was more equivocal, for the old chartered companies, notably the East and West India companies, had depended on the nomination boroughs for most of their influence in the Commons. These interests, so close to recent Tory ministries, were never again to be of such political weight. Even the increase of over 60 in the English county seats could not, in the circumstances of 1832, be seen as an asset to the opposition. The best Tories could hope then was that they would strengthen the 'independent' element in the Commons.

The implications of the changes for the relative weight of classes and economic interests had been the subject of much speculation. 'The field of coal would beat the field of barley', Alexander Baring had warned in 1831: '... the country squires would not be able to stand against the active, pushing, intelligent people who would be sent from the manufacturing districts.' Two years later Wellington gave class analysis an even more threatening dimension:

> The revolution is made ... power is transferred from one class of society, the gentlemen of England, professing the faith of the Church of England, to another class of society, the shopkeepers, being dissenters from the Church, many of them Socinians, others atheists.

Few doubted that aristocracy and Church had suffered and were likely to suffer more.

The first test of the new electoral system was even more devastating than the last of the old. The election of December 1832, the third in less than three years and hotly contested by former standards, returned some 480 Reformers and only some 180 at most for the Tory opposition, a result that would remain the nadir of the party's nineteenth-century electoral fortunes. The English counties, after years of agricultural depression under Tory governments and with the tenant farmers grateful for their enfranchisement, returned only 42 Tories among their 144 members. Again the opposition was heavily dependant on the smaller boroughs, an extra motive, if one were needed, for resistance to further reform.

There was more to the problem than the election returns. The events of 1831–32 had been a seismic shock to traditional assumptions and inevitably were regarded by many as a portent. At critical points the extent and force of popular agitation, much of it organized, had helped to sweep aside the defences of the constitution as Tories had conceived of it. The installation of an anti-reform ministry might well have precipitated something like insurrection.[1] The King and the Lords had been compelled to bend to the will of a government backed by a decided Commons majority, by an unequivocal general election result and by mass support in the country. The old tenet that one of the hallmarks of government was its readiness and capacity to resist 'clamour' had, it seemed, ceased to hold. The relationship between Parliament and public opinion seemed to have changed too. Instead of the old emphasis on 'men, not measures', one general election had been fought on a major issue of constitutional change and another had seen an unprecedented degree of pledging of candidates to further reforms. If the House of 1830 had seemed to Croker to carry 'the seeds of the most troublesome and unmanageable Parliament since that of 1640', what might be anticipated from the Commons assembled in January 1833?

To some extent the fears of Tories were the prisoners of their own rhetoric during the Reform crisis. Croker had warned Walter Scott of the consequences of 'the revolutionary Reform':

> No King, no Lords, no inequalities in the social system, all will be levelled to the plane of the petty shopkeepers and small farmers; this, perhaps, not without bloodshed, but certainly by confiscations and persecutions.[2]

Wellington too was convinced that the months of agitation, 'the general state of disorganization and contempt of all authority', would mean 'that at last we shall have a revolution gradually accomplished by due form of law'. Barriers to radical change were not easily found. Even the county constituencies, traditionally seen as the bulwark of the constitution, leaned the Reform way and seemed to be nurturing trouble for the Church. Croker feared that 'the question of *tithe* will unite them all, small farmers and great gentlemen, in the common assault upon the whole social system'. Eldon had depicted parliamentary reform itself as an assault on property in the form of the small boroughs and so opening the door to further confiscation. Even men less rigid than Eldon and less of Jeremiahs than Croker had similar fears. Arbuthnot, who had criticized the defeatists on his own side, saw the 1833 Irish Church Temporalities Bill ('the Church Robbery Bill') in this light: 'if one species of property is attacked, no other species can be secure'. Yet a Tory alternative to the Whig government was not in sight – 'the party appears for the present to be broken up'.

Yet a Conservative government with a secure Commons majority was to take office only nine years after the Reform Act. Why were the pessimists confounded? Part of the answer lay in the return to comparative normalcy after the high excitement of 1831–32. Reform had been aided by a pitch of popular emotion which simply could not be sustained on other issues. The low level of contests in the 1835 general election would show how far traditional influences and practices had been resumed. The reformed

---

[1] Despite a writer in *Blackwood's* in 1831 who had fancied settling the issue by force ('war by land and war by sea . . . there will be a bit of a dust in Manchester and it will be laid in blood'), few Tories had relished the prospect of civil war. They had, however, demanded that mob violence and illegality should be dealt with rigorously.

[2] Croker refused on principle to stand for the reformed House. Ironically he had been a strong advocate of gradualist reform of the representation in the 1820s.

system still offered considerable scope for the arts and influences of the old dispensation; in certain respects it may even have enhanced it.[3] The increase in the county seats offered scope for aristocratic reaction (as well as agricultural protectionism) to change the balance of the Commons. The tenancy qualifications which had been added to the old 40s freeholder franchise, the source of much of the 'independence' of the counties, had enhanced the influence of landlords, though also, events were to show, that of the farmers. Even without protectionism, aristocratic reaction, when it came, was bound to take a Tory turn. Old forms of borough politics had survived too. Though the indefensible cases had been excised, a large number of small boroughs remained. Some had had surrounding rural areas added in 1832 to justify the retention of seats and most were subject to some degree of influence from patrons, landlords and employers. Many small boroughs were largely agricultural in character and in boroughs of all sizes the surviving voters on the pre-1832 franchises tended to be predominantly Tory. There was also the influence which money could bring to bear. The Eatanswill element of beer, bribery and bovver has sometimes been exaggerated in accounts of this period, but it undoubtedly existed and it was an aspect which the Tory side, usually well blessed with both money and electoral experience, was equipped to exploit. Mid-century observers were agreed that the lowest (and most corruptible) classes of voters were an asset to the Tories in most constituencies.

The larger boroughs, however, particularly the newly represented ones, were less amenable to Tory influence and the majority of the seats continued to go to the Reformers down to 1841. Here frightened gentry and protectionist farmers were in short supply. In many cities the radical mood survived the Reform Bill to press for further changes, notably in religious matters, and soon the causes of further electoral reform and of opposition to agricultural protection were gaining support. Though the middling and large boroughs provided a few Conservative gains in 1841, mostly in the ports and cathedral cities, their main contribution to the Tory cause was as frightening warnings of what might happen if Whig ministries were forced further down the road of reform by their radical allies. Though there were urban Tories aplenty, notably among Churchmen and the well-heeled bourgeoisie, the generality of the large boroughs contributed little to the Tory revival beyond confirming its demonology.[4]

The Whigs had done a fair job of replacing the jumble of influences and anomalies within the unreformed system with a more uniform and rational arrangement that bore some relationship to the current distribution of wealth and property, though with a considerable weighting to great property in practice. The confusion and expedients of 1831–32 had, in the

---

[3] In one of his jeremiads about revolution Wellington had admitted, incongruously, that 'the influence of property' had not been diminished: 'the gentry have as many followers and influence as many voters at elections as they ever did'. In Ireland the 1829 suppression of the 40s freehold franchise had not been reversed in 1832.

[4] On the whole the £10 householder proved to be a tamer beast than Tories had feared. As £10 was the minimum qualification, the bulk of new borough electors were above that level. Only in some of the larger boroughs did this franchise admit many working-men, mainly artisans, to the parliamentary vote. An occupational qualification of this kind came to seem vastly safer than a democratic one. Property had not succumbed entirely to numbers.

event, married old and new with some success. Grey's claims for the conservative effect of his endeavours were to be justified in the long term. Yet, as propertied opinion began to stir uneasily, to become nervous of further radical and Irish demands and to harden its responses to continuing agitation, it became clear that the reformers had prepared the ground not merely for a future stability but also for a Tory revival more immediately.

The Conservatives were fortunate to enjoy the opportunities of three general elections within less than nine years of the assembly of the first reformed Parliament. The first one was precipitated by the King. The virtual dismissal of Melbourne's ministry in November 1834 and the installation of a minority Tory administration was a calculated putsch by William whose antipathy to Whig policy towards the Irish church had overcome his caution. The experience of office under Peel and the gains made in the election of January 1835 pulled the Tories back together and helped to re-establish them as a powerful, concerted opposition and as a potential government. The election caused by William's death in 1837 increased their seats further. Victoria's accession, however, meant that royal influence now aided the Whigs (disconcertingly for Tories who still saw themselves as in some special sense the party of the Crown) and opposed an additional obstacle to the recapture of office until the electoral tide of 1841 swept it away. In this twilight decade for its political rôle the Crown, though humiliated in 1832, 1835 and 1841, continued to play an active part which left its mark on party politics until Victoria withdrew from public partisanship after 1841. The Tories, as the party of constitutional defence, had benefited from the prerogative's exercise at a crucial moment in 1834 and the subsequent hostility of the Queen could inflict only limited damage now that the Crown could not 'make' a Commons in the old way. The weakness of executive influence by former standards now worked for the Tories in opposition and against the Whigs in office. Without the greater and more rapid impact which shifts of national opinion now had on the Commons, despite the colour of Crown and Treasury, the Tory revival would have been less swift and sure.

The Crown was not the only institution of state to operate as a bulwark of the constitution and of Tory influence in the aftermath of Reform. The House of Lords, though bloodied in 1832, remained unbowed. Its powers over legislation remained unscathed and it had suffered no large-scale creation of Reform peers. Even Tories who distrusted the inflamed truculence of the Ultra peers saw the Upper House as the main brake upon Whig legislation while the opposition continued in near-impotence in the Commons. The defence of the Lords' prerogative was confirmed among the fundamental principles and interests of Toryism. But the opposition peers lacked cohesion and agreement over strategy. Though Wellington remained widely acknowledged as Tory leader, his authority in his own House had been damaged by both Catholic Emancipation and the Reform débâcle. A body of Ultra peers promoted Lyndhurst as an alternative leader and engaged in ruthless sabotage of Whig measures both to protect threatened interests and to undermine the government itself.[5] A policy of

---

[5] The leading Ultras included the dukes of Cumberland, Buckingham and Newcastle, the marquis of Londonderry and the earls of Falmouth and Winchelsea.

sustained and intemperate confrontation with the King's ministers ran counter to Wellington's instincts and to constitutional tradition; it also risked the replacement of the governments of Grey and Melbourne with more radical, rather than with Tory, successors. Responsible Tories feared another political crisis on the lines of 1831–32 and preferred a respectable and discriminating course of opposition which would not deter conservative Whigs from moving their way. The King's commission to Wellington to form a ministry in November 1834 came opportunely. The few months of office under Peel and the increased numbers of Tory MPs strengthened Wellington's position in the Lords and ensured that the future course of opposition was better controlled, though there were still times when the Tory peers, who enjoyed a majority of some 130 over the Whigs, were the despair of the party leaders. The Upper House remained a formidable engine of constitutional defence and of Tory obstruction and politicking, its enthusiasm for rejecting or amending Whig measures now encouraged by the evidence of reviving Tory feeling in the country. Though there was less obstructiveness after 1837, when Cumberland departed for Hanover and the Whig majority in the Commons became too slender for major legislative initiatives, the Lords moved only gradually towards their mid-Victorian somnolence.

A picture confined to the relentless progress of a reviving Toryism would hardly do justice to the creativity and achievement of the ministries of Grey and Melbourne. Only from about 1839 did the government's fortunes sink so low that it depended on the Crown's support to sustain it. Paradoxically Whig success contributed to their opponents' revival by establishing a new settlement around which a conservative consensus among aristocratic politicians could form. The Whigs had produced at least temporary answers to major questions which otherwise might have embarrassed Tory politicians, among them reform of the established churches in England and Ireland, civil registration and Dissenters' marriages, an initiative in popular education and reforms of tithes, municipal corporations and the poor law. Though some of these measures antagonized certain interests, the redress of the grievances of other sections of opinion made the country an easier one for future ministries to govern. The Whigs had done something to give the 'aristocratic settlement' embodied in the constitution a more contemporary and decent face and to re-establish the conditions for political stability which Peel and Palmerston were to exploit later. It was significant how little of the Whig legacy the Tories attempted to reverse or amend after 1841. But Whig rule had still generated controversy and alarm. Much of what they accomplished or attempted damaged or threatened established interests and they had political bedfellows who kept good Tories (and some moderate Whigs) perennially alarmed. On few questions was the drift of Whig policy entirely reassuring to intelligent conservatives, let alone zealous Tories. Whigs who had once claimed credit for constructive conservatism now appeared frequently to be making indiscriminate concessions to pressure from radicals in Britain and Ireland. O'Connell remained a bugbear of much British opinion and from around 1837, as commercial depression returned, the appearance of Chartism and the Anti-Corn Law League added to the fears of conservatives. The nervousness of established interests throughout this unsettled decade was the greatest asset of the Tories.

One element of consensus between the parties remained central. From the early days of the first reformed Parliament the front benches and the mass of their respective followers took their stand on 'finality', an idea which was no invention of John Russell's in 1837 or even of the 'Tamworth Manifesto'. The word had entered the parliamentary vocabulary in late January 1833 as Whigs guaranteed no further parliamentary reform and Tories no attempt to repeal or amend the Reform Act. This agreement, itself a tribute to the Act, provided the common ground of high politics until the early 1850s. Representation had been placed outside serious controversy between the aristocratic parties and so, as the scars of 1832 healed, it was possible for restructuring at the centre of the political spectrum to occur and for moderate Reformers to cross to the Conservative side. Peel, an unyielding opponent of the Reform Bill, was to emerge within a few years as the most effective manipulator of the new consensus underpinning aristocratic politics.

Conservative Revival

From the opening of the reformed Parliament in 1833 perceptive Tories had been watching for signs of schism within the Reform coalition. The wealthy baronet Burdett, former darling of the Westminster radicals, gave them early encouragement. In February Hardinge was predicting an eventual alliance between Peel and Stanley, one of the more conservative Whigs in the Cabinet and a likely leader of a secession. The hints of incipient reaction were not confined to aristocratic parliamentarians. The City's Guildhall dinner in November received ministers with chilly silence but Wellington's name with acclamation. Though godly and nervous Tories were appalled by the government's Irish Church Temporalities Bill which proposed appropriation of the Church's 'surplus' revenues for unspecified purposes, hope and consolation came with the resignation of four of the Cabinet in May 1834, Stanley, Graham and Ripon (Goderich) among them.[6] After first Grey (succeeded by Melbourne) and then Althorp had retired, the King seized the opportunity to pronounce the ministry dissolved and to install a Tory administration headed temporarily by Wellington and then by Peel.

The subsequent general election of January 1835, with its much lower level of contests showing the ebbing of political excitement since 1832, produced Tory gains of nearly 100 seats, most coming from the counties and the small boroughs. Royal favour, Treasury patronage and Whig divisions had furthered a Tory revival already perceptible. But the Whigs, aided by O'Connell's Irish members, retained a majority and returned to office in April on humiliating terms for William after Peel's ministry had been battered by repeated defeats in the Commons. In December Peel's 'Tamworth Manifesto' had established his government's platform for the

---

[6] The measure suppressed redundant parishes and merged superfluous bishoprics in Ireland, but the appropriation clause (147) was the greatest provocation. Of the four resigners, three were to be in Peel's Cabinet in 1841. The fourth, Richmond, would emerge as the figurehead of the agricultural lobby in the early 1840s.

forthcoming elections.[7] Assertions of the finality of the Reform Act were accompanied by avowals of readiness to remedy proven grievances and to support moderate reform within the limits of the constitution. Like *The State of the Nation* more than twelve years earlier the Manifesto was issued by a government, not by a party. Indeed party was mentioned only once and then with disapprobation. It was a bid for the conservative centre ground, for a consensus embracing both aristocratic and bourgeois property and for the support of Stanley, Graham and their friends (dubbed the 'Derby Dilly' by O'Connell). Peel failed to bring the Dilly into coalition either before or after the election but he had distanced his ministry from the cruder kind of partisanship, from the irresponsibility towards the needs of government which the Ultras had shown and from the inflexibility Wellington had displayed in 1830. The Conservative party – the new name emphasized the aim of political and social stability and facilitated the recruitment of disaffected Reformers – was re-establishing itself as a party of government and as the trustee of the constitution and social order.[8]

Peel's Hundred Days and the more even balance within the Commons had a dramatic impact on both parties. Discipline tightened and, as the Stanleyites and the bulk of the Irish party were absorbed, divisions in the Commons and contests in the constituencies conformed to a much clearer two-party confrontation. In the Commons only a handful of members could not be classified with one side or the other on the main issues.[9] Irish and religious issues, often closely connected, fed this polarization. The 'Lichfield House Compact', the deal between the Whigs and O'Connell's Irish which toppled Peel's ministry in 1835 and propped up Melbourne's government thereafter, was a godsend to the Whigs but also one to the Tories. Their charge that Melbourne and Russell were in hock to Irish Catholics and that O'Connell pulled the strings of government appeared to be confirmed. Even after the suppression of the Orange Order anti-Catholic feeling continued to be a major factor in the Tory revival, although frontbenchers tried to restrain its more virulent manifestations.[10] The confrontation was intensified by the evident threat which a reviving and disciplined Tory party posed to the Whig hold on office. A Tory majority in the Commons no longer seemed impossible and in Peel the party had found a credible, indeed impressive, candidate for first minister. Once the short tenure of office in 1834–35 had established him as indisputable leader, his administrative capacity and strategic skill, his ability to speak a language that appealed to propertied opinion, non-aristocratic as well as patrician, made him a figure around whom old Tories and new Conservatives could rally. The old doubts and frictions, the old scores of

---

[7] Peel described his strategy to Croker in January: 'our main hope must be in the adhesion of moderate men not professing adherence to our politics' and 'Remember Stanley's position, and that he will subscribe himself a Whig'. The same considerations encouraged the use of the name 'Conservative' in place of 'Tory'.

[8] Three major London papers, among them *The Times*, the leading daily, and the *Morning Herald*, deserted the Whigs and moved towards the Tories in 1834–35.

[9] See D. Close, 'The formation of a two-party alignment in the House of Commons 1832–41', *English Historical Review*, 84, 1969.

[10] The Whigs suppressed the Order by statute in 1836 following allegations of an Orange plot to put Cumberland, the Order's Grand Master, on the throne in place of Victoria.

1829, were forgotten for the moment. For Peel and for his party together ambition and self-confidence revived.

The leadership continued to woo centrist opinion and to exploit the splits in the ranks of the Reformers. The Lords, now more responsive to Wellington's guidance, passed legislation of a bi-partisan character (for example for tithe commutation, Dissenters' marriages and the creation of a permanent Ecclesiastical Commission) while rejecting or modifying more contentious measures that hit at established interests. Appropriation of ecclesiastical property in Ireland and the ending of church rates in England were steps that the Upper House resisted. Indeed the Church of England, nervous of its fate after 1832, now found itself shielded by the Tory revival. On the Municipal Corporations Bill of 1835 the Tory peers reluctantly compromised, eventually accepting the Commons leadership's view that the measure must pass but, by incorporating a provision for nominated aldermen, diluting the ratepayer democracy that would elect the town councils. The Act, which established a wider municipal franchise than the parliamentary one of 1832, was a grievous blow to Tory interests. The old corporations, narrowly based and overwhelmingly Tory in character, were swept away and their influence in parliamentary elections with them. Reformers dominated nearly all the new councils and many towns experienced their first Dissenting mayors. But the medicine had to be swallowed. The Stanleyites had committed themselves to reform of the corporations and the Tamworth Manifesto had gone some way towards their position. If, in the language of that document, Conservatives were to prevent 'a perpetual vortex of agitation' and assert instead 'the respect for ancient rights, and the deference to prescriptive authority', they had to concentrate their resources on institutions and interests more defensible than the corporation oligarchies. In the event even municipal politics were not to be immune to Conservative enthusiasm, rhetoric and organization. Within a few years municipal victories were bearing witness to the party's revival, though the small boroughs provided more Tory successes than the large cities.

The 1837 election which followed Victoria's accession produced another net gain for the Conservatives, though not on the scale of 1835. The English counties continued their swing, so that the seats, evenly balanced in 1835, now went two-thirds to the Tories, but the party's performance was more chequered in the boroughs where some revival of radical feeling made itself felt. The Church interest, alarmed by many aspects of Whig policy, worked powerfully for the Conservatives. The popularity of the new Queen and her known commitment to the Whigs may have worked the other way. With Stanley and Graham now joining Peel on their front bench, the opposition was able to exploit the opportunities which even a much-whipped and well-disciplined Commons allowed them. The ministry's perennial problems with budgets and colonies were supplemented by the almost parallel rise of the Anti-Corn Law League and Chartism, both fuelled by the commercial depression which arrived in 1837. The renewed radical pressures produced strains within the ministry and policy shifts on the ballot and agricultural protection. The growing prominence of the latter question as the League intensified its activity added to the fears of the gentry, freeholders and tenant farmers of the counties and bent the Tory opposition to a more explicitly protectionist line. Chandos, who had refused to serve in 1834 because of differences over the malt tax, had long been playing the 'Farmers' Friend'; Peel and Graham, now the leader's confidant, were more circumspect but committed themselves, like most prominent figures in both Houses, to adequate protection for agriculture on the basis of the sliding scale.

Along with the surge of protectionist sentiment there came a reaction against an increase of disorder in Britain and in Ireland. Though firm against the Chartists in 1839, the Whigs were not firm enough for the opposition. In a Commons debate early in 1840 Tory critics hounded the government for their supposed encouragement of Chartist agitation and lawlessness – John Frost, the leader of the Newport rising, had been appointed a magistrate by the Whigs – and for their softness towards O'Connell's movement for the repeal of the Union. Peel alleged

> that this country is now convulsed with political disorder, that a spirit of insubordination is spreading far and wide, nay, that rebellion and insurrection are rearing their heads. . . . Instead of being a control over evil passions, and a check upon unruly acts, you make the Government and the magistracy the actual fomentors of disaffection and insubordination.

Pressing the charge that Whig government was now increasing instability rather than counteracting it, Graham directed an appeal to 'all men on that [Whig] side of the House, who were bound to prevent dangerous changes, and who were anxious to preserve to property its influence and security . . .' The party of order was demanding its chance again.

Victoria's truculence (the 'Bedchamber Crisis') helped to prevent the formation of a Conservative ministry in 1839 after the government had been defeated on a colonial issue in the Commons. Peel may have felt that a minority ministry was both risky and premature. The many Tories avid for office had to restrain their impatience. Seeking to repair a crumbling position Melbourne dissolved in the summer of 1841 and, aided by an assertive display of royal support, fought on the platform of a fixed duty on grain imports in place of the sliding scale. The decisive majority returned for the Conservatives made royal confidence a minor issue. Ironically it was this triumph of the Tories, the more monarchical of the parties, that persuaded the Court to avoid the dangers of further public partisanship.

The victory of 1841 was based primarily on the English counties and small boroughs. Despite the confidence which Peel had laboured to inspire in business and financial circles – the Tories won two of the four City of London seats – it was the alarm of the landowning classes, of the Church of England and of protectionist agriculturalists that brought the great majority of the 368 seats. Of the 144 English county seats, of which the Whigs had won 102 in 1832, 124 now fell to the Conservatives.[11] The parties were about evenly balanced over the rest of the English seats, though most of the large boroughs had remained with the Whigs. The strength of the interests ranged behind the Conservatives, the effectiveness of their electoral organization, the talent and experience available to a Conservative Cabinet and Peel's personal standing, all these were beyond question. Even most Whigs seemed to accept the inevitability of Tory government with

---

[11] The party also made useful gains in Scotland and Ireland, though it still held a clear minority of the seats in both countries.

equanimity. Yet, in the moment of triumph for a party that had overcome its humiliation over parliamentary reform, Peel, newly installed as first minister, chose to make a unilateral and quite gratuitous declaration of independence. Turning to his own followers in the Commons, he warned them that

> no considerations of mere political support should induce me to hold such an office as that I fill by servile tenure, which would compel me to be the instrument of carrying other men's opinions into effect.

Government and Disintegration Again

The ministry of 1841–46 was a pivotal experience for the Conservative party. The cataclysm of its ending, though less shattering in its immediate electoral consequences, was to be even more decisive than that of 1831–32 for the party's prospects of office. Conventionally the episode has been seen as a triumph of constructive statesmanship and, more improbably, of liberal values, so that the central protagonist, Peel, appeared as a moral hero more readily to future Liberals than to Tories. But the fundamentally conservative objectives of the party and of the government it sustained should persuade us to see these years as the triumph of the 'friends of order' and of the authority of the state over radical challenges. The long industrial depression was weathered, social unrest contained, Chartism in its most dangerous phase put down and the Anti-Corn Law League trumped and outwitted. Yet it was a victory for conservatism rather than for Conservatism, for government rather than for party, for aristocratic centrism rather than for Tory partisanship. It stands as a reminder that the Tory party, under whatever name it fought, was only one variant of conservatism or, rather, was an uneasy coalition of a variety of the conservative interests and opinions current within British and Irish society. Its relationship to other interests within the political nation and to government itself remained ill-defined and uncertain.

Though among the most talented of the century, the ministry formed in 1841 was dominated to an unusual degree by its head. Peel, who had achieved a standing and indispensability perhaps unprecedented in an opposition leader, had a clear strategic vision and drove his ministry hard towards it. His formidable Commons presence and administrative capacity daunted many among both friends and foes, though he suffered from a degree of nervousness about social order unusual even among Tory politicians.[12] The experiences of 1828–32 seem to have convinced Peel that issues which jeopardized political and social order should be settled when opportunity offered. Letting sleeping dogs lie was too dangerous. Better to anticipate inevitable change, so that the terms of adjustment were controlled by the 'friends of order' rather than dictated to them by opponents. The danger was that Peel's tendency to see change as inevitable before his

---

[12] Twice, in 1831–32 and 1842, Peel fortified Drayton Manor and prepared to fight it out with anticipated insurgents from the lower classes of neighbouring industrial districts. His insistence that government must move rapidly to stabilize the constitution was clearly influenced by these fears for life, family and property. Wellington noted this element of 'panic' in Peel's responses in 1845–46.

followers did and to buy off opposition by more generous concession than circumstances absolutely required would meet the entrenched resistance of diehards within his own party and provoke vested interests powerful enough to undermine him.[13] His style of opposition in the late 1830s, when he had backtracked on some of the reform commitments of the Tamworth Manifesto, had entailed firm resistance to agitation and radicalism. In office, however, he soon seemed to be pursuing a policy of graduated concession to precisely those forces he had resisted before. By 1844 Disraeli in his novel *Coningsby* was able to mock 'sound Conservative government' of the kind Peel and his colleagues purveyed as 'Tory men and Whig measures'. Part of the problem was the pace of change that the ministry forced upon its supporters. In certain areas, notably finance and trade, their approach involved a vigorous resumption of the policy directions of Liverpool's ministers two decades earlier. But Peel was more of a driver than Liverpool had been, his Cabinet was more cohesive and disciplined (and so less representative of opinion in the lower reaches of the party) and events, particularly those of 1842, suggested the need for greater urgency than ministers had felt before 1827.

Financial stabilization was one of the priorities. In 1842 the income tax was revived, a bold though supposedly temporary move which ended the unbalanced budgets that had harassed Whig ministers. In 1844 the Bank Charter Act brought the banking system and note issue under tighter control. These victories for direct taxation and tight money harked back to the controversies of Liverpool's day when ministers had displayed similar preferences. Income tax facilitated moves, modest when taken singly but considerable in the mass, to liberalize trade by reducing tariffs and prohibitions, the aims being the lower domestic prices, freer trade and increased consumption which Peel regarded as crucial to both economic well-being and social stability. The measures of 1842 included a reduction of the protection the sliding scale gave to domestic grain producers, despite the resignation of Buckingham, the Cabinet's 'Farmers' Friend'. In the context of the long trade depression which climaxed in ugly fashion that year the message was clear: the good conservative should encourage trade revival and prosperity in order to take the wind out of the sails of radicalism and lower-class discontent. That was the way to secure the constitution, social order and the rights of property.

The ministry moved to secure law and order more directly too. Graham, continuing the Tory stance in opposition, was the most suspicious and repressive Home Secretary since Sidmouth. With none of the relaxed faith in 'the good sense and virtue of the people of England' professed by his Whig opponents, he viewed disturbance as virtually inevitable among the lower classes of the depressed industrial districts and so 'the law and civil rights must be upheld by power'. There was a whiff of Peterloo in the responses of Graham and of Wellington, the Commander-in-Chief, to the events of the summer of 1842 when government seemed to be facing what Melbourne called 'certainly very near, if not actually, a rebellion'. Graham exhorted magistrates to 'act with vigour and without parley' against mobs.

---

[13] In 1828 Croker had noted of Peel that 'it is the turn of his mind to get over adversaries by concession. He always gives more importance and weight even, to a public enemy than to his own supporters'.

Military commanders were rebuked or replaced for insufficient zeal, the commander of the Northern District being subordinated to a tough Tory general after he had advised magistrates to 'temporize with the people where they feel themselves quite unequal to enforce the law'. Though less militaristic than Wellington, Graham recommended the suppression of large public meetings regardless of their character and was astringent with the Commons when taxed on the niceties of magistrates' powers and on his authorization of the opening of private correspondence.[14]

Apart from this authoritarian tendency, the nervousness and distrust of mass (particularly lower-class) opinion was revealing of the government's instincts. Most Tories had no complaints over its performance on this score.

Initially Ireland produced a more complex pattern of response. Before 1841 the Tory mood had been strongly anti-Catholic and bitterly hostile to O'Connell's brand of radical patriotism. Indeed Peel, taunted in the House about the attitudes of other Tories, had needed to confirm his commitment to the Emancipation Act of 1829. Now in office he could hardly give his zealots all they wanted. Government in Ireland had to fight on too many fronts to risk antagonizing the Catholic bishops gratuitously. The government's own councils were divided. The Lord Lieutenant, De Grey, who identified with the Ascendancy interest and was hard for law and order, was balanced by the Chief Secretary, Eliot, who was more conciliatory towards Catholics and concerned to establish the administration's reputation for impartiality. The first phase of the ministry's policy was one of benign neglect, but by 1843 the growth and significance of O'Connell's Repeal movement could no longer be ignored. Pressed by Wellington, *The Times* and a body of Irish Protestant peers, the government moved to put down organized agitation and to strengthen military provision in Ireland. The Irish Chancellor, Sugden, dismissed pro-Repeal magistrates. O'Connell's great meeting planned for Clontarf in October was banned and he was arrested, convicted and imprisoned. At last the government had lived up to the hopes of some of its most committed supporters.

But Peel's prudent instinct was for conciliation alongside coercion and once De Grey had been succeeded by Heytesbury in May 1844 the Cabinet began to take initiatives to woo Catholic opinion. Peel argued

> the necessity of disuniting, by the legitimate means of a just, kind and conciliatory policy, the Roman Catholic body, and thus breaking up a sullen and formidable confederacy against British connection . . .

It could be done by 'weaning from the cause of Repeal the great body of wealthy and intelligent Roman Catholics'. A Charitable Bequests Act was passed in 1844 to make it easier for Catholic institutions to receive endowments, but an attempt at Irish franchise reform failed largely because of opposition from the Tory right. The report of a Commission appointed under the Earl of Devon to consider Irish land law led to the introduction of a Compensation to Tenants Bill in June 1845, but its provisions for compensation for unexpired improvements and the

---

[14] F. C. Mather, *Public Order in the Age of the Chartists* (Manchester, 1959), is the standard study of this aspect. He suggests that 'anti-Jacobin alarm' remained a factor in Tory responses. The ministry also started a campaign of prosecutions of 'blasphemous' publications in London.

appointment of a Commissioner of Improvements to oversee its operation and to maintain a register of estates led to such resistance in the Lords, backed by *The Times*, that Peel was forced to withdraw the measure. Once again the intractability of his party's right wing – in this case a body of hardline peers and Irish landlords in the Upper House – had shown itself on Irish issues. Even without an atmosphere poisoned by the Maynooth controversy, the tactical flexibility and political sensitivity that ministers believed they needed to govern Ireland were likely to hit the rocks of interest, emotion and 'principle' within their own party.

Maynooth was a Roman Catholic seminary that had long received a public grant. Peel's decision to make the grant much larger and permanent was intended to sweeten the Irish Catholic bishops whom he saw as the key to effective conciliation. But if the measure made sense for the government of Ireland, it made none in the contexts of British politics and of the Conservative party. Gladstone, with conscientious angularity, resigned from the Cabinet, petitions flooded in (from Dissenters as well as from the established churches) and the ministry found itself at odds with a large part of its own following. Peel's assurance to Croker that the opposition was mainly from Dissenters betrayed a profound insensitivity to British opinion in general and to that of his own party in particular. The anger of many Tory Churchmen was all the greater because the government had failed to give the Church of England the degree of support over church extension and factory education which they had expected. In the greatest revolt of the Parliament to date 149 Conservative MPs voted against the Maynooth grant and 148 for. The measure was passed with the aid of Whig votes. The betrayal of 1829 was on men's lips again. The National Club 'in support of the Protestant principles of the Constitution' and with eighteen Tory MPs on its committee was founded by a secession from the Carlton Club led by Winchelsea. Ashley headed a Protestant Association dedicated to the repeal of the Maynooth Act and in Ireland the Orange lodges revived. By March Graham felt that 'the country gentlemen cannot be more ready to give us the death-blow than we are to receive it' and the diarist Greville concluded that

> the Tory party has ceased to exist as a party; . . . Peel's unpopularity is at this moment so great and so general that there is no knowing where to find any interest friendly to him.

Maynooth showed the readiness of Peel, Graham and most of their colleagues to flout the sensitivities of their supporters in the interests of what they intended to be strong government and political stability. The same motives contributed to the final crisis over the Corn Laws. Peel had never viewed agricultural protection as a matter of absolute principle, but from 1838 onwards he had committed himself in public to the maintenance of a sliding scale of duties and his moves towards freer imports in 1842, 1843 and 1845 had been sweetened by assurances to his followers that these relaxations were the surest way to preserve protection itself. By 1843, however, he had probably decided on repeal of the Corn Laws at an opportune moment. The events of 1842 had suggested that high food prices during an industrial slump and mass unemployment were a threat to the constitution and to social order. By this time the Anti-Corn Law League was exerting pressure on the Whig leadership through propaganda and electoral organization and, through the rhetoric of Cobden, directing an impassioned assault against the aristocratic constitution itself. The Corn Laws had become a hostage to fortune. Peel and Graham were to argue that agriculture could flourish on increased urban consumption and on greater capital investment ('high farming' the phrase went) but their primary reasons for repeal were political rather than economic. The stability of the constitution, social order and security for great property were more important to them than the profitability of certain kinds of agriculture.[15] From the standpoint of a far-sighted conservatism, it made some sense; for certain major interests represented within the Conservative party it made little or none. Peel's seizure of the opportunity afforded by the Irish potato blight in late 1845 and by the challenge of Russell's Edinburgh Letter to announce not only the suspension of the Corn Laws but also the impossibility of re-imposing them seemed to much of his party to be yet another betrayal.

Even by 1841 the bulk of protectionist interest and sentiment had become concentrated on the Tory side. Though some Whig landowners favoured protection, the weight of urban opinion and pressure from the Anti-Corn Law League pushed the Whig Cabinet in 1841 into a commitment to replace the sliding scale with a small fixed duty. Protection was a major issue in many constituencies, particularly the English counties, in the general election and the decisiveness of the Conservative majority owed much to the alarm of the gentry, clergy, freeholders and tenant farmers at the Whig proposal.[16] Peel's subsequent steps towards freer importation revived the worries of the agriculturalists and caused a group of some sixty dissident MPs, knights of the shires prominent among them, to watch his course with suspicion and increasing hostility from the backbenches. In the country a movement to establish county agricultural protection associations culminated early in 1844 in the formation of the Central Agricultural Protection Society with Richmond as its president and an array of Tory peers and MPs in support. This time protectionism commanded prestigious and influential patronage of the kind that had eluded George Webb Hall earlier. Here, ready to hand, was the instrument of resistance to the party leadership.

The Corn Law crisis, like that of Maynooth, was shaped by Peel's personality and purpose. That he eventually lost only one senior minister, Stanley, despite the lack of enthusiasm for repeal among many of his colleagues, spoke volumes for his dominance of the 'official corps'. But his relations were much less close with the greater part of his party. He believed that he was serving the interests of the gentry by protecting them in a dangerous and changing world, but he had little respect for their intelligence, opinions or policy preferences. A quintessential ministerialist, he had spent most of his political life on the front benches, either in office

---

[15] After discussions with Peel in December 1845 the Prince Consort summarized his purpose as 'to remove the contest entirely from the dangerous ground upon which it has got – that of a war between the manufacturers, the hungry and the poor against the landed proprietors, the aristocracy, which can only end in the ruin of the latter'.

[16] The Anglican clergy had a substantial stake in agricultural fortunes through their leasing out of glebe land and through tithes which the 1836 Tithe Commutation Act had pegged to the average level of corn prices.

or in opposition, and he lacked much experience of genuinely representative politics. (Oxford University had been the nearest thing to it.) He despised and feared populist politics and had a touch of the conviction, common among old Tories, that good government sometimes had to be unpopular, at least temporarily. He had little more patience with 'clamour' from the county electorates and from the 'country party' in the Commons than he did with that of O'Connellites, radicals and Chartists. Socially too Peel did not fit easily into the familiar categories of Tory politics. The Peels had never been ordinary squires; they had moved straight from the industrial plutocracy to landed magnate status. For the mere gentry, the most significant force in the counties and on the Tory side of the House, Peel had little feeling. Formidably wealthy, formidably intelligent, formidably experienced in office, he felt something like contempt for the backwoodsmen on the benches behind him, men of great 'principle' and pretension whom he saw as ignorant, bigoted, narrowly self-interested and blind both to the dictates of office and to their own long-term security. Seeing his immediate followers this way, he could not bring himself

> to be the tool of a party – that is to say, to adopt the opinions of men who have not access to your knowledge, and could not profit by it if they had, who spend their time in eating and drinking, and hunting, shooting, gambling, horse-racing, and so forth . . .

He could turn and hector such men just as easily as he spoke for them.[17] Peel was also a good hater. He had clashed with Orangemen in Ireland and with the 'Protestants' among his own followers, most spectacularly in 1829; over two decades he had tangled with the agricultural lobby over issues like the currency and the malt tax. He was not inclined to let enemies off lightly.

Behind these aspects of personality and background there were more fundamental disagreements over both the function of the party and the nature of conservative strategy. The Conservatives found themselves in a novel position. No longer the 'party of the Crown' to the extent Liverpool's followers had been, the party had won its way into office through long endeavours in opposition and by the verdict of the electorate (or rather, given the low level of contests in 1841, by the verdict of the dominant interests within the electoral system) against the influence and personal preference of the monarch. The organization and loyalties of the party, hardened by the experience of opposition, had filled the vacuum left by the decline of Crown and Treasury influence. Here were the means by which Commons majorities could be delivered and government could be carried on. But was party to be anything more than disciplined support for the Queen's ministers? How far should a party determine the direction of the ministry it sustained? Constitutional theory gave a negative answer to these questions; as yet political case-law hardly gave another. Peel and his colleagues had developed no new theory of the relationship between party and government. Though subsequently labelled 'the first modern party leader', Peel preferred to speak in the name of government rather than that of party, as he had done in the Tamworth Manifesto. He recognized

---

[17] The almost comic priggishness and arrogance shown here (in a letter to Hardinge in 1846) were characteristic of Peel's comments on the Tory squirearchy.

the value of party for the pursuit and maintenance of office, but it existed for the defence of the constitution, not to exploit it for sectional ends. Party was to serve government, not vice versa. The interests of aristocracy and property which Peel saw so strongly represented among his followers were ones which he believed it legitimate, indeed essential, to protect, but they were to be served as government (in the shape of a small executive élite) determined, not as they themselves thought fit. In a favourite metaphor of his, the 'head' of a party should direct its 'tail'. The social assumptions of most Tories were similarly hierarchic and they assumed that authority came naturally from above, not from below. In 1841 few men had believed that the party should determine its own policy and mandate a government to follow it, though numbers of Conservative candidates had pledged themselves, under pressure from their constituents, to maintain the Corn Laws. Even the increasingly vocal critics of Peel who held that leaders owed a debt of honour to their followers normally stopped well short of arguing that the former should simply represent the latter, though the emotions of 1846 pushed some closer to such arguments. The weight of convention and theory on the side of the Cabinet was one reason why the Conservative party took its time to break up. Most Tories felt a deep respect for government (and a deep fear of political instability) and they did not oppose the Queen's ministers without good cause when those ministers wore their own colours. The habits of party discipline acquired since 1835 worked in the same direction, as did the sense of personal loyalty and honour. Tories who had willingly acknowledged Peel as their leader were not anxious to turn and rend him. If the party faithful bore many blows that the ministry inflicted upon them, it was because they feared the alternative of a Whig government (conceivably with Cobden included) and because they believed that on issues of domestic order, constitutional defence and the security of property Peel and his colleagues were still with them. Parliamentarians, unlike the farmers in the constituencies, were also inhibited about displaying their own sectional and material interests. They preferred to depict and defend (perhaps to perceive) the ascendency of the landed aristocracy in higher terms than the level of agricultural rents and prices. Politics, at least for gentlemen, should be a matter of principle, of public duty and public interest, not of private gain and material self-interest. The constitution was sustained by its moral legitimacy. Hence the reluctance of many Tory parliamentarians of the landed classes to identify themselves with the narrow case of agricultural protectionism. When eventually they felt forced to renounce Peel's leadership, the publicly stated grounds were more likely to be those of personal consistency (their own) and inconsistency (his), breach of faith, gentleman's honour or moral duty, than simply sectional, personal or party interest.

Also at issue was the strategy that the Conservative party should pursue in the circumstances of the 1840s. It was the dilemma that predecessors had faced in the 1820s and left unresolved. Were the interests that the party served best protected by an implacable resistance to the forces of change or by a policy of tactical concession to the inevitable? Should prudent conservatives seek confrontation with 'agitation' or seek to placate it with a show of modernity and legislative activity? Peel's instincts were for prudent concession at a safe moment. Men of property needed strong government and so they were wise to make society easier to govern. Many of his Cabinet were for a constructive conservatism which distinguished the negotiable from the non-negotiable and which would command the centre ground of parliamentary politics. Few responsible Tories sought the fate of Wellington in 1830. They recalled how loyal Tories had resisted Catholic Emancipation and parliamentary reform, yet had been forced to swallow both eventually amidst the triumph of their enemies and disaster to themselves. Now the reformed electoral system gave even less encouragement to Ultra politics. On certain issues it might be wiser to concede in good time and gain the credit rather than to suffer humiliation at a later date. Men like Graham and Ripon, whose shifts and turns had helped to shape the restructurings of parties and majorities since 1827, had an instinctive feeling for the centre ground which they almost personified. It was natural for such men to believe that the aristocratic constitution defended itself best by flexibility, not by rigidity. Property served its own ends best by a display of public responsibility, not by a crude assertion of self-interest. A ration of legislative gestures that did no major harm to the constitution would, at the very least, direct public opinion away from the more dangerous issues like parliamentary reform and established churches. Men too rich to worry about agricultural rents could see the Corn Laws as a worthwhile sacrifice to protect these more fundamental interests. But within the 'confederacy' of the Conservative party there were others less protected against the realities of economic depression and social change. Interests which found themselves being sacrificed as part of the concessionary policy of the cabinet felt entitled to resist. Tories had feared the Whig ministries of the 1830s which they had believed to be on the slippery slope of concession to radicalism and agitation and they had celebrated the victory of 1841 as the end of such proceedings. The circumstances of the mid-1840s argued against the policy of concession and conciliation as much as for it. The concessions of 1828–32 had not stilled agitation in Britain and Ireland. The aristocratic constitution found itself under more pressure than it had experienced under Liverpool. Why should concessions over Catholics and corn still agitation now?[18] Why concede readily what you might defend successfully with determination? Did Conservatives in office really need to play the Whig? Tories who thought this way were alarmed, not delighted like the Queen, to find in December 1845 that Peel 'was immensely cheered at Birmingham – a most Radical place'.

There was another question associated with the problem of strategy. Was the conservative cause identical with the interests of the Conservative party or was the party only one possible means to the desired end? Might the party as presently constituted even be an obstacle to an effective conservative strategy? If the party was indeed essential to stability, then Peel's critics were amply justified, for he broke up the party, in the end almost wilfully, and condemned it to nearly three decades of minority status. If, however, the party was, at best, only one of the means to conservative ends, then Peel had a case and the two decades of relative stability which followed 1846 might be seen as his justification. Over that

---

[18] Richmond, for example, pressed this argument in the Lords in January 1846: 'The Government comes and asks us to make a sacrifice to popular clamour, while we find ... that the concessions of Sir R. Peel in 1829 have been soon forgotten, and that they have not produced tranquillity in Ireland'.

period parliamentary politics were mediated from the centre ground by men who, in essentials, were intelligent conservatives. If politics and the constitution were best managed by aristocratic centrists, with Ultras and radicals being confined to the margins of influence, then perhaps a firm two-party structure was unnecessary. If that structure placed leaders at the mercy of their more uncompromising followers, it might even be a menace. The polarization of politics which it encouraged might tend to destabilize the whole political system. Arguably a more flexible structure which facilitated centrist mediation, perhaps through the construction of coalitions or other alliances as had occurred between 1827 and 1837, would serve better. Peel did not design this outcome at the start of the Corn Law crisis – he sought to do something similar within the two-party framework – but he had settled for it by June 1846 when his ministry fell. But to party loyalists and traditionalists like Croker and Wellington, to men who had laboured for the party as the main bastion of the constitution and social order, as well as to men whose personal interests and ambitions depended on the party holding office, this sacrifice of a then majority party to a strategy of concession which as yet had no track-record of success was both a betrayal and a folly.[19]

To many Tories there was one major concern which united the arguments about constitution, strategy and economics. If agricultural prices were exposed to the full competition of the world market, what would become of a landowning class mainly dependent on agricultural rents? Could the aristocratic constitution survive if much of the aristocracy went under? If government encouraged trade and industry at the expense of the landed interest, would not the business plutocracy soon replace the territorial aristocracy as the ruling class? To many landowners rubbed raw by the hostility of the assault on their position pressed on the platform and in the press by radical Leaguers like Cobden, the arguments were not simply about economics but also by clear implication, about the nature of the constitution and class relations. The League had injected an element of class war into the debate about protection, revived the Tory fears of 1831–32 over the political influence of the industrial cities and raised the level of political emotion among their Tory opponents. The Corn Laws now stood not simply as a regulation of practical utility to the landed interest but also as a symbol of an aristocratic constitution apparently threatened by an alternative system which Disraeli labelled 'the thraldom of Capital'.

Fears of this kind moved Edward Stanley, the most important of the Whig seceders of 1834, to lead the opposition to Peel and Graham within the Cabinet in November 1845 and to bring about its resignation the following month.[20] Stanley, who as Colonial Secretary had been little

---

[19] Goulburn, though eventually supporting Peel, had argued that repeal would break up the party and that then the full revolutionary consequences of 1832 would follow – 'the exasperation of class animosities, a struggle for pre-eminence, and the ultimate triumph of unrestrained democracy'.

[20] Initially Peel and Graham had found only two supporters in the Cabinet of fourteen, but by early December only Stanley and Buccleuch still held out against repeal. After Peel's resignation Russell failed (or perhaps chose to fail) to form a government and the Conservatives returned to office, though without Stanley.

involved in domestic strategy, now committed himself to protection more for political than narrowly economic reasons. He held agricultural protection to be crucial to the position and influence of the landed classes whose role was central to the constitution and who were entitled to regard their own interests as being more than merely selfish or sectional. A conservative Reformer who had intended the 1832 measure to usher in tranquillity, not inspire perpetual agitation, Stanley had been driven out of the Whig ministry by the threat of O'Connell and his followers in Ireland and of radicalism and militant Dissent in Britain. He became convinced that the constitution and social order were endangered and that a party of resistance was essential. Though his attempt to hold the parliamentary balance with his 'Derby Dilly' in 1834–35 had failed, his presence on the opposition front bench beside Peel from 1837 had added immense force and prestige to the Conservative revival. But the activities of the Anti-Corn Law League, centred in his own county, Lancashire, added to Stanley's alarm. Unlike Peel, whose family background helped to persuade him that the business plutocracy, properly cultivated, would be no threat to the aristocratic constitution but rather a powerful force for conservatism, Stanley saw it as a threat to the constitution and to his own class.[21] Restive in the Commons, where he found himself playing third fiddle to Peel and Graham, and uneasy with the prime minister, he had chosen to move to the Lords after the 1844 session. Already that year, however, when he quelled a dangerous backbench rebellion against Peel's authoritarianism, he had had evidence of his standing and popularity among Tory members.[22] By 1845 Stanley was a solid and self-consciously aristocratic conservative who saw Peel's latest ploy as an unnecessary and reckless gamble with the future of the constitution and of the aristocracy. Where Peel and Graham feared an assault on the constitution from without, Stanley saw the greater danger as self-destruction from within. He had not joined the Conservatives as the indispensible barrier to 'the brawling torrent of agitation' only to have them reproduce the recklessness in concession for which he had disowned the Whigs. Nor did he intend to let Peel and Cobden create a 'pauper and dependent aristocracy' humbled by agricultural collapse and humiliated by the industrialists of the League. The Conservative party and the Corn Laws together symbolized a political order for which Stanley intended to stand and fight.

By early 1846 when protectionist Conservatives were already looking to Stanley for a lead (in February Wellington offered him the leadership of the Tory peers), there were several perceptions in play among Peel's critics:

---

[21] Stanley's hostility towards the 'middle classes' organized in the League was combined with a distrust of industrialism which he held to be chronically unstable and so a threat to political stability. As he argued in the Lords in May 1846, 'Do nothing ... to check the prosperity of your manufacturers; but do not let us, by unwise legislation, promote and pamper an unwholesome increase, which, when the bubble bursts, involves all in serious evils'. Compare Peel's conviction that Britain's future prosperity and stability depended on the encouragement of manufacturing and commerce.

[22] Peel, by threats of resignation, forced his men to reverse two votes (on sugar duties and factory reform). As well as falling foul of the West India interest, he antagonized or alarmed many of his supporters by his insensitivity and acerbity when confronted with dissent. Some saw the performance as a deliberate humiliation of the House of Commons. Ashley wrote to him to warn that his style was 'tending to a dictatorship under the form of free Government'.

a sense of great damage being done to agriculture and the landed interest, a sense that the party's instincts, principles and interests were being betrayed, and a sense of danger to the aristocratic constitution itself. For the moment the first of these was the most powerful. The Agricultural Protection Associations threatened and coerced the county members who were not already in revolt (some MPs resigned their seats under the pressure) and worked to break down the bonds of loyalty to the ministry among Conservatives in the country. The county electorates did not let gentlemanly scruples and conventions stand in their way, though it was a very Lockean form of resistance: rebellion from below was justified by prior betrayal by rulers. Stanley, despite his prominence as the sole Cabinet dissentient, hardly shaped the break. It was the raw anger of the agriculturalists that did so. Though the old agricultural lobby in the Commons was marshalled by William Miles (Somerset East), the mass of the Tory backbenchers were rallied by Lord George Bentinck, a close friend of Richmond and a personification of integrity on the turf, who now emerged as their effective leader. Bentinck, like Stanley, was an ex-Reformer with no reputation as an Ultra maverick and he had the prestige of a great ducal family behind him. But it was also as the embodiment of honour, something Peel had conspicuously betrayed and forfeited, that Bentinck stood tall. (Stanley had warned his Cabinet colleagues that they could not 'do this as gentlemen'.) Disraeli meanwhile taunted Peel mercilessly, giving a voice to the bitterness of the less articulate. But Peel showed no inclination to make amends. In fact his attitude hardened in the face of opposition. His repeal bill now included no substantial compensations for the landed interest of the kind he had suggested earlier and the eulogy of Cobden which he was to deliver in the Commons in June was a deliberate rubbing of salt into his party's wounds. In the crucial division in late February 112 Conservatives voted for the government and repeal and 231 against, the measure passing with the aid of Whig and radical votes. The Lords, assured by Stanley that it was their right and duty to 'interpose a salutary obstacle to rash and inconsiderate legislation', remained the best bastion of Tory resistance. Though Stanley laboured mightily in the debate in May, urging his House to 'protect the people . . . against the treachery of those whom they have chosen to be their representatives' and, by forcing a general election on the issue, to 'give time for the intelligence of the country to act upon the public mind', Wellington put his immense prestige behind the government and the bill passed 211–164. The day after the Corn Importation Act entered the statute book in June, the government resigned following a defeat on an Irish coercion measure, some seventy of its own side having voted with the opposition and about the same number having abstained.

Protection and Popery

Even then the permanent nature of the schism in the party was not clear. Stanley was keen for reconciliation. Peel, however, ignored a move to have Graham and himself resign to give a replacement leader the opportunity to reunite the party in office. He worked to keep the party divided and the Protectionist rump as weak as possible. Despite his disclaimers of further ambition as a party leader, his whips worked to take as many Conservatives with them as possible. The Peelite ex-Cabinet aimed to control events in the Commons until emotion over protection had subsided and a general election could be held safely.[23] The Protectionists' problem was that the politicization of the agricultural constituencies rose and fell inversely with prices. The 1847 general election was held when corn prices were good and the farmers were contented. The great majority of Peelites were un-opposed by Protectionists and the results hardly changed party numbers. In fact the number of contests was the lowest the reformed Parliament would ever experience. Most Stanleyites found that Maynooth and No Popery were more effective cries than corn. Their great hope, a general election when agricultural prices were at rock bottom, was never to be realized. The truth was that agriculture had not collapsed dramatically enough to salvage Protectionist fortunes. That reckoning was to come three decades too late. Even the financial and commercial crisis of the autumn of 1847, which undermined confidence in the programme of measures passed by the late ministry, came too late for the election. But gut feelings about Ireland and Catholics did not depend on the vagaries of harvests and markets. One lesson of the Parliament of 1847 was that, to the discomfort of Whiggish figures like Bentinck and Stanley, new Protection-ism was often little more than an adjunct of old Toryism.

Bentinck, a religious liberal without the tact to dissemble, fell foul of these sensibilities. His vote for the Jewish Disabilities Bill of 1847 angered his followers, most of whom had been in the other lobby, and forced his resignation as Commons leader ('I am a most unnatural leader for a high Protestant Party'), so ridding Stanley of a coadjutor he could hardly control. After attempts to plug the gap with a reluctant Granby, heir to a great Tory dynasty, and then with an ill-assorted triumvirate, by 1849 the improbable figure of Disraeli had emerged as Tory leader in the Com-mons. At least his ability to sustain debate was not in question. Nor did anyone doubt that the Protectionists were Stanley's party. Their tragedy was that their one leader of commanding stature was marooned in the Lords when the Commons situation demanded his presence. Disraeli's promotion reflected the paucity of Tory talent in the Commons ('a terrible want of officers', he called it) except that on the Peelite benches. Nearly all the office-holders of 1846 had followed Peel into what amounted to an alternative Conservative party, free-trading, relatively liberal on religion, self-consciously centrist and balance-holding, but assertive enough to press its claims to legitimacy upon wavering Protectionists. Reunion of the old party remained an influential ideal, even a goal for some figures on either side, and Stanley's tactics were often influenced by this objective. But while Peel remained a dominating figure in the Commons and protection the policy of most of the Stanleyites, there was little chance of reunion. Though after Peel's death in 1850 his heirs were divided between those who wanted and those who resisted reunion, the dominant pattern of the twenty years after 1846 was to be Whig-dominated administrations supported by

---

[23] Peel, in this respect a traditionalist, had insisted that the corn issue should be decided by Parliament and not by the electorate. The Protectionists had demanded a general election on the issue and had berated both Houses for their failure to stand by the expression of public opinion in the 1841 election. Here the Tory right stood for the 'modern' ideas that Parliament ought to represent opinion 'out of doors' and that major issues should be put to the electorate.

Peelites and with the influence of radicals confined to the margins. It limited the scope for a recovery by the main Conservative party by ensuring a centrist domination of parliamentary politics in place of the two-party polarization of the 1830s and early 1840s. The Peelite group, though almost more chiefs than Indians after 1852, embodied many of the traditions of an earlier front-bench Toryism, particularly their commitment to a strong and stable executive (an ideal they placed above partisan interest), financial reform, administrative efficiency, moral high-mindedness and economic liberalism. This Pittite strain of conservatism, which carried with it considerable support in the press, the intelligentsia and the City, was compatible enough with Whiggery. Though the strong High Churchmanship of some of the younger Peelites jarred with the more latitudinarian and secular instincts of the Whigs, they shared a distaste for the virulently anti-Popery feeling that flourished on the Tory side. Their common purpose was the maintenance of the aristocratic constitution by providing it with a modern, reasonably liberal, vaguely reformist and benevolent face.

Much of this would not have been beyond the capacity of a Conservative party reunited under Stanley's leadership, even if the No Popery atavism and the diehard element among the gentry would still have presented problems to a leadership attuned to the demands and responsibilities of office. But the issue of protection remained an obstacle to reunion down to 1852 and the incompatibility of personalities even longer. Disraeli was, as Stanley saw, 'the most powerful *repellant* we could offer to any repentant or hesitating Peelites' and his leadership in the commons was always unacceptable to ambitious men who viewed themselves as senior to him in official experience and credibility. Some Peelites did drift back towards the main party, Ellenborough, Hardinge, Pakington, Northcote and the aged Wellington among them. The Lords indeed never suffered a party schism on the scale or with the bitterness experienced in the Commons. But the Lower House was the arena that mattered. There the remnants of the Peelite leadership, including Gladstone, the main object of Stanley's pursuit, were to merge with the Liberals of Russell and Palmerston in 1859, an outcome foreshadowed by their coalitions under Aberdeen in 1852 and, more briefly, under Palmerston in 1855.

The continuities of the post-1846 Tory party with its predecessors are evident in everything except its ministerial-level leadership. Only in its loss of nearly all the official talent and experience in the Commons did it command less legitimacy and credibility than the Peelite minority, though the weight conservative opinion attached to a capable and experienced executive made that a serious deficiency. Stanley's position as a potential first minister and the continuity he represented with past administrations and the resurgent Conservatism of 1837–41 were invaluable assets, but his ascendency in the Lords hardly solved the problems in the Commons. There, behind the shattered front bench, remained the substance of a party of government. Some 240 members, about two-thirds of the Conservatives, had acknowledged the leadership of Stanley and Bentinck. The 1847 election left around 230 to set against some 90 Peelites. Though some city seats were lost, the party had suffered nothing like the electoral smash of 1832. Soon, as the government's radical supporters went their own ways, the Tories were the largest single grouping in the House and a relatively cohesive one at that. The disaster that had befallen the old party was not its collapse but its division on lines made inevitable by Peel's handling of events in 1846. Even thereafter, protection and personalities apart, there might have been scope for Stanley within a fundamentally conservative Parliament. The faultline, the division between essentially incompatible attitudes, ran not between Whigs and Tories, not between free-trading and protectionist Conservatives, for all three offered versions of aristocratic conservatism, but between the Whigs and the radical left-wing of their own party. But, as the radicals became neutralized in the years after 1846, the Conservatives could do little to disrupt the centrist consensus around Whigs and Peelites once the possibility of an electoral triumph on a protectionist platform had passed. The frontbench strength of the Whig/Peelite ministries of 1852, 1855 and 1859 and the largely conservative tenor of Whig policy left the Tories little to bite on, so that, though Peelite seats were gradually absorbed by the two main parties, they went disproportionately the Whig way. Stanley and his party had to compete not with a Liberal party radicalized by Cobden, Miall and O'Connell but with an aristocratic, reassuring and decently up-to-date leadership which satisfied most opinion in and out of Parliament. Until the Liberals initiated a new phase of political polarization, the Tories stood little chance of reoccupying the conservative centre ground.

It is often argued that the Tories lost credibility as a party of government because they became too identified with the landed interest and so lost the support of industry, commerce and the city constituencies. According to this interpretation the problem was the alienation of the urban middle classes whom Peel had wooed effectively. If 'landed interest' is interpreted to mean the agricultural lobby and protectionist policies, the argument has some justification. The call for a return to agricultural protection was divisive of the nation and would have become more so had it approached closer to success. Outside the agricultural constituencies it was widely perceived as subservience to one economic interest at the expense of the rest. But the most significant objection at the parliamentary level was not that of the urban bourgeoisie but that of sections of the landowning classes who declined to present themselves in this light. From both high-mindedness and prudence they sought to appear as promoting the general well-being, not as fighting their own corner at the expense of other interests. Higher food prices were not the most comfortable cause. Even men who were scandalized at the element of class warfare the Cobdenites had brought into Parliament hesitated to retaliate in kind. A high-minded if limited paternalism, politics that were clean as well as slightly progressive, were what the aristocratic constitution needed to project to the nation. That remained one of the strengths of the Peelite position. Many Tory parliamentarians, moreover, had been uneasy with the surge of protectionist fervour in 1846. It had been populist and often non-deferential, too much a revolt of the freeholders and the tenant farmers for the taste of patrician politicians accustomed to settling the counties themselves. Ashley, given his marching orders by Farquharson, 'King of the Dorset farmers', had resigned his seat rather than obey. Though some Tories lamented the supineness of the county electorates in 1847, others were relieved that the fury had subsided. Once again contests were being decided (or avoided) among the aristocracy and gentry, just as ministries were to be largely made and unmade in the Commons and not by the electorate in this period.[24] In the counties and small boroughs the old politics of influence and deference revived. This stability was not unwelcome. Though protectionist sentiment persisted in many constituencies, the Tory leaders who had abandoned protection without undue sorrow in 1852 declined to stir the issue further. The defence of the aristocratic constitution did not lend itself naturally to populist politics.

If, however, 'landed interest' means the landowning classes, the Tory problem after 1846 was that they did not command enough of them. The Whigs had checked the drift of patrician support in more overtly conservative directions and the Peelites had detached from the Tories a sizeable body of landowning opinion together with the balance of the Commons and the party's ministerial élite. The key to a restored Tory majority lay not so much with the cities, where the party never flourished under the 1832 system, but with the counties and small boroughs where property and influence had their sway and here the Whigs and their allies were able to maintain or re-establish themselves sufficiently during the 1850s.[25] The Tories needed more, not less, of the 'landed interest' in this sense. They needed to re-identify themselves with a broad aristocratic conservatism rather than with an agricultural sectionalism that had its most direct appeal to the rural middle classes. But even when protection was dropped, the Conservative party – Stanley had insisted on readopting the name 'Conservative' early in 1848 despite protests from Bentinck, Disraeli and Manners – found itself as only the most sizeable of several conservative groupings.

Though the party had not gained enough of the county and small borough seats in 1847, it remained heavily dependent on those constituencies for its 230 members, most of whom had fought on a protectionist platform. The two Conservative parties retained a majority of the English seats between them, while Russell's supporters won clear majorities of the Scottish and Irish seats. Though there was some blurring of the line between Peelites and Protectionists both in Parliament and in the constituencies, the two categories of Conservative hardly co-operated in the Commons outside limited areas of religion and foreign policy despite Stanley's conciliatoriness and the continued membership of the Carlton Club by most of the Peelites. The Whigs too were wooing Peelite support and the Peelites themselves were determined never to permit the formation of a Protectionist ministry. In the country protectionist feeling see-sawed with agricultural prices. At times the cause seemed all but dead, but the onset of an agricultural depression in 1849 gave the Conservatives by-election triumphs in both Britain and Ireland and discouraged the leadership from seeking an alternative platform. In February 1850 Disraeli's motion on agricultural distress pressed the government hard and found the free-traders in some disarray. But agriculture's depression was not shared by the rest of the economy, by-election gains were confined to agricultural constituencies and the nervousness which centrist opinion

[24] The six general elections 1847–68 showed a notable stability in patterns of representation. The largest shifts occurred in Ireland.
[25] In 1857 the Whigs won 53 English county seats, the Peelites four and the Tories 87. Contrast this with the 1841 result of 20 Whigs and 124 Conservatives.

displayed about likely popular reaction to a Protectionist government undermined Tory credibility within Parliament itself. The party made few inroads into centrist opinion, partly because Russell, dependent on Peelite votes for his majorities, gave the opposition little opportunity to re-occupy the centre ground. In 1848, when revolts flared up across the continent and Chartism revived at home, the government staged an elaborate show of confronting and overawing the Chartists, even mobilizing the aged Wellington to command the capital. A grip was kept on Dublin too and the Young Ireland revolt put down. Civil order and resistance to 'democratic' agitation were being denied to the Tories as issues. So was patriotism. Palmerston's conduct of foreign policy, though displaying too much liberalism for the Tories and too much 'bluster' for the Peelites, was gaining for the Whigs and himself in particular the patriotic, though still progressive, identity that Macaulay was appropriating for them in literature and historiography. Though both Tories and Peelites opposed Palmerston over Don Pacifico in 1850 and Derby won a vote of censure in the Lords, the Foreign Secretary's triumph in the Commons left little scope for the opposition.

Nor could the Conservatives control legislation as much as they wished. The passage of a Ten Hours Act in 1847 with the aid of many Protectionist votes gave the satisfaction of revenge on the Anti-Corn Law League, on factory owners and on Peel and Graham, who had restrained their followers over factory reform in earlier years. The Jewish Disabilities Bill, passed in the Commons despite major Protectionist resistance, fell foul of the party in the Lords. But on issues more central to the party confrontation the record was poor. The government's decision to repeal the Navigation Acts gave the protectionists the opportunity to fight on a broader front than just agriculture, for there was substantial support for the Acts in the shipping and colonial trades. During 1849 the Central Agricultural Protection Association was merged into a National Association for the Protection of British Industry and Capital which, though under Richmond's presidency, had a Limehouse shipyard-owner, George Frederick Young, as its driving force. But even this collaboration between agricultural and business protectionism failed to halt the march of free trade, Derby's resistance in the Lords achieving no more than holding the repeal bill down to a majority of ten on the crucial division. Even with the electoral system itself 'finality' seemed to be crumbling. In 1850 the government pushed through an Irish Franchise Bill which the Tory peers were able to modify only by limiting the reduction of the franchise qualification. Even the Upper House was proving to be less of a Tory weapon than Stanley had hoped. At the end of the 1850 session the leader shared his gloom with Croker: 'the *gentlemen* of the country ... apathy is fast destroying them'.

All the tendency of our legislation and of our proceedings in Parliament is towards the lowering of the weight, in the social scale, of the proprietors of the soil; ... I have never before taken so gloomy a view of our position; ... I see few, if any, young men coming forward or taking an interest in public affairs imbued with *Conservative* principles and ready to stand by and with 'their order'.

But hope and opportunity were at hand. That autumn the Pope's restoration of the Roman Catholic hierarchy in Britain ('Papal Aggression') provoked an explosion of Protestant outrage. Russell, perhaps fearing Tory exploitation of the issue, responded with a 'Durham Letter' which condemned both the Catholic move and the influence of Puseyites within the Church of England. Catholics, Irishmen, and Peelites were all offended. The prime minister promised legislation which, with the aid of Tory votes, materialized as the 1851 Ecclesiastical Titles Act. Though it damaged Russell and divided his supporters, the episode confirmed the Tories as the party of what Beresford, the Commons whip, had called 'the proper and just old No Popery cry'. By March Stanley was proclaiming 'an utter break up of all parties, except the Protectionists' and planning to 'consolidate . . . the now awakened spirit of Protestantism, and at the same time keep the latter within reasonable bounds' in anticipation of an election. The 'evocation of the Protestant spirit' appealed to Dissenters in radical constituencies as well as to Anglican opinion and would surely 'neutralize the cheap bread cry'.[26]

By then Stanley had already received (and eventually declined) his first commission to form a government, Russell having resigned in February 1851 after a defeat in the Commons. Whigs, Peelites and the Court had all encouraged fears that a Protectionist ministry would occasion civil disorder. (Disraeli, anxious to drop protection, had predicted 'the manufacturing masses . . . would be arrayed against us'.)[27] But a breach between Russell and Palmerston occasioned a second opportunity and led to the formation of a Tory ministry under Stanley, now Earl of Derby, in February 1852. Though well manned in the Lords, the new government was woefully weak in the Commons where Disraeli, Chancellor of the Exchequer and Leader of the House, was faced by an array of Whig and Peelite talent. Attempts to buy in conservative Whig support, including Palmerston, had failed and Derby had extracted from the Peelites only Aberdeen's assurance that there would be no 'factious or obstructive' opposition. The general election, which was held in July, again did not coincide with low agricultural prices like those which had buoyed up the party's hopes and fortunes in 1849–51. Already the leadership had started to distance itself from the commitment to protection. Disraeli was foremost in this, too much so for some Cabinet colleagues. Derby insisted that they should play the game 'honestly and manfully' and not repeat the betrayal of 1846:

> . . . to take office with the purpose of throwing over, voluntarily, the main object of those who have raised us to it is to follow too closely an *exemplar vitiis imitabile*, to which I can never submit . . .

---

[26] He added that 'the real battle of the Constitution' remained 'whether the preponderance, in the legislative power, is to rest with the land and those connected with it, or with the manufacturing interests'.

[27] Stanley's reluctant attempt had been doomed by the refusal of leading Peelites to serve. Without them his party had no hope of commanding either a majority or much front-bench talent in the Commons. But Wellington, hearing of Russell's resignation, 'expressed his regret and his dread of a Protectionist Government with a Dissolution, which might lead to civil commotion'. The Queen and Albert were similarly apprehensive when Stanley announced his resolve, if he took office, to introduce a fixed duty on corn imports.

Disraeli blamed Derby's persistence on the influence of Beresford and of Young, whose National Association had made its mark in the days of the by-election triumphs. But soon Derby himself suspected that leaving the verdict on protection to the general election, as the ministry had agreed to do, would yield a negative result: 'it is well to let down the Agricultural body as easily as we can'.

Initially Derby, like many Tories, had been shaken by Russell's promise in his last days of office to take up parliamentary reform again. 'Finality' was a posture on which Tories could unite more easily than protection. The *Quarterly Review* sought to rally to the new administration, as 'our last chance of escape', all those 'desirous to avert a democratic and socialist revolution'. Wellington's last days were made fearful by 'the ruin that is gathering around us'. But the tone that Derby and Disraeli set for their front benches was more accommodating and flexible than these calls to fight in the last ditch. The previous autumn Derby had warned Croker of the danger of committing the party to resist all change, both 'because a change *may* have a real Conservative tendency' and because the party could not afford to dispense with tactical flexibility when an issue had gained momentum. Here, prompted by the need to win over Whigs or Peelites, was a reassertion of the importance of pragmatism and calculation against the probably self-defeating negativism of more atavistic or 'principled' Tories. But, unlike Peel earlier, Derby intended his pragmatism to strengthen the party, not to deny its claims.

In the 1852 election the party at least had the advantages of office. Perhaps it made too much use of them. A scandal over the use of Admiralty patronage for electoral purposes burst over the government and refurbished the party's image of Old Corruption. The returns, however, showed only modest Tory gains and left the ministry still in a minority, its 280–290 seats requiring assistance from the Peelites who themselves had lost seats in some number. Though there had been Tory gains in Ireland, where protectionist sentiment and Russell's offending of Catholic sensibilities had helped Derby's candidates, a more significant portent was the strength of anti-Catholic feeling in Britain where traditional hostility had been sharpened by the heavy Irish immigration since the Famine. Beresford and his fellow-whip Newdegate were more passionate on this issue than any other. Despite its attempts to woo Irish opinion, on the eve of the elections the government had issued a royal proclamation to reinforce a prohibition of processions in the 1829 Emancipation Act by banning the display of Catholic vestments and ornaments in public. Now 'civil commotion' did occur in both Ireland and Britain, the worst outbreak being anti-Catholic riots at Stockport. Indeed popular 'Protestantism' appeared strongest in the industrial North West where anti-Popery leaders were emerging like the Evangelical clergymen M'Neile in Liverpool and Stowell in Salford. For many Tories in constituencies elsewhere, as in Parliament itself, Maynooth remained an open wound.

One consequence of the election results was the dropping of protection, though hopes of 'compensation' were held out to the agricultural interest. The government was committed to bringing in a budget before the year's end and Disraeli's longstanding concern to 'devise a scheme, which will rally the landed party, and yet be suited to the spirit of the age' was further complicated by current controversies about the balance between

direct and indirect taxation and by the hostility recently evinced in the
Commons (not least among Tories) to the extension of the income tax.
Disraeli had little room for manoeuvre once the service ministries, backed
by the Cabinet, had raised their estimates and thwarted his plans for a
tax-cutting budget. His attempts to do much with little gave opportunities
to adversaries all to ready to maul such an unlikely figure at the Exchequer.
His proposals to halve the malt tax and the duty on hops, to reduce the tea
duties, to increase the house tax and to introduce graduations into the
income tax (in effect differentials between earned and unearned income)
appeared to be slanted too much the ways of the agriculturalists, to
abandon fiscal orthodoxy and to reflect on Peel's legacy. Gladstone savaged
the technical detail. But the budget debate was a highly political occasion,
both in the character of the proposals and in the hostility displayed by the
Whigs and Peelites who, brought closer together by their taste of Tory
government and now ready to evict the trespassers, were in for the kill. The
government was defeated 305–286 and Derby resigned to be succeeded by
Aberdeen at the head of a Whig/Peelite coalition.

Palmerston and Equipoise

The experience of office had had its value. It left Disraeli more secure as
Derby's lieutenant and he was now able to rid himself of Beresford as chief
whip. The dropping of protection had left the party looking less sectional,
self-interested and backward-looking and so better fitted to pursue that
'spirit of the age'. Old fears had been laid to rest. Conservative government
had shown itself to be feasible, no-one had risen in revolt and Derby and
his Cabinet had governed at least half-respectably. Opponents who had
previously predicted Conservative rule would be doctrinaire, rigid and
dangerously provocative had changed their tune. One Whig peer had
complained that 'the only principle' adopted by the government was 'that
everything in the world is a compromise'. Among the verdicts of a
predominantly hostile press was that of *Frazer's Magazine*:

> Their three most conspicuous articles of faith – Protection, Protestantism and
> resistance to democracy – have been abandoned in a moment of power. . . .
> Where they did not actually deceive their party, they disappointed them.

The hard-liners in the party had not been amused. Old Croker, disappointed again in a Tory leader, ceased to correspond with Derby. But
compensation came elsewhere. Almost in the moment of the ministry's fall
the Whig diarist Greville wrote 'I believe, if the country were polled, they
would as soon have these people for Ministers as any others'. Pragmatism,
however, could be carried too far. Disraeli's appetite for office had led him
into negotiations with the 'Irish Brigade' and even with John Bright,
alarming colleagues and impelling Derby to stamp on the intrigues. It was
also clear that tolerance of Tory government had its limits. Relations with
the Court had remained uneasy and the Commons majority the party
sought had never looked like materializing either through the elections or
through the dealing and shifting of parliamentary factions. Even though
the Tories had abandoned protection, the Peelites had remained elusive,
particularly once the idea of a coalition headed by Aberdeen became
current, and now had thrown in their lot with the Whigs. Tory reunion

now seemed like the remotest of possibilities. In the long term the Conservatives stood to gain from the absorption of the Peelites by the Whigs, but the party's immediate prospects were worsened. For the moment, though the experience of office had done something to re-establish the Tories as a party of government and though the fruits of office had been tasted again, to the reward and delight of the faithful, the experiment was widely regarded as a failure. Derby felt it as such and Hardwicke, lately a ministerial colleague, wrote that it 'seems to me to settle so clearly the question of a Conservative Government, that I no longer think it possible. . . . I think the Conservative party beaten out of the field'.

The danger of the tactical flexibility which the Tory leaders had reasserted was that the party lost something of its distinctive identity and purpose. Though the maintenance of the aristocratic constitution and of social order remained the ultimate objectives, Whig/Peelite governments were visibly capable of such achievements themselves – Hardwicke's conclusion that 'We must now depend on the moderation of the movement party for the safety of our firesides' had had the character of prophecy – and the relatively settled economic conditions of the 1850s did not generate any serious political challenge to the style of government. Only on religious issues, particularly the defence of Church interests, did the parliamentary party maintain a distinctively Tory identity, though even this was compli-cated by the factional strife within the Church which made it a less coherent and cohesive force than in the 1830s. Whigs and Peelites could fish in those waters too. The High Churchmanship of some of the younger Peelites – Malmesbury had dismissed them in 1852 as 'Puseyites, Pedants & crotchety' – and the encouragement of the Evangelicals by Palmerston under the guidance of his son-in-law Shaftesbury left the Tories with little to bite on beyond their resistance to regular private members' motions for the abolition of church rates. Only when the Liberal party took up the remaining Dissenting and Roman Catholic grievances and put 'The Church in Danger' again would there be a political resurgence of Anglican-ism behind the Tories.

In 1855 Derby turned down an opportunity of office when the Aberdeen coalition collapsed under the pressures of the Crimean War. He believed that war required stability at home and that a Palmerston ministry was an inevitable successor to the government lately toppled with Tory help and he himself had no taste for another short-lived minority administration. Disraeli resented the decision bitterly. The emergence of Palmerston as premier, patriotic hero (the war was triumphantly concluded) and Whig top dog left a dire situation for those Tories who, like their Commons leader, longed for office. The ebbing of radicalism in both Britain and Ireland had left established institutions without immediate threat. The reformed electoral system had settled down into remarkable consistency, politics had restabilized, the social order no longer seemed to stand on the brink of a precipice. Now, in the Palmerstonian 'Age of Equipoise', what was the need for a professed party and government of order? How far were the Conservatives the party of order any more than the Whigs whose hold on office with only one major interruption since 1830 had begun to seem the very essence of stability? With Palmerston in charge even the patriotism which had once served the Tories so well was no longer theirs to command.

The general election of 1857 which the Tories, allying in the House with

Cobden and the radicals over policy towards China, had forced upon Palmerston only strengthened his position. It was a victory for Palmerston, patriotism and Whiggery in general, a battering for Tories, Peelites and radicals, particularly those who had opposed the Crimean War. Of all general elections it was perhaps the one to which the Conservative party had least relevance. It lost more than twenty English county seats to the government and consolation resided only in the defeat of figures like Cobden and Bright. Yet within the Commons itself discipline on the government side remained loose enough to leave the Tories some scope. In 1858 they joined with the Peelites (no longer in coalition) and the radicals to bring Palmerston down for his alleged servility towards Napoleon III. This time Derby did not scorn the opportunity. The ministry he gathered was rather more impressive than that of 1852 and at junior level figures like Hardy and Northcote indicated that young talent was again gravitating the Tory way. Derby himself was less hesitant than in 1852. This time he had opted to play the Spirit of the Age, though it was an act which sections of his party found it hard to applaud.[28] But Derby, whether from a restored faith in modernity or from desperation after recent reverses, had decided to up-date the image of his party.[29] The fluid situation in the Commons and the impending appeal to the electorate encouraged the Cabinet to play the Whig. In the Lords, in language that alarmed conservative Whigs, Derby asserted that a Conservative ministry was not necessarily 'a stationary Ministry':

> We live in an age of constant progress, moral, social and political. . . . Our constitution itself is the result of a series of perpetual changes. . . . in politics, as in everything else, the same course must be pursued – constant progress, improving upon the old system, adapting our institutions to the altered purposes they are intended to serve, and by judicious changes meeting the demands of society.

Certain Whigs, Russell foremost among them, had been pressing the idea of a further instalment of parliamentary reform. Now Derby sought to pre-empt a Whig measure and to display his own party's empathy with the present by producing his own Reform Bill. The measure, introduced in the Commons by Disraeli in February 1859, was not a surrender to radicalism and democracy but rather a piece of partisan fiddling with a system which many Tories had always felt their opponents had designed to spite them. The measure proposed a uniform rated franchise for counties and boroughs (a lowering of the county qualification, no change in the boroughs), votes for wealthy lodgers, the exclusion of borough inhabitants from the county electorates, a redistribution of seats slanted towards the counties and some gerrymandering of constituency boundaries. Though enough to divide Conservatives, the measure was too partisan in its implications to sway Whigs and radicals, who mocked the 'fancy franchises'

---

[28] At this time the revamped Tory newspaper, the *Standard*, which aimed to appeal to the metropolitan bourgeoisie, announced that it stood for 'politics . . . of the age – enlightened amelioration and progress', though it still upheld 'staunch Protestantism'.

[29] Derby's friskiness may have been a response to serious criticism of his leadership within the party in 1857, but Malmesbury, Disraeli and the premier's son Edward Stanley took a similar line on parliamentary reform.

the bill proposed.[30] The opposition forces regrouped to pass a resolution hostile to the government and to force Derby to a dissolution. The outcome of the general election was the Conservatives' best performance between 1841 and 1874, some 290 seats which included a majority of the Irish seats for the only time between the rise of O'Connell and the end of the Union.[31] But it still fell short of a majority. Russell and Palmerston reunited the Whigs and used the issue of Italian unification, towards which the Tories had been largely unsympathetic, to bring the Peelites and radicals into the fold. A meeting of these forces at Willis's Rooms, which is seen traditionally as the foundation of the Liberal party proper, led to the replacement of the Conservative government by another Palmerston administration in June 1859.

For the moment that was that. Though Palmerston had his problems with the Queen, Gladstone and Bismarck, he could not be ousted. For much of the Parliament of 1859–65 there was an informal arrangement for Derby to use his votes to prop the ministry up, if need be, against its own radical wing. Here was a centrist coalition of minds, if not of men. Tory opposition to the Reform Bill which Russell pressed, particularly to its £6 householder franchise in the boroughs, helped the Whig element in the government to stifle it. In 1860, when Gladstone sought to cheapen newspapers by repealing what was left of the old paper duties, Palmerston enlisted the support of the Tories against his own Chancellor of the Exchequer.[32] To many Conservatives Palmerston looked like the best prime minister they had. In 1863 Edward Stanley recorded 'The truth is, no one wishes to replace Lord Palmerston. . . . Half the country gentlemen would refuse to join in an attack on him'. The Tory whips complained of his popularity with their backbenchers; Derby complained of his inability to command a regular majority in the Lords, an invidious position for a Tory leader. Walter Bagehot congratulated the country on being ruled by 'the like-minded men of both parties'. When the government was humiliated over the Schleswig-Holstein question in 1864 and suffered a vote of censure in the Lords, Derby's inclinations as well as his ill-health held him back from the kill. Bismarck apart, it was almost the Golden Age restored. Some Conservatives, Disraeli inevitably among them, resented the longeurs of seemingly perpetual opposition, but conservatism of a kind was reign-

---

[30] Robert Cecil later portrayed this moment as the Tory leaders' apostasy on opposition to democracy. Disraeli, however, had protected his back in the Commons. After a few bland comments to the lower classes on their orderly and patriotic disposition, he argued that 'If you establish a democracy you must in due course reap the fruits of a democracy', which included sharp increases in public expenditure, 'wars entered into from passion', 'property less valuable' and 'freedom less complete'. The bill, however, provoked the resignation of two Cabinet ministers who were supported by some forty Tory rebels. The ministry did pass the abolition of the property qualification for MPs.

[31] Since 1846 the Tories had been helped in Ireland by protectionist feeling, but the 1859 gains owed more to the Italian issue. Conservative opposition to government policy towards Italian unification was welcomed by the Papacy and by Catholic opinion at home. The Tory leaders kept the party's anti-Catholicism under wraps better than in 1852.

[32] Though the measure passed the Commons, Derby had it defeated in the Lords. Gladstone had it passed in a different form in 1861 but admitted 'We live in anti-reforming times'.

ing. While Palmerston lived, radical change and the Tory party marked time together.

The 1865 general election, a low-key affair, confirmed this stability. The Conservatives fell back from the high point of 1859, most of the seats lost being in London, Scotland ('All influence appears to have slipped away from its proprietors,' grieved Disraeli) and Ireland. Derby told Disraeli that 'a purely Conservative Government is all but hopeless, until, upon Palmerston's death (for he will never resign), Gladstone tries his hand with a Radical Government and alarms the middle classes. Then there *may* come a reaction . . .'[33] Within two months Palmerston had died, a more significant event for the Conservatives than anything their own leaders could stage. Now Russell was premier again, Gladstone led the Commons and in March 1866 the government introduced a Reform Bill. Its nature, particularly the proposal to reduce the borough £10 householder qualification to £7, alarmed both the Tories and a conservative section of the Whigs. A revolt of the 'Adullamite' Liberals assisted the Conservatives, solid this time, to defeat the ministry and in July 1866 Derby headed a minority administration for the third time.

---

[33] Note that Derby, who had feared the political influence of the 'middle classes' so much in the 1840s, had now come to see them as a force for stability and even, perhaps, as potentially Conservative.

4

A Mid-Century Perspective

Party and Politics

The nature of a major political party is rarely simple. It is partly the product of the systems and structures, both social and political, within which the party operates, partly the result of the peculiarities that distinguish it from other parties and from the non-partisan. A party may also be shaped by its reaction against the character of opposing or rival parties. Over time major events and changes in circumstances leave their mark too, so that the party carries the impress of its own history. The importance of circumstances between the French Revolution and the mid-Victorian period means that any understanding of the Conservative party involves a major element of narrative.

It makes sense, nonetheless, to stand back at some point and to assess the party's character and construction. One starts with the recognition that, for all the changes over the period, the party operated within a well-established and widely admired framework of constitutional monarchy and aristocratic parliamentarianism. Conservative politicians were committed to uphold that constitution and did indeed help to do so. The party remained self-consciously traditionalistic with its main focus in Parliament and government. A major change, however, had been the decline of the influence of the Crown between the 1780s and the 1840s. The consequences for parliamentary politics had been immense, particularly for the Tory party which had developed initially as an extension of the old Court party. Though an attachment to monarchy as a pillar and symbol of the constitution and of social order survived among Tories, loyalty to the person of the monarch had become a minor factor and, with executive influence over the Commons and over elections almost gone, the party could no longer rely on the Treasury. Once out of office in 1830, it had to learn how to be effective as an independent opposition as well as a potential government. The notable success achieved in this respect between 1835 and 1841 was not, however, to survive the strains of resumed office. Two crucial components of the party, the substantial cadre of experienced office-holders and the majority of the landed gentry, once the basis of the eighteenth-century 'country party' and now with additional county seats and a much-enlarged county electorate behind them, were not easily compatible. They had divergent views of the rôle and strategy of Conservative government in the circumstances of the time and there was no consensus on the appropriate relationships between party and government, between Parliament and social interests in the country and between leaders and followers within the party itself. Schism and disintegration followed once the loyalty of followers had been worn thin and Peel himself had decided against trying to hold such a party together any further. Though the issues were not entirely resolved by the crisis, the tensions within the party were never to flare up so violently again. A leadership unable to come to terms with the party it had helped to create had been replaced, while the years of minority status gave the mass of the party time to digest the lessons concerning the consequences of schism. The caution and sensitivity Derby displayed before dropping protection was one sign of the change; the degree of cohesion and discipline displayed by the party during its long sentence of opposition was another.

Organization and ideology are two of the most obvious features of party inviting the historian's attention. The first, however, is not one of the most helpful approaches for an understanding of the Conservative party in this period. Though management had long been an ingredient of parliamentary (and to a lesser extent local) politics, the parties were still light on formal institutionalization by twentieth-century standards. The Reform Act had not suddenly produced a 'modern' type of party. Indeed in its immediate aftermath the Tories had no recognized leader in the Commons, apparently no whip and even, some suggested, little that held together like a party at all. That was a temporary and untypical condition but it was still revealing. What mattered more than formal organization were states of mind, complexes of attitude, loyalty and 'principle', modes of behaviour and practice, interests and relationships. Tory sentiment in the country, though damaged electorally, largely survived the parliamentary disintegration of 1830–34 and provided a base for the rapid revival of the parliamentary body afterwards. Here, at the centre of things, the party was built around the parliamentary classes, their London clubs and residences, their families and country houses, their estates and spheres of influence. At certain levels Toryism had an almost dynastic character. But the party also needed to command competence and commitment – frontbench weight and talent and backbench commitment – within the context of the parliamentary sessions. It depended on the willingness of sections of the aristocracy, gentry and others of influence and property to spend time, effort and money for the cause, particularly in the periodic general elections.[1] Then the party became temporararily more a matter of the constituencies, less a matter of metropolitan and parliamentary life.

Thus the party was not simply a body of ideology or high theory any more than it was primarily an organizational structure. Nor did it exist as a tug-of-war between ideology and pragmatism, though this antithesis has been a common analytical device for the study of the modern Conservative party. Both ideas and pragmatism were shaped by the material interests

---

[1] Throughout our period Parliaments had a maximum life of seven years, but general elections were more frequent than that in practice. The 64 years of Victoria's reign saw 15 general elections; the 32 years 1820–52 experienced ten.

which the party served. Theory, to have much appeal or meaning, had to relate to social realities and to political context. Though there were always Tory philosophers and ideologues from Burke onwards, they flavoured the party's rhetoric rather than altered its fundamental purpose and direction. Pragmatism too was limited by that framework of constitutional forms and social structure. Men of business who saw government as their trade and politics as a practice of mediation and who consequently tended to dislike the sectionalism and rigidity they met within their own party still derived much of their purpose from the interests and causes they shared with their supporters.

Those interests were not very different in mid-century from what they had been in Pitt's time. Rank, property, wealth, status, privilege, power and authority were the essence of the party and its purposes. It represented a significant part of what G. M. Trevelyan called 'the enjoying classes', people with much to lose combining to defend their common interests against real or perceived dangers. The 'property versus numbers' view of the party remained as valid as it had been for Burke or Sidmouth, though now, as then, Toryism enjoyed substantial support outside the ranks of great property. Anti-Catholic sentiment was one factor in this support, as patriotism had been before 1815. But the party was not inclined to trust to that wider support and its instincts and calculations remained fundamentally anti-democratic. Certain of the interests represented in the party were more central than others. There were times when Tories presented the rights and interests of landowners as the main cause the party served. This view, sharpened by the anti-aristocratic tone of the Anti-Corn Law League, derived support from traditional social theory, was embedded within the constitution itself and was congruent with the background of most of the parliamentary élite. The prominence of the protection issue had given an additional economic dimension to this concern and in the debates of 1846 Conservatives on both sides of the Corn Law issue had proclaimed their devotion to the cause of the 'aristocratic constitution'. But land was only one of the interests which identified with the party. The interests of the established churches, though related to, were not identical with those of landed property. The chartered corporations and funded and commercial property had also added depth and breadth to the Tory cause. Wellington had included the clergy and the 'great Merchants and Bankers' in his *parti conservateur* in 1827. Graham saw the party in 1837 as 'the best portion of the entire Community which claims to itself a great preponderance of property, of learning, of decent manners, and of pure religion'; in 1866 Derby, with similar vagueness, thought it composed 'in a great measure of men who have the greatest interest and the largest stake in the country', adding that they were 'the least likely to be carried away by ... popular enthusiasm and ... popular impulses'. In 1883 Salisbury supplied more detail, listing 'Churchmen, landowners, publicans, manufacturers, houseowners, railway sharehol- ders, fundholders' among those who looked to the Conservatives for protection because 'their most vital interests are at the mercy of some move in the game of politics'. Though the list reflected certain developments since 1827, the interests and personnel of Toryism always defied precise sociological analysis as it did precise institutional definition. One assump- tion among contemporaries, though, stood out clearly. The Conservative party was about the defence of established interests against their enemies, even if the shape of the threat perceived changed in certain respects decade by decade.

This socio-economic base gave the party its backbone and it always influenced, positively or negatively, the governments the party maintained. It dictated much of the ideological content of Tory politics and bound men to the defence of those aspects of the constitution – such as the prerogatives of the Lords, a limited parliamentary franchise, the maintenance of the established churches and the assertion of property rights – which embodied or sheltered those interests. The pragmatism displayed by Tory ministers or politicians rarely went far beyond what these considerations permitted. But the very interests that gave weight to the party and exerted influence within it generated problems of their own. For one thing not all interests pointed in the same direction. For another, the best strategy for a particular interest was not always self-evident. Was it more prudent for the landowning classes to uphold or to repeal the Corn Laws in 1846, for example? Gentlemanly politicians, moreover, had reservations about the more overt kinds of interest-group politics. The parliamentary culture and tradition worked against a frank recognition of the element of material interest in Westminster politics. The upholders of the Corn Laws in the 1840s had suffered from the difficulties and embarrassments of a case too easily depicted as one of class interest. Virtually every interest had its critics and opponents and so could cause problems for Tory governments anxious to maintain social order and political tranquillity. In consequence ministers had often done very much less for their supporters than the latter had expected. The Anglican clergy and the protectionist gentry were only two interests that constantly felt let down by Tory ministries, even when not utterly betrayed. As the Catholic issue had shown in 1829 and 1845, ministers might become convinced that, for the good of the interests they served, they should enact measures which the great majority of their partisan supporters anathematized. The interests which normally gave the Tories their strength had, temporarily, become its weakness. The 1840s, like the 1820s, had shown that Toryism in office was likely to exacerbate the problems and uncertainties of its own interest-group politics.

Nor was the parliamentary party a microcosm of either the Tory interests or Tory opinion in society at large. The party had evolved out of the shifting groupings of Westminster politics, itself the politics of a relatively small élite within the larger body of patricians and substantial property-owners. Parliamentary politics were the sport of a minority of a minority. In 1861, admittedly a low ebb of political excitement, Edward Stanley reckoned that at most 93 peers out of some 380 eligible for the Upper House 'take part in public affairs, or are in any way before the public', and this number included Whigs and crossbenchers as well as Tories. Among such modest numbers it was easy for the zealous, active or ambitious to make their mark, all too easy for individual leaders of standing and influence to determine much of their side's political direction, particularly in office. There had been times, latterly under Liverpool and again under Peel after 1841, when Tory cabinets had led in directions that were unwelcome to most of their followers. High politics were thus never a simple manifestation of class or group interest. There was a further complexity too. The Westminster parties, led by men of similar social character, were part of a system of adversarial politics with all its confrontations, rivalries and competition for the fruits of office. The courses that leaders pursued were sometimes influenced by that 'game of politics' in ways that appalled many of their supporters, though the length to which Conservative leaders might be driven by the exigencies of adversarial politics still awaited the illustration of 1867. Leaders who told themselves and the faithful that they personified 'property against numbers' and the defence of the aristocratic constitution were still capable of bidding for support outside the ranks of the patrician and propertied and of playing to the gallery of 'public opinion' and the press. The backbenchers too could be swayed by the emotions engendered by adversarial politics and in the constituencies not firmly controlled by 'influence' party rivalry was often the very stuff of politics and fed upon its own practice. Peel's hope that parties – his own at least – might transcend partisanship and sectional interest and sustain a ministry more executive in its style and operation was asking too much. The danger, as some reflective Tories saw it, was rather that the Tory party, now released from the shackles of Peel's authority, might allow its adversarial instincts to overwhelm its prudence and so imperil its mission to maintain order and stability.

The emergent parties of the century's first half had organized themselves for certain, largely familiar kinds of activity, which included the making and unmaking of ministries within Parliament, competition for patronage, the conduct of parliamentary business during sessions and the contesting of elections and of election petitions. Because little of this was dramatically new, the institutional elaboration of party, even after 1832, had been modest. Parties were not primarily bodies for the evolution of policies and for the implementation of major legislative programmes. Legislative initiative was accepted as lying with ministers once they found themselves in office and with private members (whose bills and motions still took up much of each session) and major legislative proposals from whatever source were likely to find Tories in one or both of the Houses divided. Only on major divisions involving confidence was the party expected to be a monolith. Ministers who tried to turn their followers into a legislative machine and to change the line of demarcation between issues of confidence and normal legislative proposals, as Peel did after 1841, were likely to find themselves in trouble. Most contemporaries saw parties as standing for generalized 'principle', vague stances on major issues, rather than for detailed policy. This was one of the strengths of the parties but also, when major issues became too pressing to ignore, one of their weaknesses, for there were no established mechanisms outside Parliament itself for parties to decide and legitimize policies. At such moments of strain the quality and sensitivity of party leadership were crucial.

Leadership

Leadership in two senses – the few prominent individuals whom we can recognize as leaders in virtually the modern sense and the much larger cadre of the actual or potential holders of major offices, the patrons and magnates – was an essential feature of parliamentary politics. Frontbench quality and experience were needed in order to win and maintain office and, when in opposition, for the composition of a credible ministry-in-waiting. The character of Parliament and government determined the nature of this leadership. The constitution as patrician politicians understood it did not permit extra-parliamentary party organizations to force their leaders upon Parliament and the Crown. In fact leaders were most often installed and their rôles defined through the holding of office. A ministry required a leader in each House, one of them serving as first minister (First Lord of the Treasury) and acting as chairman of the Cabinet, the main line of communication with the Crown and the main source of major patronage. Standing achieved in office might carry over into opposition, though inevitably leadership in opposition lacked the definition and support given by the structures of government. Several *de facto* leaders of the emerging Tory party, Pitt, Liverpool and Peel among them, had had reservations about the legitimacy of party leadership as such and at certain points had declined to present themselves (perhaps even to recognize themselves) as primarily partisan leaders. The acceptance of the fact and of the idea grew only slowly out of older notions of the relationship between government and Parliament, of loyalty to the Crown and of the 'independence' appropriate to gentlemen politicians. On the Tory side the development of a party leadership distinct from the ministry had been held back by the long hold on office of the 'friends of order', though brief experiences of opposition in 1806–7 and 1827–28 had helped to sharpen men's perceptions and to identify Perceval and Wellington respectively more clearly as party leaders when they returned to office. Yet Wellington continued to view his primary loyalty as to the Crown and to the public service rather than to a body of partisan support. The nature of leadership among the Tories was hardly clarified initially by the loss of office in 1830. Wellington, soon under challenge himself in the Lords, could hardly control the Commons, where Peel, the former leader, now refused to serve. For some four years there was no established Tory leader in the Lower House and Wellington and his party experienced all the difficulties of a leadership poorly defined in its authority and functions and poorly supported institutionally. But the disintegration of the party had underlined these deficiencies and in late 1834 William and Wellington between them took steps to remedy them by installing Peel as first minister. As the Tamworth Manifesto clearly signalled, Peel insisted on presenting himself as the King's minister first and a party leader only second, if at all, but in opposition over the next few years he acted, with Wellington's support, and became accepted as overall party leader. He rallied support in the country as well as in Parliament, his name was used by the majority of candidates in 1841 and he was the inevitable first minister when the Conservatives returned to office. The problems, however, soon returned. Peel's leadership after 1841 was a remarkable combination of a harder driving and whipping of his MPs than ever before and of a blank refusal to accept that his position at the head of a party should determine anything of his course as minister. Indeed he argued that the royal commission put the ties and obligations of party into abeyance for a minister. His evident distaste for party except as a useful bulwark against radical change and as a bloc of votes supporting a ministry helped to produce the party crisis of 1845–46 and it was perhaps only through that experience that a leadership emerged in the persons of Stanley, Bentinck and then Disraeli that fully recognized its own party status and responsibilities and incorporated those interests and commitments into its ministerial ambitions. Though inevitably tensions between leaders and followers continued (and tended to be accentuated whenever the party took office), the shock of 1846 and the years of opposition that followed ensured that there was to be no return to the uncertainties and ambiguities of the style of leadership provided by Wellington and Peel.

Those two figures, however, had shown one potentiality of personal leadership – its capacity to project something of party and government well beyond Parliament and the great houses. Both men, like Pitt earlier, had been national figures widely written and talked about. That 'public opinion' which worried thinking politicians needed identifiable figures of a kind the press and the provincial public could recognize and relate to. Leadership nonetheless remained primarily parliamentary in purpose and character. In the last resort it depended upon the willingness of parliamentarians, both peers and MPs, to follow. Except when the royal commission made someone *de facto* leader, the installation and acknowledgement of leaders was only modestly formalized. The normal ritual was the issuing of invitations to party meetings before or early in the session by a whip or whips in the name of one or both of the foremost figures in the two Houses. Such meetings might ratify the emergence of one of the leaders as an overall leader in opposition, but they did not elect to a formal position that limited the royal choice if a government were formed and leadership remained more defined and expressed through parliamentary convention and practice than by the party's organizational structure or formal constitution. (The latter was in any case entirely lacking.) There was certainly no formal mechanism for getting rid of a leader, a circumstance that added to the uncertainties and embarrassments of 1846.

But whether a single leader or a dual leadership was acknowledged, there had to be collaboration between the senior figures who commanded experience, parliamentary weight and ability and electoral influence. A team had to be collected that could command wide support, particularly in the Commons, and a man who could not form a Cabinet from among his virtual equals was no leader at all. (In opposition occasional meetings of former senior office-holders might constitute something like a 'shadow Cabinet'.) Party leadership was thus always more diffused and collective than modern perspectives might suggest. The influence of Wellington and Stanley in supporting Peel in 1837–41 had shown that and Peel's problems in the Cabinet crisis at the end of 1845 did so again.[2] Stanley's weakness after 1846 was that he had virtually no other figures of real standing around him and that in the Commons the Tory front bench was scarcely recognizable as such.

Though virtually all MPs and many peers had accepted party designations and had become used to a degree of discipline, they did not take easily to leaders who tried to command them military-style. Both Wellington and

---

[2] Despite Peel's dominating style as premier, the collective element in the leadership showed once the Corn Law crisis broke. The dissent of two Cabinet ministers produced the Cabinet's resignation in December 1845 and the outcome of the subsequent negotiations depended on the interaction of Peel, Wellington, Stanley and the otherwise more marginal figure of Buccleuch, the party's leading magnate in Scotland. It was the agreement of the two dukes to continue to serve that enabled Peel to isolate Stanley and to continue in office for the moment.

Peel had alienated supporters with their authoritarian brusqueness. One of Stanley's virtues was that he saw his party as a body to be rallied when occasion required it rather than to be commanded. Gentlemen preferred to be treated as more than lobby-fodder and expected their leaders to behave like gentlemen too. Party leadership was now a complex exercise in personnel management (of both colleagues and followers), in parliamentary tactics and performance and in the manipulation of identity and image for attentive audiences within but also beyond Parliament. A proper collective leadership could increase the sensitivity of the strategists' antennae to party opinion, while the whips and other party managers could help to keep leaders and followers responsive to each other's needs, but the parliamentary sessions were still hard graft for the few leading figures who bore the brunt of the speaking in the two Houses and who had to keep their colleagues and backbenchers sweet. The professionalism of Disraeli's long commitment to the business of the front bench was to be a sign of the times as well as a major factor in his eventual success. One aspect of management, though, had become less of a problem: the enforced withdrawal of the Crown from overt political influence after 1841 meant that it could never again be the menace that George III and his sons had often been. The Tories did not enjoy the sympathy of Victoria and Albert after 1846 and they found the Court unhelpful in 1851–52, but there were limits to the damage it could inflict now. The royal prerogative of choosing (or attempting to choose) the first minister remained a potential problem for both parties, but the Conservatives never offered Victoria any choice while Derby remained active.

The normal prerequisites of leadership included the social station and means to sustain a major parliamentary career. Most Tory leaders were men of wealth themselves or came from families that owned property on a scale that overawed even the knights of the shires.[3] (Here Disraeli was an exception, as also in respect of his lack of patrician standing, but a loan from the Bentincks set him up as a country gentleman at Hughenden and enabled him to acquire the status of a county member.)[4] The peers and squires looked for a 'high tone' in their leaders such as Pitt, Castlereagh and Wellington had provided and Derby did now. Canning's less gilded origins had been among his handicaps and, despite his formidable wealth, Peel's family background in manufacturing was a disadvantage in his dealings with the squires, with some of the peers and with Stanley himself.

---

[3] Though the squirearchy were so numerous and influential in the Commons party, they figured little among its frontbenchers. Of the official leaders only Hicks Beach in 1885–86 was anything like a typical country gentleman. The inability of the country gentlemen in the Commons to produce leaders of frontbench calibre was one of their weaknesses. It left them with at most a power of veto over the policy of the party leaders.

As for the wealth factor, Peel's income was over £41,000 p.a. (Multiply by twenty to approximate to 1980s values.) Derby's was at least £60,000 p.a., though some reckoned it was much higher. Wealth on this scale was a tremendous asset for a political leader, not least in helping to confer a reputation for disinterestedness. Peel and Derby could pursue political success with a material independence and self-confidence very different from the financial worries and temptations that beset Russell and Disraeli.

[4] Disraeli's enemies, however, could exploit his origins. In 1868 his enemy Cranborne could inform a Conservative association that he was not 'identified by birth or property with the Conservative classes . . . he is an adventurer: & . . . without principle or honesty'.

Because social standing meant so much, a great grandee in the Lords like Wellington or Derby could exert some sway in the Commons too. Twice it was a factor that helped to save the party from worse disintegration. With the few exceptions when orators or men of business from more modest backgrounds proved their indispensability, the Tory leadership was essentially and naturally aristocratic and not merely plutocratic and this feature may even have become more important in mid-century when sections of the party saw their mission as the defence of the aristocratic constitution against a rising business class. The jibes about the 'Hotel Cecil' during Salisbury's leadership towards the century's end were novel only in being jibes.

This patrician character reigned perhaps even more evidently among the broad collective leadership. In metropolitan political society the party resembled a club of territorial magnates. The importance of Buccleuch to Peel's survival in office at the start of 1846 and the impact of Richmond's desertion to the Whigs in 1830 and of his return to the Tory colours by 1841 had many parallels. When three Cabinet members resigned over parliamentary reform in 1867, Derby could assert his Tory credentials and his support among his fellow-grandees by appointing two dukes among their replacements. It was normal anyway for Tory cabinets to draw half or more of their members from the Upper House. Most of them were magnates with considerable social and political influence in their parts of the country and with connections and influence in the Commons too. But there were limits to what even blue blood, great titles and vast rent-rolls could achieve against the grain of political change. Grandees like the dukes of Newcastle and Buckingham (and the royal duke of Cumberland) and the marquis of Londonderry had remained essentially maverick figures confined to the margins of influence by the official leaders whom they plagued. The aristocratic frondeur was a familiar figure of Tory politics and a party of government had to keep him in his place.[5] For office the party needed not just a patrician ambience but also a central élite capable of holding its own in debate and of conducting parliamentary, administrative and legislative business. It was usually well enough blessed on these scores in the Lords but there were times, most of all after 1846, when its front bench in the Commons was poorly staffed and suffered in comparison with the luminaries opposite. Early in the century the party's long hold on office and its inheritance of the official element left over from the eighteenth-century Commons had given it a near-monopoly of the 'men of business'. The wide appeal of its conservative purpose and its almost guaranteed occupation of office had helped the recruitment of ambitious young men from aristocratic, professional and even business backgrounds. Even so, debating ability was among the rarer qualities and at times the front bench in the Commons had been deficient in it. As Commons divisions were likely to decide the fate of ministries ('a Government cannot go on without the gift of the gab', Croker had written), the need for debating talent ensured the indispensability of Canning and later of Disraeli. It was the vast

---

[5] Disraeli's comment in 1880 on the diehard Earl of Redesdale, Chairman of Committees in the Lords and frequent chairman of the Carlton committee, summed up the frontbenchers' view of such men: 'many excellent qualities and talents, but . . . narrow-minded, prejudiced, and utterly unconscious of what is going on in the country, its wishes, opinions, or feelings'.

haemorrhage of debating as well as administrative talent in 1846 that diminished the Protectionists' credibility as an alternative government and the poor prospects of office handicapped the recruitment of new talent. Men of obvious frontbench ability were highly transferable. The restructuring of 1827–37 had included an element of competition to secure the available talent, as the politics of the 1850s would do too. Stanley and Graham had brought an immense accession of debating ability as well as ministerial experience to the Tories in the Commons in 1837; the Peelites Graham, Gladstone, Herbert and Cardwell returned it with interest to the Whigs in the 1850s.

These men were not mere officials like the working placemen of the old Court party – the latter element were now classed as civil servants and separated from Commons politics – but gentlemen politicians of social standing who could run a ministry, handle a brief in the House, deal with the Court and shoulder public responsibility. They provided the core of a credible ministry and much of its public profile. Certain kinds of competence, though, tended to be in short supply, particularly when the placemen had departed from the Commons. Both parties felt themselves to be short of expertise in finance and trade and the rapid rise of Peel and Gladstone reflected their ability and self-confidence in these areas. It was not expertise the backbench gentry could supply and Tory leaders were painfully aware of their deficiency after the loss of so much ministerial talent in 1846. Witness Bentinck's frenzied efforts to master the statistics of trade and finance in 1846–48, Derby's later attempts to recruit Thomas Baring, head of the family Bank and chairman of Lloyds, as his Chancellor of the Exchequer and later still the rapid rise of the ex-civil servant Northcote. It was not simply a matter of debating competence. Conservative governments, despite or because of 1846, would need to inspire confidence in the City and among mercantile interests. Despite its commitment to the 'aristocratic constitution', there were limits to how far the Tory party could press its claims to office simply on the grounds of pedigree and broad acres.

The Parliamentary Party

Early in the century business confidence in Tory government had come more easily. Financial and commercial interests had feared both the French and domestic radicalism and had rallied to Pitt, patriotism and order. The property rights which Toryism upheld embraced commercial and funded property as well as land. The war governments had enjoyed close relations with the Bank of England and the Indies companies, even when the Orders-in-Council rendered relations with provincial manufacturers and merchants acrimonious. But the post-Waterloo revival of Whiggish reformism in the City, the Tory loss of office in 1830 and the growing influence of the agricultural lobby weakened these ties. The City showed its nervousness at Tory anti-Reform truculence in 1831–32 and the Reform Act almost eliminated the once-extensive electoral influence of the pro-Tory Indies companies.[6] Though the Tory success in two of the four City

---

[6] In 1846 Bentinck estimated the Indies interests in the Commons at 16 members, mostly West Indians. In 1802 one reckoning had put the East India interest alone at 95 members.

of London seats in 1841 was a token of their leaders' standing and of City impatience with Whig financial management, these seats were otherwise dominated by Whigs and Liberals between the two Reform Acts, the Tory position collapsing after 1846. But Toryism was never extinct among the business classes. Family tradition, Churchmanship, protectionism and social-climbing aspirations all helped the party's appeal to sections of the propertied bourgeoisie. There was always at least a sprinkling of financiers, brewers (though not on the later scale), merchants and shipowners on the Tory benches in the Commons, among them Baring the banker, the elder Peel the cotton spinner, Cobbold the brewer, Hudson the 'Railway King', the Gladstones for the West Indies interest and Young the shipyard owner who attempted in 1849 to unite the commercial and the agricultural protection lobbies. Some of these men sat for towns where they had interest and influence, others were prepared to spend their money on the smaller and more amenable boroughs.

At times, though, particularly when the party's fortunes were down and its borough representation suffered, parliamentary Toryism represented a club for the aristocracy and gentry. Aristocratic self-consciousness was a feature of Toryism at this level. Here, in Westminster, in the clubs and in high society the peers and the gentry mixed and mingled much as they did in county society. The peers were always a considerable force, both collectively and also through the capacity and influence of individuals. The Tory phalanx in the Upper House exercised an influence upon the leadership, upon legislative policy (for example in checking Peel's attempts at Irish land reform after the Devon Commission) and upon the Commons party where so many scions and connections of the peers sat. In the early 1830s and again after 1846 the party's centre of gravity had lain in the Lords, though on the latter occasion Stanley's influence had at least ensured that the party's two parts kept reasonably in step. The Commons party was inevitably less homogeneous in social composition than that in the Lords, where only the odd arriviste lawyer, banker or military man diluted the strength of landownership, but the former was still heavily dominated by the gentry and connections of the peerage. The domination was a matter both of numbers and of the prestige of the county seats which the 1832 Act had increased in number. In the division on Disraeli's budget of 1852, when all the other parties opposed, the Tory minority of 188 included 149 county members, 113 of them English, with only 29 in the majority. Though there are various and differing estimates of the economic interests represented in the Commons, they all agree on the dominant weight of landownership. One puts the ratio of landed to business interests among Tories in 1833 at 8:1 (when it was 6:2 among the Reformers) and still at 9:2 in 1865. Another reckons that the Commons party of 1865 included nearly 200 landowners against about 110 men of business backgrounds. It was not surprising that both opponents and supporters of the party identified it with the maintenance of the aristocratic constitution and with the interests of landownership. If anything this identity was even stronger in respect of Ireland, where the landed classes faced serious challenges, than for England or Scotland. Many of the British aristocracy owned Irish land and the Union with Ireland had also brought numbers of Irish peers and gentry to Westminster to swell the Tory ranks. (The representative peers for both Ireland and Scotland were Tory-controlled blocs.) Even on the Tory side landownership was never monolithic – there were differences of outlook between the magnates and the mere gentry, between frontbenchers and the perpetual backbenchers and between the proponents of class interest and those of party advantage – but the conclusion that it was part of the essence of parliamentary Toryism was almost unavoidable in mid-century. When in 1850 Stanley lamented the shortage of young men entering politics to defend 'their order', he intended that phrase to signify 'the proprietors of the soil'.

At least down to the 1850s Tory leaders sometimes used the phrase 'the country party' for a section of their Commons following. The 'country gentlemen' in this narrower sense were usually county members and, responsive to some extent to the freeholders and tenant farmers among their electorates as well as to their fellow-gentry, they tended to constitute themselves the spokesmen for agricultural interests. Though staunchly conservative on issues like religion and Ireland, their notions of 'independence' made them difficult to discipline by the party managers and they tended to have minds of their own on issues of retrenchment, taxation and agriculture. They had helped to abolish the income tax in 1816 and to keep Liverpool's government under pressure over retrenchment and in later years they had given trouble over currency questions and the malt tax. Though they responded to the tighter party discipline after 1834–35, the Tory government's drift towards freer trade after 1841 was soon countered by the truculence of the agricultural gentry, some sixty of whom constituted a lobby for the defence of the Corn Laws. In the end their loyalty to the ministry and their fear of resumed Whig government were outweighed by their resentment of Peel's style of leadership and by their growing concern for agriculture and their constituencies. The last point was not unimportant. The natural inclinations of Tory members were sometimes reinforced, sometimes modified, by the constituencies they represented – predominantly the counties, the small and often agricultural boroughs and the universities. The counties, with their strongly representative politics, were recognized as having particularly strong claims upon their members. Peel's contempt for the 'blockheads' betrayed his blindness or indifference to this representative element among his parliamentary followers. 1846 showed its importance and future Tory leaders, whatever their private reservations about the 'country gentlemen', their instincts and their grumbles, had to pay them some heed.

Next to land the most important interest represented within the parliamentary party was the established churches, above all the Church of England. In the Lords the government-nominated bishops were overwhelmingly pro-Tory until 1830 and predominantly Whiggish in mid-century, but the lay support for the Church was always weightier than the clerical. Virtually all Tory parliamentarians were of one or more of the three establishments, the church of England accounting for the great majority, and they accepted that the interests and the constitutional position of those institutions were properly among their main concerns. Certain peers could be Churchier than some of the bishops and in the Commons there was a 'Church party' which took its lead from the members for the universities (nearly always Tories), particularly during the 1830s and 1840s from Sir Robert Inglis, member for Oxford University. This group of about fifty, which overlapped with the 'country party', was drawn mainly from the gentry and aristocracy, many of them patrons of Anglican livings, though it also had support among the professional and business men. From 1829 onwards Tory governments usually disappointed these zealots. Though kinder towards the Church than their Whig counterparts, Tory ministers found that there were political limits to the positive assistance they could render the Church. Religious issues, moreover, like those of agriculture, could divide Tories as well as unite them. The problems Peel's ministry experienced with the 'Disruption' in the Scottish kirk and with the growth of Puseyism (and of the reaction against it) in England added, as did Maynooth in 1845, to the divisions among Conservatives at Westminster.[7] The party split of 1846 also divided Anglicans and contributed to a weakening of the cohesion of political Churchmanship. By 1850 the Church interest in the Commons was less united than it had been formerly and there was never to be another leader as readily accepted as Inglis. Though Conservatives (and Peelites too) could usually unite when the Church's interests were obviously at stake (for example in opposing motions for the abolition of compulsory Church rates), it was clear during Palmerston's ascendency that the Church interest, though still powerful in both Houses, no longer provided a clear direction for the Conservative party. The latter was something rather more and rather less than the Anglican Church at politics.

One major religious issue, namely the confrontation between Protestantism and Popery, was not simply a question of establishment. The two greatest revolts among Tory parliamentarians, 1846 excepted, were over Catholic Emancipation in 1829 and Maynooth in 1845. Many Tories, among them Beresford and Newdegate, the Protectionist whips from 1846, saw the defence of Protestantism as central to the Tory mission. Inglis was a scourge of Papists as well as of religious liberals[8] and the capacity of the party for outraged 'Protestantism' was to be shown again by Papal Aggression in 1850–51. Though the Irish peers and MPs had added to the virulently Orange element at Westminster, many of their British counterparts needed little prompting. The secession of the Peelites in 1846 had left the Tory rump with less restraint upon its instincts, but there was another factor at work. Even those Tories who disliked religious emotion at Westminster and who recognized government's difficulties with Ireland's Catholic majority had to concede something to anti-Catholic feeling in the constituencies. The elections of 1847 and 1852 showed that anti-Popery had a stronger hold among the electorate than protectionism did and that it remained a major part of the Tory appeal. A largely aristocratic parliamentary party which saw the protection of the Church of England as its main religious cause was finding that No Popery enlisted a breadth of popular support, including that of many Nonconformists, which the Church itself could hardly command.

---

[7] The schism in the Church of Scotland in 1843, which arose from controversy over the rights of appointment to the ministry, was not mainly of the government's making, but the Free Church which resulted from it was to be a fierce opponent of the Conservative party in Scotland.

[8] After Inglis had led the opposition to the admission of Jews to Parliament and so helped to end Bentinck's leadership, Peel wrote 'I hope to see Inglis in his proper place as the leader of a real old Tory, Church of England, Protectionist, Protestant party'.

Constituencies

Though the parliamentary sessions provided the main arena of party politics, the constituencies mattered too. Inevitably their influence was felt more in general elections (sometimes in by-elections too), but even between elections MPs felt the pressure of local interests and of constituency feelings and might feel it their duty to represent them. It was a factor which differentiated Commons politics from those of the Lords, though peers sometimes cultivated opinion in the constituencies where they had influence. The county constituencies had been central to the Corn Law crisis of 1846. In 1845–47 and 1850–52, as on earlier occasions, constituency opinion firmed up the anti-Catholicism of parliamentarians. Few members wished to risk their seats or contests that might entail considerable expense. But the diversity among constituencies, even those that returned Conservatives, ensured that the pressures did not all operate in the same direction. Some members had to heed even Nonconformist or free-trade sentiments that were influential in their constituencies. Tories who sat for large boroughs could easily find themselves pushed in directions different from those taken by colleagues attuned to the counties and agricultural boroughs. If constituencies influenced MPs more, patrons now did so rather less than before 1832, partly because there were fewer seats subject to direct nomination. Though magnates like Newcastle, Lonsdale and Londonderry still had their nominees in the Commons and expected a degree of deference from them, influence of this kind was in retreat before the growth of party loyalty and discipline, factors that also limited the impact of the constituencies on the House. But even the party managers recognized members' right to represent the interests of their constituencies, particularly the more 'independent' kinds like the county divisions and the large boroughs. Some constituency interests were broad and general, like agricultural protection or the Church; others were more specific, like a concern for a particular trade or a town's ambition to obtain a railway line.

The character and composition of Toryism in the constituencies are rarely easy to establish, though naturally they were less aristocratic than the Westminster equivalent. Despite the spread of Conservative and Constitutional clubs in the boroughs during the late 1830s, there was still no formal party membership as we would understand it. Contested elections at least revealed something of the scale of Conservative sentiment, but certain kinds of constituencies, notably the county divisions, were not regularly contested. Even the pollbooks, the best source for voting patterns until the secret ballot ended them in 1872, were published mainly for the small and middling boroughs and rarely for other kinds of constituencies.[9] They can tell us nothing about opinion when there were no contests or about the significant part of the adult population which was unenfranchised. But the evidence that we do possess shows that Toryism, even in the troughs of its fortunes, enjoyed substantial support within the great majority of constituencies. Some of it, admittedly, was an extension of the influence of the gentry and aristocracy. There were county divisions where dynasties like the Lowthers, the Manners, the Cecils, and Stewarts and the Pelhams would, if forced to a contest, bring their tenants and dependants to the poll

---

[9] See J. R. Vincent, *Pollbooks. How Victorians Voted* (Cambridge, 1967).

in traditional fashion. In many of the small boroughs that had survived 1832 the influence of landowners and employers underpinned the Tory position similarly and, as the old kinds of negotiation for seats had died out, party managers had come to rely on the 'natural' influence of local property. But Toryism was always much more than matters of influence and deference, even when the patriotism and loyalism of the war period receded and when fears about social stability lessened. This support had, however, fluctuated over the decades. The enthusiasm of the minor gentry, freeholders and tenant farmers of the counties for Tory governments had been hit hard by agricultural depression in the 1820s, but support for Peel's party had then benefited mightily from the prominence of the protection issue from the late 1830s, by which time the tenant vote had been much increased. Much of this agricultural support stayed with the party even after 1852 and, except where Nonconformity had made inroads among the farmers, the agricultural societies and farmers' clubs remained bastions of Toryism throughout the Victorian period. Religion too sustained the party in the constituencies. The clergy and committed laity of the established churches provided a Tory potential nearly everywhere. (Though some Wesleyan Methodists were Conservatives and were responsive to the No Popery cry, the party had virtually no other support from Protestant Nonconformity.) The party's anti-Catholic identity supplemented this support and gave it a popular dimension it might otherwise have lacked in many urban constituencies. 'Protestantism', with its patriotic and moral connotations, transcended class and sectional interest more effectively than the church establishments did, though its force fluctuated with the prominence of the Catholic question. The Tory identification with resistance to parliamentary reform antagonized many electors (and presumably many non-electors too) but also won the party many friends, not just among cautious conservatives who feared the radical consequences of further reform but also among surviving voters on the pre-1832 franchises and among small boroughs nervous about their own prospects in a further redistribution of seats. The pre-1832 voters remained an influential body in a number of constituencies for some time after the Reform Act, particularly where there had been a freeman franchise, and they were often active in the foundation of Conservative clubs and Constitutional associations in the boroughs in the late 1830s. The Tory oligarchies that had been entrenched in the old municipal corporations also continued as a substantial party interest in many boroughs after 1835. In fact, despite the party's image as one of landed gentry and county divisions, few boroughs lacked a Tory interest of at least moderate significance and there were some, notably among the ports and cathedral cities, where it was a majority interest with an appeal little dented by the reforms of the 1830s.

The pollbooks show us something of the breadth and depth of this support in the small and middling boroughs. The extent to which it cut across class and occupational boundaries can be explained partly by religious factors and partly by networks of influence and patronage. Occupation and social status were still, however, among the palpable influences on political behaviour. The Tories were usually in the majority among the 'gentlemen' and the professions but weaker than the Reformers or Liberals among the shopkeeper, tradesman, artisan and other industrial categories. (Even among the shopkeepers, though, there were countervailing influences: butchers were more likely to be Conservatives, grocers Liberals, probably because the former depended more on the custom of the wealthy.) The party's candidates often attracted most support among those of the unskilled ('labourers' and so on) who had the vote, maybe because of the strength of deference among them but more likely because of their responsiveness to the beer, bribery and bovver that the Tory side often provided generously. (Nonconformity with its Liberal disposition was also weak among the unskilled.) For obvious reasons voters in occupations connected with horses or carriages tended to vote Conservative. In the ports the party derived considerable support from its connections with shipping interests, the colonial trades and protectionism and it often had the majority of votes from the merchant class and others with maritime connections. In places like garrison and dockyard towns where the government had influence, the Tory interest weakened during its years of opposition after 1830 and again after 1846, though there was some compensation for the loss of office in boroughs where the party could pose as the defender of local 'independence' against Whig governments and centralizing bureaucrats of the Chadwick variety. But even when borough Toryism had some popular vitality, it tended to look to prominent men of local influence and wealth to give a lead and provide finance.

Local diversity, though, often defied neat generalization. Totnes in Devon, for example, had formerly been a Tory-dominated corporation borough where money played a major part in elections. The Reform Act had brought the estates of the Whig Duke of Somerset into the extended constituency and now he was normally able to control at least one of the seats. As Totnes was not particularly agricultural or protectionist, there was little to sustain a Tory challenge beyond the readiness of many electors to sell their votes and the enthusiasm of several local attorneys for forcing a contest by finding a Tory candidate with a long pocket. Here the struggle, such as it was, was between Whig influence and Tory money, though money from outside the town. Religious affiliation probably determined some votes but national issues had at best a modest impact on the borough's elections and its reputation for venality helped to produce its disenfranchisement in 1868. Though its party colour had changed, Totnes had remained defiantly traditional. In contrast the county town and cathedral city, Exeter, had a strongly entrenched Toryism which, even after the 1835 Municipal Corporations Act had shaken its grip on the corporation, competed vigorously with the Reformers so that the seats were shared between the parties, five times without a contest, in eight of the nine general elections between the Reform Acts. The party depended on a substantial Church interest, on the support and patronage of neighbouring landowners, on the influence and commitment of a number of business leaders, bankers and builders prominent among them, and on those shopkeepers and tradesmen who catered to the 'carriage trade'. Despite its Barchester flavour, Exeter displayed a diversity of interests and cross-currents of opinion well beyond the scope of Totnes. It was also rather more responsive to the issues and developments of national politics. But the even larger borough constituencies sustained party politics that were still more recognizably modern in their admixture of local and national conflicts and controversies. For example Liverpool, where the defeat of the Peelite Cardwell produced a Tory (and Protestant) triumph in 1852, had contests in eight of the nine general elections, Birmingham (where the Tories were the normal minority party) five and Marylebone seven.

Most constituencies had leading figures who sustained the party interest. In the counties they were usually peers or substantial gentry, as they might be in the smaller boroughs, but in the middling and larger borough constituencies they were likely to be professional men (particularly lawyers or bankers) and local employers (shipbuilders and shipowners, brewers, manufacturers, merchants). Occasionally men of this kind stood for the House themselves; more often they found suitable candidates from among the traditional parliamentary classes and worked for their election. The party's central managers could not afford to ignore these figures. The Conservative whips in the two Houses had a worried exchange in 1841 when a Mr Lawrence of Gloucestershire East applied for a public post:

> Our position in this division of the county is mainly owing to his exertions, & he has spent a good deal of money in the canvass . . . He is known all over the division, far better than Codrington or Charteris [the members], and both certainly in a good degree owe their seats to his efforts. He has some influence in Cheltenham & the late good fight there . . . was greatly promoted by his exertions.

The importance of local 'exertions' meant that the party managers had to work with the grain of constituency politics. Conservatism, as it manifested itself in elections and as it reached the Commons, was a complex of localized forces and interests which only occasionally were swept along or aside by the emotions generated by great national issues like Catholics, corn or parliamentary reform.

But influence did not flow only one way. The impact of Westminster politics on the localities had increased during the century's first half. The localism of the constituencies was being aligned with national causes, adopting the labels of parliamentary parties and electing (or accepting) candidates attached to those parties. The King's Friends and the parliamentary independents had been almost eliminated by the 1830s and, though party splits like those of the Derbyites and the Peelites could still cause some stirring and blurring of identities, there was never to be any wholesale revival of traditional forms of connexion or of old-style independence. Though the Toryism of Totnes and the Toryism of Birmingham were not identical, they were on courses of convergence. Though there were occasions, as in 1831–32 and 1846, when Commons politics were wrenched into new forms by the force of opinion in the constituencies, the long-term trend was the disciplining of localism by the growing strength of the parliamentary parties. The parties were instruments by which Westminster politicians, themselves largely drawn from the central élites of national life, imposed themselves upon the constituencies and channelled the diverse aspirations, discontents and interests within British society into constitutional forms. In this way, though the parties helped to transform certain features of the constitution, they did more to stabilize it.

Management

One element in this process, party management, was certainly not an invention of the post-1832 period. In one form it had enjoyed a heyday in the late eighteenth-century Court party and the Treasury had long been the seat of management, much of it discreet in character. Men like Holmes, Planta and Arbuthnot had played a central rôle in the consolidation of support and the management of constituencies, particularly the small boroughs, for early nineteenth-century ministries. As government became more identifiably Tory, in contradistinction to Whig, these men had become in effect party managers and not simply Treasury functionaries. But it was the loss of office in 1830 which put matters to the test. The virtually clean sweep of office-holders by Grey put these 'men of business' into opposition where they promptly started to work for the return of their friends and themselves to office. The informal committee established in 1831, the 'Charles Street Gang', though it gained backing from Wellington and financial assistance from Tory magnates, owed more to the second-rank administrators than it did to the great names. From its activities developed both the Carlton Club and a permanent system of electoral management.

The management of the parliamentary personnel remained, however, a crucial part of party organization. Despite the innovations after 1832 the familiar post of the parliamentary whip remained an integral part of the party's operation, just as the two Houses remained the primary forum of party politics. (It was a comment on Tory disorganization that the party apparently had no Commons whip in 1833.) Though normally appointed by the recognized leaders, the whips could be influential in their own right. In 1846 the Protectionist MPs in revolt against Peel elected their own whips. The senior figure, Major William Beresford, was, from Bentinck's resignation, which he helped to secure, until his own fall after the 1852 election, as influential and assertive in the Commons party as any of its nominal leaders. Normally, however, whips were discreet and subordinate figures who accepted that their task was to serve the recognized leadership. Old-style Commons management had included the dispensation of Treasury patronage as well as the supervision of the placemen and by the 1830s the post of chief whip in government was combined with that of patronage secretary to the Treasury. Though the shady side of the work was still regarded as something of a disqualification for the very highest offices, the whips' posts in the Commons were becoming more gentlemanly in their occupants as the Tory ranks were stripped of their placemen and became dominated by the county members. The typical Tory whip would henceforth be a country gentleman himself and fitted to manage others of his kind. Peel was well served by one of this type, Sir Thomas Fremantle (whip 1837–44), as Disraeli was to be even more notably by Sir William Jolliffe (1853–66). Such men – affable clubmen but firm with dissidents, loyal to the front bench and with no axes of their own to grind, efficient as channels of communication and influence to and from the back benches and, to some extent, the constituencies – could be the making of the better-known leaders. The very survival of a ministry or the morale of an opposition might depend on their success, not least in persuading the country gentlemen to attend early in the session and to stay late.

Perhaps the main novelty of the situation after 1830 was that Tory organization now had to establish itself in opposition to the Treasury, but another feature was that aspects of constituency liaison began to separate out from the work of the whips. This development was far from clear-cut and there was never any complete separation between parliamentary and extra-parliamentary management. Bonham, a significant figure in the development, was himself an assistant whip in the 1835 parliament and held minor office in Peel's two ministries. But the need for constant attention to the constituencies even outside the sessions, the more gentlemanly character of the whip's office and the lack of support from Treasury officialdom meant that some bureaucratic back-up was needed for the party managers that was obscure enough to be at a safe remove from the recognized leadership. The new premises of the Carlton Club in Pall Mall provided a centre away from the Palace of Westminster and the Treasury where party business could be transacted while peers, MPs and other men of position mingled socially. By the late 1830s the phrase 'the Carlton Club' was being used to denote the party organizers. But the new management represented no sharp break with the old. The whips from the Commons and, in the persons of first Rosslyn and then Redesdale, from the Lords were closely involved and the central group, which seems to have constituted a permanent committee from 1835, remained closely identified with the parliamentary leadership. There were limits to the rôle of Bonham, the figure usually associated with the Tadpole and Taper image of what Disraeli called the 'unseen management' of the party. Bonham's main concern was with the boroughs, the smaller ones particularly, and he was little involved with the county divisions where the landowning classes continued to provide their own style of direction. Scotland and Ireland, moreover, were run separately from the English organization. The central rôle of the territorial grandees in Scotland and of the Protestant gentry class in Ireland had survived 1832. The central finance of the party was also kept under the control of the whips and of men like Rosslyn and Hardinge who combined social standing with closeness to the party leaders.

The Carlton, though founded only in 1832, could itself be seen as a reaffirmation of a traditional feature, the political club. Though the old Whig club, Brooks's, had kept its party identity, that of its former Tory equivalent, White's, had become obscured by decades of parliamentary groupings and regroupings. The Carlton clearly met a need. The increase of its original membership limit as early as 1833 and the long waiting lists thereafter showed how well represented Toryism was among gentlemen capable of entry fees and annual subscriptions of ten guineas a time. A home-from-home for the whips and managers, the Carlton helped to pull the party together after the Reform Act, to bridge any gulf between the Lords and the Commons and between 'men of business' and the country gentlemen and to replace the old ethos of 'independence' with party loyalty. In these years the club was a force for conformity rather than backbench rebellion, though it felt the strains caused by Corn and Catholics, as the secession to form the National Club showed in 1845. (In 1851 the latter's membership included 45 MPs, mostly hostile to Disraeli's lead in the Commons.) The Carlton had been unmistakably Tory from the start, so that Stanley and Graham had signalled their accession to the party when they joined it, but it provided no organizational model for the new-style Conservatism. Its committee had no official chairman, though Redesdale chaired it often in the early decades, and not until 1912 did it adopt a rule that applicants had to be members of the Conservative party. The contemporary phrase 'club government' overstated the significance of the Carlton and of its adversary, the Reform Club, in the developments that followed 1832. The Carlton's success was created by as much as it contributed to the Tory resurgence after the disasters of 1829–32 and that success faltered when the party itself experienced setbacks. The schisms of 1845 and 1846 and the uncertain status of Peel's followers subsequently (Gladstone did not resign from the club until 1860) seem to have reduced the Carlton's political effectiveness and this may have influenced Disraeli's decision in 1853 to vest the party's electoral management in his solicitors' firm.

The party management which went beyond the whips' familiar work was concerned primarily with the development and tuning of the election-fighting capacity, a preoccupation which the series of general elections in the 1830s had encouraged. Working on constituencies and their patrons, finding candidates for constituencies and vice-versa, encouraging contests (which meant persuading supporters to spend their money and to 'break the peace' of their localities), advising the leaders on tactics, patronage and dissolution prospects, promoting or opposing election petitions (the petition against O'Connell's return for Dublin in 1835 inspired a major Tory effort) were all part of the work. The rejigged constituencies and enlarged electorate of 1832 had outdated much of the old expertise and had put a premium upon hard work to master the new; the system of registering electors introduced by the Reform Act had necessitated central encouragement of local supporters, particularly in the boroughs, to keep the registers up to date and to work the revising courts in the party's interests. But this relationship between the parliamentary party and the localities was not essentially new. Management remained, as it had long been, part of the texture of political life, whether Conservatives were in or out of office, and Parliament could hardly have operated in its familiar ways without it. At times – the early 1830s were an obvious case – the managers worked to hold the Tories together with little or no help from a recognized leader in the Commons. The loss of the prominent frontbench names in 1846 was compounded by that of the party organizers. Granville Somerset, a major figure who combined frontbench status with a central role in the organization, Young, the chief whip, and Bonham all remained loyal to Peel.[10] In Scotland many of the influential magnates were lost by the Protectionists, though in Ireland the Protestant Ascendancy gave a backbone to native Toryism and the party organization was relatively little damaged by the Peelite schism. But for years the Tories in England and Scotland found themselves shorn of the old organizational expertise and it was not to be easily replaced.

The relationship between the recognized leaders and the party management was not entirely stable. Liverpool, Wellington and, at certain times and in certain respects, Peel had taken management for granted and given it encouragement and recognition. After 1846 and the loss of the official men neither Bentinck nor Stanley took a particular interest; the neglect into which management fell was the despair of Beresford who carried its

[10] For the party organization see Norman Gash's chapter on Bonham in *Temporal Pillars* (a revision of an article originally published in *English Historical Review*, LXIII, 1948) and his two articles on 'The Organization of the Conservative Party, 1832–1846' in *Parliamentary History*, I, 1982, and II, 1983.

main burden. Though Secretary-at-War, he managed the 1852 general election for the party. The defeat of the Peelite Cardwell at Liverpool was a Tory triumph, but the aggressive and anti-Catholic tone of Beresford's campaign disturbed some parliamentary colleagues as well as worsened relations with the Peelites. The over-indulgence in official patronage and influence was perhaps a reflection of Tory perceptions of the party's weakness. Beresford had strained the system's tolerance without achieving efficiency or success and this was serious for a party which, if it failed to achieve a reconstruction within Parliament, could look only to electoral gains for its recovery. Malmesbury, perhaps with exaggeration, urged on Disraeli

> the absolute necessity of reforming our personnel and getting matters into an administrative form. . . . It is better to fail in orators to back you by words than in men to back you by votes. *We lost the Elections from bad management* and are out in consequence.

Beresford's condemnation by the House for 'reckless indifference to systematic bribery' gave Disraeli his chance. He appointed his solicitor, Philip Rose, who was to be aided by Markham Spofforth, as party agent and henceforth, with Jolliffe now chief whip, party management found itself on a broader and firmer basis. But even Disraeli, an enthusiast for electoral management despite his comments in *Coningsby*, had to distance himself from its details. As Beresford's fate showed, management often involved the dubious and the shady – financial transactions that sailed close to the wind of corruption, patronage negotiations of potential embarrassment and dealings with the constituencies that sometimes provoked local resentment, as those of 'the Carlton Club' had often done in the 1830s. There remained an appearance of separation between the parliamentary leadership and that 'unseen management' by obscurer men which usually belied the realities.

Finance

Finance was a necessary preoccupation of party management. Parties needed money; even more, they required men with money. Parliamentary politics were rich men's sport (a circumstance which both limited the discipline which party leaders could hope to exert over their wealthier followers and helped men of wealth to maintain their political influence and position when they changed parties) and it was often the task of party leaders and managers to encourage the sport, particularly to persuade men with local influence to contest seats at what might be considerable financial sacrifice. The readiness to contest seats in the party interest was an index of zeal, morale and resolve. When in 1850 Stanley sought to 'rouse the gentlemen of the country from ... apathy', he noted that 'desertions and defeat have at once reduced their means and depressed their spirits; and they neither can, nor will, make the pecuniary sacrifices and exertions'. Problems of this sort were often the nub of party management. A parliamentary career itself was a considerable expense – estimated at an average of £800 per annum upwards for a county seat and from £400 for a borough seat,[11] even without the costs of living in London during the

---

[11] M. Pinto-Duschinsky, *British Political Finance 1830–1980* (1981), ch. 1.

session. Expense might be reduced by a series of unopposed returns at general elections but could be increased significantly by contests and petitions. The major cost was not always bribery and corruption; the expense of politics was usually more a matter of legitimate than of illegitimate expenditure as electoral law defined the latter.

The common view that early Victorian politics were prey to the 'corruption' inflicted by the wealthy misses several points. One is that legitimate 'influence' was usually far more important than cash, though there was certainly a class of borough where money spoke very loud. Another is the fact that few men of means bled themselves gladly for political purposes and that 'corruption' was fuelled by an importunity which came from much lower in the social scale. The third is that the more obviously partisan kinds of expenditure were only part of the total investment in political influence. There were many kinds of expenditure and transaction – for example the purchase of estates and properties, the negotiation with tenants over rents, patterns of custom and patronage – which had political purposes or implications. Party politics were naturally interwoven with other aspects of social and economic life and would remain so while there was no secret ballot to give confidentiality to voting behaviour. Perhaps we should simply accept that the parliamentary constitution in which parties and elections had become central features operated through extensive subsidy out of private pockets and could hardly have developed such vigorous party politics without this access to private capital.

Though most expenditure was local or private and relatively little came from central party funds in this period, there were such funds in existence. Early nineteenth-century administrations had had available to them the civil list and the secret service money, the traditional resorts for official 'influence'. The Crown, in both the personal and the institutional senses, was the great paymaster. Yet, though its origins are obscure, a regular party fund seems to have existed by Wellington's premiership and, after being taken into opposition in 1830, to have been used extensively in 1831. The Tory experience of opposition in 1806–7 and 1827–28, the barring of direct government purchase of seats by Curwen's Act (1809) and the increasing pressure upon and inquiry into the civil list by a retrenchment-minded Commons after 1815 may all have encouraged the separation of certain aspects of political finance from Treasury management and the loss of office in 1830 inevitably completed this process. Though the existence of a Tory party chest was sometimes denied, it is clear that there were such funds and that Rosslyn, later Hardinge, was the main distributor among candidates and constituencies, usually in consultation with the whips, managers and leaders. Though the permanent chest was minimal, each general election saw a fund-raising effort, the largest contributions normally coming from the wealthier peers. In 1831 Buccleuch was the largest contributor with some £10,000, in 1837 Newcastle with £2000. Derby, who had been criticized earlier for his backwardness, gave £20,000 to party purposes in 1859. The Tories, who even in their worst moments commanded great support among the wealthier classes, were probably always better financed than their opponents and there were Reformers who talked (misleadingly) as if the electoral forms of 'Old Corruption' were virtually a Tory prerogative.

Only a small minority of candidates and constituencies received help from central funds and the transactions were usually kept confidential. Disraeli was aided with sums of £300 and £500 for borough contests in the mid-1830s. The £2000 which Ashley was offered from the pockets of leading ministerialists in 1846 if he stood for re-election as a Conservative free-trader in Dorset was a remarkably large sum. Even after general elections further funds were required (they were often raised by subscriptions at the Carlton) for the promotion or defence of petitions alleging corrupt practices. The effort to unseat O'Connell as MP for Dublin in 1835 may have cost the Tories over £5000. But usually central funds could do little more than pump-priming and the party's fortunes depended much more on the 'exertions' that men of wealth and position were willing to make for it. Thus the loss of the modest central chest controlled by the party managers in 1846 damaged the Protectionists much less than the loss of a body of support among the magnate and gentry classes who provided most of the finance for party purposes.

Place and Patronage

Patronage was both a lubricant of the workings of party and a cement of its structures. Though the early nineteenth century had witnessed a steady reduction of the patronage, particularly sinecure places, available to government, the surviving political correspondence of the period shows no corresponding decline in the appetite for place and pension, profit and honours. Indeed the diminution of certain kinds of patronage (and possibly an increase of the contenders for it) put the remaining resources under increased pressure. It was no coincidence that government chief whips came to serve as patronage secretaries to the Treasury. The parliamentary parties were among the main providers of patronage both in actuality and in anticipation. Had they not been, they would have commanded much less support. The Tories experienced sharply contrasting fortunes: first the near-monopoly of public patronage down to 1830 and then exiguous rations for the greater part of the following decades. Though so much depended on the holding of office, there were also forms of private or semi-public (notably ecclesiastical) patronage which continued to serve party purposes even when there was no Tory government.[12]

The command of public patronage enjoyed by the Pittites and their successors down to 1830 had been bitterly resented by the Whig opposition and by radical critics of the system of government. But what enemies saw as 'Old Corruption' was valued highly by its beneficiaries and helped to bind many individuals, families and interests to government and to consolidate its support inside and outside Parliament. Liverpool was more cautious and abstemious in his dispensation of patronage than many contemporaries, though he bought off the Grenvilles lavishly in 1821–22, and he was less prodigal with honours than Pitt had been. Both men had been willing to consult the efficiency and credibility of government itself as well as more crudely partisan considerations. Yet the importance of patronage was

---

[12] On aspects of this question see W. D. Rubinstein, 'The End of "Old Corruption" in Britain 1780–1860', *Past & Present*, 101, 1983, pp. 55–86. The view that patronage as a major force expired with the eighteenth century has also been challenged by J. M. Bourne, *Patronage and Society in Nineteenth-Century England* (1986).

never in doubt. The Union with Ireland, for example, had been pushed through the Irish Parliament in 1800 by Castlereagh's distribution of places, pensions and peerages on an enormous scale and the subsequent Tory ascendency in Ireland continued to derive nourishment from the patronage system. Nor was the largesse confined to Parliament and the parliamentary classes. The extension of patronage into the law, the churches and the armed services helped to tie sections of the professions to the defence of the constitution. Yet soon the supply of rewards and favours was falling short of what the whips and managers claimed they needed to sustain a government and the disintegration of Wellington's support in 1829–30 showed the limits of what the slimmed-down system could do for a ministry in trouble. The further disintegration of the Tories once out of office showed, however, that their leaders were weaker still when deprived of the command of public patronage. The subsequent Tory revival owed little directly to patronage, except during the brief ministry of 1834–35, and much more to the enhanced solidarity among men of property alarmed by events, but the anticipation of good things to come sweetened and encouraged exertions in the party's cause. The Tory return to office in 1841 was an improvement on Whig government, but in this respect, as in others, Peel was a reluctant partisan and a disappointment to many expectant supporters. He claimed that the reward for the 'toil and care and drudgery' of a minister's life was

> not patronage, which imposes nothing but a curse, which enables him to do little more than make *dix mécontents et un ingrat*; not ribbons or hopes of peerages, or such trumpery distinctions . . .

His view that 'the strengthening of the Administration' was the only justification for honours was a political criterion indeed but with an emphasis different from that given by party managers and zealots. For example the attempts of Graham and Peel to push magistracies and minor offices the way of Irish Roman Catholics antagonized many Tories. Here were additional reasons why many Conservatives did not love Peel by 1846. It was an attitude to patronage that carried over into the Peelite group, perhaps to their detriment. When in 1847 Peel announced that he would not hold office again, Bonham predicted that this would not help Peelite candidates 'as . . . Constituencies have at least as keen a relish for "favours expected" as their Representatives'.

Peel's successors as Tory leaders rarely emulated his mistake. The exclusion from office for long periods after 1846 left the appetite of the faithful for the loaves and fishes chronically unsatisfied. There were elements in what Malmesbury in 1865 called 'a numerous and hungry Conservative Party' who looked for office at every opportunity. Derby's lack of interest in taking office in 1851, 1855 and 1864 angered sections of his support, among them Disraeli who not only longed for the pleasures of giving and receiving but also, as Commons leader, knew at first hand the importance of public patronage in consolidating the party and improving its electoral fortunes. Salisbury commented later that a leader who declined office while in a minority and instead supported a Whig ministry against the radicals 'is blamed by his party as a failure, and he is almost eaten up alive by the hungry camp-followers who depend upon the loot of a parliamentary campaign'. Here the leader was caught, Salisbury felt, between 'the incompatible claims of his principles and his adherents – the immediate objects of his party as candidates for political employment, and the great enduring interests which that party exists to defend'. Most Tories, though, probably ignored this theoretical problem. Derby himself, though distant from the frenetic exploitation of minor public patronage to which Beresford and others resorted in 1852, dispensed the loaves and fishes enthusiastically when in office. He seems to have pioneered something like the resignation honours list and by devoted attention to aristocratic honours in particular he not only served his party but also built up a loyal personal following within it. Disraeli, who had himself been granted a public pension on leaving office in 1859, wrote when 'the Chief' was near retirement, 'You have done very well for your friends: 3 Garters, 4 Bishoprics, 8 Lord Lieutenancies, and almost the whole Bench [of magistrates] in the three kingdoms'. Even then, in 1868, Derby was planning more peerages ('we must have a batch') just before the impending general election. It was not simply that party served as a vehicle for the pursuit and distribution of patronage at many levels, much of it less aristocratic than the kind that engaged Derby, but also that leaders understood, if they were wise, that the 'exertions' which followers made for the cause had to be recognized and rewarded. As the party which after 1846 could not take office for granted, the Tories seem to have understood that lesson supremely well.

The Press

Conservative politicians, Derby among them, were less interested and accomplished in the management of the press, that 'fourth estate' which had become a major element in political life by mid-century. The reaction of the 1790s had included a strong distrust of and hostility towards an independent press. Two measures of 1792 – Fox's Libel Act, which moved the responsibility for deciding on seditious libel from judges to juries, and the Royal Proclamation against 'criminal and seditious writings', which was a call to battle against the radical press – set the scene for three decades of struggle between ministries and the opposition press, prosecutions for seditious libel reaching peaks in years of political tension like 1817 and 1819–20. Government had other ways of limiting the press too. One was to force prices high through stamp, advertising and newsprint duties so that only a 'respectable' readership could afford newspapers. Taxation of this kind reached its peak in 1815–36, after which Whig and Liberal governments began a whittling away that was completed in the early 1860s. Early nineteenth-century governments had also tried to sway the London press by subsidies and by the concentration of advertisements in loyal publications, the latter practice being followed by their provincial supporters too. The former approach was largely ineffectual. A paper with healthy sales needed no subsidy, a struggling paper could not gain readers by receiving one. In any case the secret service funds available for the purpose were inadequate for the metropolitan press, let alone for the burgeoning provincial press which governments largely neglected. That provincial press was soon predominantly reformist in tone, though Tory papers like the *Leeds Intelligencer* (Tory from 1805), the *Sheffield Mercury* (1807) and the *Manchester Courier* (1825) contrived to flourish, often in opposition to established local rivals. Despite the bitterness which many Tories felt towards the opposition press and which Southey and others writing in the *Quarterly* and *Blackwood's* often generalized into hostility towards a free press altogether, the government ceased its campaign of prosecutions from about 1824 and accepted that an independent press was a cross it had to bear. As Peel had seen in 1820, 'newspaper paragraphs' would henceforth figure in everyone's conception of 'public opinion'. Several ministers had already been active in trying to revive the flagging pro-government press. The tub-thumping weekly *John Bull*, started by the journalist Theodore Hook in 1820, took the radical press on at its own game and the government's pamphlet *The State of the Nation* in 1822 reflected a sensitivity to its image with a reading public. The *Quarterly* continued to give a direction to the Toryism of the intelligentsia, while from 1824 the monthly *Blackwood's Edinburgh Magazine* contributed to the periodical press a high, even romantic tone appropriate to a city captivated by the novels of the (now) Tory Walter Scott.

But the balance of opinion and circulation in the daily and weekly press remained adverse. Governments did little to cultivate even the metropolitan press now. Liverpool tended to regard it as following rather than forming opinion; Wellington's aristocratic hauteur kept editors and journalists at more than arm's length. As the ministry tottered in November 1830, Ellenborough complained

> The press is turning against us. . . . We have neglected the Press too long. The duke relies upon the support of 'respectable people' and despises the rabble; but the rabble read newspapers.

With *The Times* and the *Morning Chronicle*, the foremost metropolitan papers, pro-Whig and with the *Courier* lost too, Wellington himself soon admitted the folly of neglecting the press ('We ended consequently by having the whole of it against us, and against the solid institutions of the Country') and urged 'great monied People' and 'the great landed Proprietors' to 'set to work regularly' upon it. It was one of the first matters given the attention of the 'Charles Street Gang' of displaced party managers and when Wellington resumed office in November 1834 he negotiated for the support of *The Times*. Though he failed, the paper was to follow the Stanley Whigs over to support the Conservatives. Though the party's own attitudes towards the press remained lukewarm and ambivalent, by the time of the electoral triumph of 1841 Peel and the party had a significant body of press support behind them. But the gains were to be dissipated by the outcome of 1845–46. The initial Tory opposition to Peel had included a group of metropolitan papers – the *Standard*, the *Morning Chronicle* and the *Morning Post* – but the second was lost to the Peelites, who also commanded the sympathies of *The Times*, and the third to Palmerston. Stanley, who initially disliked the ultra-Protestant line of much of the surviving Tory press, was uninterested in its management and even Beresford and Disraeli, who showed more concern, had fallen out with the strongly protectionist *Morning Herald* by 1849. Croker kept the *Quarterly* committed to Stanley, but it was less of a force than in earlier years and by the 1850s the traditionalist flavour of Croker's political articles made it seem old-fashioned. But the periodicals were not the main problem. With the daily press Conservative interests languished. According to Edward Stanley, the leader's son, in 1851

> the party in general seemed to regard the newspaper interest as their natural enemy, and any attempt to turn it into a friend as a mere waste of time: my Father sympathized in this view . . . The actual state of Conservative journalism is as low as it well can be.

When the Tory ministry of the following year found itself battered by the greater part of the press, particularly the Peelite *Morning Chronicle* and *The Times*, Derby himself came to 'admit more than I ever did, the possible powers of the press in a crisis'. But the bickering between Derby and *The Times* throughout the decade showed little yielding on either side. Malmesbury reflected in 1857

> Lord Derby has never been able to realize the sudden growth and power of the Political Press, for which he has no partiality, which feeling is reciprocated by its members . . . Lord Derby is too proud a man to flatter anybody, even his greatest friends and equals, much less those of whom he knows nothing.

Derby's hostility to Gladstone's 1860 budget, which proposed repeal of paper duties and which he helped to defeat in the Lords, showed the gulf between the old and the future styles of politics. It was not a stand by which the Tory hierarchy would win the gratitude of most proprietors and editors. Admittedly Disraeli, anxious to return to the Peelites some of their own medicine, had founded *The Press* in 1853 with the support of Malmesbury and Edward Stanley; until he sold his interest five years later it was regarded as his mouthpiece (and distrusted accordingly). But its circulation of perhaps 3000 scarcely dented the Liberal/Peelite dominance of the national newspaper press which in 1852 had been estimated as divided 2:1 against the Tories.

But what was cause and what effect? If, as Disraeli claimed with exaggeration in 1853, 'the whole ability of the country is arrayed against us', there were other reasons than the indifference of leading Tories to press management. Though Derby's mixture of pride and animus did not help, the problems had originated long before his leadership. The commitment of most Conservatives to a traditionalistic, restrictive, exclusive and sometimes repressive conception of the constitution was bound to jar upon the enterprising and rapidly growing newspaper industry once loyalist influences upon the latter had weakened after 1815. The press – largely urban and bourgeois in its readership as in its ownership and authorship – was almost inevitably unenamoured of Tory restriction and repression of its activities and of what Huskisson, complaining of the subversion of the 'yeomanry' by 'the low periodical press', had called in 1818 'the old Tory interests and principles which are prevalent in the Nobility & Gentry'. Relations between the press and leaders like Wellington and Derby reflected the realities of the situation and more strenuous management might have made only marginal difference. If the press indeed followed opinion more than it created it, then the prerequisite of the enhanced newspaper support for which mid-century Tories were beginning to yearn was not an improvement in efforts at management but a profounder change in sentiment towards the party among the purchasing public. The rapid revival of the Tory press from the late 1860s onwards would show that, once political circumstances changed, problems with the press would largely solve themselves.

Principles

The press was one contributor to a larger area of ideas, attitudes and 'principles'. We have seen how political developments since the 1790s had involved enhanced elements of ideology, argument and polemic. Though most politicians remained well aware of those 'great enduring interests that the party existed to defend', they still required modes of discourse that were appropriate to parliamentary and public debate. Toryism was never simply and mindlessly 'pragmatic'. Even hard-nosed defenders of material interests sought to argue their cases in ways that were both coherent and honourable. Privileged minorities had to convince others, as well as themselves, of the legitimacy of their privilege. The parliamentarians who gave much of the tone and lead to the political nation were anyway mostly educated men who wanted to see themselves as enlightened, civilized and intellectually and morally consistent. The crudities of material self-interest normally had only a limited rôle in parliamentary debate and in the intellectual periodicals. Most people expected Westminster politics to provide a show of 'principle' and 'honour'; 'unprincipled' remained a term of opprobrium. Honourable conviction, even if balanced by prudence, was expected of leading politicians.

It is not easy, however, to define a single, neat Toryism of ideas. It was always a complex of attitudes, moods and interests rather than a hard-edged political or social philosophy. It was also in a process of adaptation. Since the century's early years emotional commitment to the Crown had come to play a more modest part in the Tory consciousness, though republicanism remained an anathema, the strain of coercive authoritarianism had weakened, and party itself had become more readily accepted, so that party loyalty sometimes served to unite Conservatives when they failed to agree intellectually. But there had also been continuities in mood and belief. There remained a yearning for social order, harmony and stability that was natural to people who enjoyed the existing order of things and who stood to lose from its dissolution. People who wilfully disrupted this order were cast as enemies. Most Tories would have said that they stood for monarchy, aristocracy and property, all comfortably hereditary in character, and they opposed democracy and 'levelling'. 'Order' in all its connotations appealed to them, 'disorder' appalled them. Hierarchy was of the nature of things. Mostly members of the established churches, they disliked and distrusted religious nonconformity almost as much as they did political radicalism. Roman Catholicism remained a particular bugbear. They agreed that the constitution should be upheld. This last stance, however, had become less straightforward than in earlier years. The major changes that had been forced through since 1828 meant that to many Tories the reformed constitution was much less sacrosanct than that of 1820 had been. Many continued to resent the reforms of 1829 and 1832 deeply, even when they recognized their inability to reverse them. The constitution had also become much harder to define in its essentials as a result of the process of reform. The nature of the relationship between Church and State, for example, was now much more obscure than it had been before 1828. Some thinking Conservatives were coming to feel, moreover, as they witnessed the rate of change in society around them, that an element of constructive adaptation was prudent if the constitution was not to be left behind by the times.

Tory principles beyond a few basic propositions were thus not entirely settled or straightforward. No thinker had provided the party with a satisfactory and sufficient ideology or even with an approach to the problems of government that commanded broad assent. The natures of British and Irish society, of the larger political culture and of the Conservative party itself precluded anything like unanimity. The exposure of Tory ministries and majorities to the problems of the 1820s had produced doubt and confusion. Even the bitter experience of Whig government in the 1830s had not reunited Tories in much beyond a determination to restore their own leaders to office. Indeed the 1830s had witnessed some further fragmentation of Tory thinking through the impact of the Oxford Movement within the Church of England, through the differing reactions of Tories to certain Whig legislative initiatives and through the growing prominence of issues of protection. The traditionalism that came easily to frightened conservatives was complicated by the cross-currents of interests and pressure-groups and by the tension between a backward-looking romanticism fed by the writings of Scott and Southey and a more utilitarian conservatism embodied in the party's administrative élite and strengthened by the accession of ex-Reformers like Graham and Ripon. The question whether a government supported by Tories was to pursue romantic reaction or a tempered and controlled modernity was scarcely settled by the electoral victory of 1841 and it remained to be resolved by the party conflicts and schisms of the years that followed. So there was never any settled ideology, whether of Toryism, Conservatism or conservatism. A cause which numbered Southey, Coleridge, Croker and the young Gladstone and Disraeli among its theorists and polemicists did not lack intellectual vigour or pretension, but no one voice predominated, despite the standing enjoyed by the *Quarterly* until mid-century. As for the practising politicians of the parliamentary classes, there was no established mechanism like those available to modern parties by which the party as such could define and decide its stance on current issues. Policy, like theory, was inevitably a matter of argument and of circumstance. Most Tory parliamentarians had to decide for themselves, often in response to constituency pressures, what stance to take on the questions of the moment. Inevitably, once office was regained, it would be the small leadership group on the front benches that would decide the policies and responses of government.

Certainly the different levels of the Conservative party in 1841 – the ministerial élite, the supporters in the two Houses and the much more diverse mass of support outside Parliament – were in broad agreement on a number of matters. They were set against O'Connell and his demands for further Irish church reform and for the repeal of the Union. They were set against Chartism and other forms of radicalism and they asserted the 'finality' of 1832. They would maintain the constitution against 'agitation' and the social order against the disaffected. They would maintain the privileges and property of the established churches, all the more so because of the unsettling legacy of Whig government in these areas. Beyond this differences of emphasis emerged. The backbench and constituency support was pervaded with anti-Catholic sentiment, but the frontbenchers tended to play it down in the interests of the government of Ireland. The party, notably the county members and the agricultural constituencies, had become more self-consciously protectionist and it was fearful and resentful of what the Anti-Corn Law League represented, but its leaders were wary of offending industrial and commercial capital and nervous about the impact of high food prices on the populace during trade depressions. The most common factor was simply the defence of the existing order. Nothing united Conservatives so well as conservatism. Even the *means* of upholding the existing order divided them. The party was united by basic purpose, not by the subtleties of pragmatism or philosophy. In *Coningsby* Disraeli contrasted 'high philosophy' (of which he claimed to approve) with 'low practice' and argued for a 'Creed' rather than a 'Confederacy' of interests as the basis of true Toryism. But that sort of line appealed to malcontents and to the literati more than to ministers. Gladstone, a more obvious 'rising hope of those stern and unbending Tories' and now a minister, was already in evolution away from the high-flown propositions of his *The State in its relations with the Church* (1838). Even when the 'Confederacy' broke up in 1845–46, it was not replaced by anything that could be called a Creed and Disraeli himself scarcely attempted to give it one. The party was simply not quick on its feet when it came to ideas. It was above all a parliamentary party of landed gentlemen. Both theorizing and pragmatism had to be filtered through the social assumptions common to the kind. The outcome of this process tended to be a matter of convention and style rather more than of ideology. Leaders who offended against standards of honour and principle (the latter term here signifying gentlemanly integrity rather than high theory), as Peel did flagrantly, courted danger. At least Derby had the advantage that, as the personification of the patrician ideal, he was beyond serious damage by accusations of dishonour and duplicity, despite his inconsistencies of practice and approach.

The language and argument of Toryism, whether the public versions in parliamentary debates, the periodicals and the newspaper leaders or the private discourse and correspondence of politicians, were inevitably to some extent reactive. The pressures of current issues did much to shape them. Even long-established attitudes could be given a new and sharp focus by events, as concern over Catholicism was by Maynooth and by Papal Aggression. Church and State employed the minds, tongues and pens of so many Tories in the 1830s not because they found the question of ecclesiastical establishment difficult in itself but because the established churches in two countries (and soon in the third too) were under challenge. Answers had to be found because questions were being posed by troublesome people who would not go away. If clear answers rarely emerged, it was sometimes because of the insoluble nature of the questions but often because the character of the Conservative party itself was hardly conducive to intellectual clarity and consensus. Disraeli was right about the 'confederacy' aspect of his party. It was a coalition of sections of the great aristocracy and of the gentry, of the establishment clergy and of other professional men, of religious zealots and of occasional conformists, of Irish Ascendancy Protestants and of the rather more liberal establishments of Scotland and England, of instinctive authoritarians and of equally instinctive constitutionalists, of protectionist agriculturalists and business-men and of others from an assortment of backgrounds who were per-suaded by economic liberalism, of parliamentarians and backwoodsmen, of frontbenchers and backbenchers. What held this potentially ramshackle collection together was, perhaps above all, a fear of what would happen if they did not hold together. The Whigs and their more radical fellow-travellers provided the cement of the Tory coalition. The Conservative party would not have existed without the threat perceived on the other side of the political divide.

Protectionism was an illustration of the relationship between party politics and theory. Protection, historically, had not been essentially Tory. The political and economic circumstances of 1815 had added the Corn Law to the legacy of commercial protection and regulation which the 'party of order' inherited. The additional weight given to the counties and to the tenant farmers in 1832 increased the potential for protectionism at the same time as the growth and enfranchisement of the industrial cities strengthened the free trade and cheap food lobby behind the Whigs. Soon, with the appearance of the Anti-Corn Law League, the political system faced the prospect both of an intellectual polarization between protection and free trade and also of a battle of interests between land and manufac-ture. Yet even during the period 1838–52, when the Conservatives were most committed to protection, its theory was poorly developed within the party. Few Tories claimed to be protectionists on grounds of high principle and those who did were usually hesitant and ambivalent in their commit-ment to state intervention in the economy. Most Tories argued that the Corn Laws were simply an expedient warranted in particular circum-stances of economic interest and political prudence and claimed that those circumstances existed. The split within the party in 1845–46 was less one between rival philosophies, more one between alternative understandings of advantage and sense. Though the outcome of 1846 committed the rump of the party more clearly than ever before to protection, its leaders started to wriggle free of the commitment when it proved to be electorally unprofitable. After 1852 the party's leading parliamentarians and intellec-tuals were predominantly free-traders, though their language usually paid some deference to the protectionist sentiment surviving among sections of their backbenchers and even larger parts of their constituency support. In the end the removal of the Corn Laws and the Navigation Acts from the statute book only assisted the progress of (by now commonplace) *laisser faire* attitudes among Tories. But at no stage of this process could the whole party be identified with any one position on questions of trade, of tariffs and of interference with the free market. Indeed one lesson of 1846 had been the very danger of explicit commitments to a party which was a confederacy in itself and which depended on even more diverse forces for its chance of a parliamentary majority. During the 1850s and 1860s political commentators frequently noted the difficulty of identifying any consistent line pursued by the parliamentary Conservative party.

Other areas also showed the blurring of Toryism's intellectual compo-nent. Though most Conservatives were committed to ideals of social harmony and stability, their perceptions of the appropriate nature of the social order and of its relationship to political practice showed no consen-sus. Some Tories, particularly the literati, chose to depict society in terms of more-or-less fixed hierarchies in which deference and subordination below were rewarded by the practice of *noblesse oblige* above. During the century's early decades a cult had developed among Tory writers and theorists romanticizing and idealizing medieval chivalry, quasi-feudal paternalism and ancient religious faith as central features of Toryism. These enthusiasms, largely anti-liberal and anti-modernistic in tone, found expressions like the Eglinton Tournament in 1839, the Oxford Movement of ecclesiastical Ultras, the Young England côterie of backbench frôndeurs and Disraeli's novel *Sybil*. Lord John Manners in 1841 published an unfortunate couplet in a slim volume of verse: 'Let wealth and commerce, laws and learning die, But leave us still our old nobility'. But other Conservatives mocked these fantasies, knew the importance of 'wealth and commerce' to Britain's social stability and well-being, believed that a buoyant economy was the best recipe for social order and held that an element of social mobility was a crucial and beneficial element in society. A host of arriviste Tory families could hardly hold otherwise. Peels and Gladstones were among them, but these views were by no means confined to the Peelite secessionists. Most thinking Conservatives saw that new wealth derived from commerce, industry and the professions had to be attached to the constitution and, preferably, to their own party. A cult of patrician pedigree and chivalry might affront people who, alienated, would be a threat to the constitution but who, conciliated, might even become good Conservatives. 'Old nobility' has its uses but scarcely as the party's sole identity. A prudent aristocracy would identify its interests with those of substantial property in general, enlist allies among other significant interest-groups and work to cultivate non-aristocratic but respectable opinion. Some Tories even felt that the leaders of patrician society should put themselves at the head of a moderate but modernizing movement that brought other classes into a significant but subordinate position in the constitution and gave some recognition to their economic weight. Perhaps only in this way could the cities and industrial districts, still growing disturbingly fast, be tamed by the 'aristocratic constitution'. By the mid-1840s Peel personified this approach, as the young Edward Stanley did later, but most Tory leaders were capable of gestures in the same direction. Derby's 'spirit of the age' stance in 1858 contrasted with his embittered patrician negativism of a decade earlier. Here, in the spectrum of opinion between a Manners and a Peel, were divergent views on the character and direction of British society, on the means to social harmony and stability and on the practice of party politics. Even social conservatism had to be argued out amongst Tories.

The same blurring had occurred in Tory attitudes to public disorder and the authority of government. Either side of 1841 Tory responses to agitation in both Britain and Ireland had shown the old instinct for coercion and authoritarianism still alive. But attitudes had changed too since Sidmouth's time. By mid-century Tories generally accepted the inevitability, even the normality, of an independent press as few had done in 1820. The old commitment to constitutional government and to 'the liberties of the subject', never totally absent even in the darkest moments of repression, was now enhanced by the liberal drift of opinion during the century's second quarter. Admittedly Ireland still strained this tolerance. Confrontations with emancipated Catholicism, militant nationalism and peasant violence could provoke hardline responses from Tories of a kind rarely seen on non-Irish issues. But Ireland was also a severe test of the cogency and practicability of Conservative attitudes. It was capable of forcing responsible Tories, though not perhaps their constituency following, to expedients that British conditions would hardly have dictated. If Ireland often found Tories at their most coercive, it could also find them at their most pragmatic and concessionary. The contrast was illustrated when Inglis, once Sidmouth's secretary and now opposed to the Maynooth grant, told Gladstone in 1845 that he would have sent Cumberland and an army of 30,000 into Ireland in 1829 rather than concede Catholic Emancipation. Now he only strengthened the younger politician's determination not to lead the opposition to Maynooth. Whatever the integrity of their principles, men like Inglis were discrediting themselves in the eyes of more realistic and sophisticated Conservatives by the illiberalism of the practical consequences of their views.

Though Gladstone regretted it as much as anybody, even in the 1840s high Tory principle, inspired by that sense of the constitution's almost religious sanctity which Burke, Sidmouth, Eldon and Inglis had all felt, was in retreat before a more prudential, secular and utilitarian style of conservatism which Pitt and Liverpool would have recognized. Perhaps views of the authority of government itself were changing. If many Tories were still distrustful of the propensities of the enlarged electorate, they were now also distrustful of the rightness of central government. Mid-century Tories, influenced by the periods of opposition since 1830 and realistic enough to see that Whitehall would often be in the hands of their opponents, were more distrustful of government and its claims to authority than their equivalents of 1820 had been. The elements of localism and particularism which had always been present among Tories had now been strengthened by the experience of opposition and of Whig government, by the intellectual advance of free-market economic theory and, perhaps ironically, by a more general spread of liberal attitudes. The idea of strong and active central government which the panicky Southey had advocated in the 1820s to maintain social order in troubled times was left with few sympathizers outside the romantic fringes of Toryism.

Religion

Perhaps no issue during the century's second quarter had attracted the attention of Tory theorists so much as the relationship between the state and Christianity and, more specifically, the question of church establishments. A commitment to the establishments was a hallmark of contemporary Toryism and ideologues like Burke, Coleridge and Gladstone had written powerfully and feelingly on the relationship between secular authority and religious duty. On practical matters involving support for the establishments Conservative governments were usually much friendlier than their Whig equivalents. The party was rewarded by the loyalty of the majority of the clergy of the three establishments. Churchmen both clerical and lay knew that most of the convinced opponents of their churches were concentrated on the left wing of the Reform party.

Yet Tories were often more uncertain and divided on religious matters than the Church of England's later description as 'the Tory party at prayer' would suggest. There were both practical and theoretical problems in the commitment to the establishments. That commitment could hardly be isolated from the realities of the substantial support enjoyed by the non-established faiths in Ireland, England and, after the Disruption of the early 1840s, Scotland too. Anglican theorists sometimes ignored these unpalatable realities, but governments of all complexions had to accommodate the influence of Roman Catholicism in Ireland and that of Protestant Nonconformity in Britain, each of which had become stronger and more assertive during the century's second quarter. Though most Tory politicians wished to assert the peculiar status and privileges of the establishments, there was little sense in outraging the sensibilities of other denominations by measures that could be depicted as discriminatory against voluntarist Christianity or as restrictive of civil and religious liberties. (Tory squires and magistrates, among the latter large numbers of Anglican clergymen, faced similar dilemmas in their localities. Some resisted the encroachment of Dissent fiercely; others learned to live with Nonconformity.) Though most Tories continued to distrust arguments for 'religious liberty' and even more those for religious equality, the party's office-holders usually gave some weight to political expediency and prudence. The government of Ireland would suffer if the Catholic bishops were alienated; government in Britain was wise to heed Dissenting anger like that which compelled Peel's ministry to retreat over the pro-Anglican education clauses of Graham's Factory Bill in 1843. Similar considerations persuaded Peel against proposing a new parliamentary grant for Anglican church extension, a measure for which Inglis and the 'Church party' had lobbied hard. The party managers were well aware of the importance of Wesleyan Methodism, the largest of the Nonconformist denominations and one which had long provided a degree of support for the Tory cause, particularly from its clergy. This support could easily be alienated by partisan and discriminatory proposals that threatened Nonconformist interests, as Graham's measure did, though Wesleyanism, strongly anti-Catholic in sentiment, also reacted angrily against the Maynooth grant. What all this meant, though it disappointed Anglican zealots, was that Conservatives in office could do little to promote the Church's interests positively as opposed to simply defending its remaining privileges. (Perhaps the most effective aid now was to shape the system of grants-in-aid of lower-class schooling, which the Whigs had established in the 1830s, in order to help Church schools.) Nor was there always electoral mileage in the cause of the establishments. In 1847 and 1852 many Tory candidates and their constituency supporters were happier beating the anti-Popery drum than asserting the privileges of the Church of England.

The other side of the problem was one of constitutional theory. Recent legislation, notably the measures of 1828 and 1829, had liberalized some of the central features of the relationship between the state and its established churches. The kingdoms were now in constitutional law multi-confessional states which conceded to subjects not only an advanced degree of religious liberty but also, for most political purposes, religious near-equality. The high-principled view, which Eldon had upheld in 1829 and which Gladstone had restated in a different form in 1838, that the constitution (in England anyway) was essentially Anglican in its Christianity ran up against the legacy of legislative change inherited by the 1841 and subsequent Tory governments. Precisely what the new theoretical basis for Church/State relations was remained far from clear – the survival of established churches linked to a confessionally liberal state was explicable politically but hardly in theory – and it was to be a bone of contention among Conservatives as well as between them and their opponents. The fragility of the surviving relationship was illustrated when what seemed to be a minor legalistic problem within the Scottish Church erupted into the major crisis of the Disruption which split the Kirk and damaged both the Tory cause and government itself. In England too the eddies of controversy and theory which circumstances had generated left Churchmen themselves divided in their understanding of and attitudes to the Church/State relationship. Some worked to restore its closeness, others distrusted what survived of it. The process of church reform in Ireland, particularly the contentious Temporalities Bill of 1833, and the measures of modernization imposed upon the Church of England by the Whigs helped to convince some Anglicans that a close relationship with a liberal, progressive and now Whig-dominated state was dangerous to the spiritual integrity and material interests of the Church. Keeping legislative reform away from the ancient universities, which remained confessional in character, became a major objective of Tory Churchmen.

The Oxford Movement, which began in 1833 in reaction against Irish church reform, fed upon this distrust of Erastianism among many of the clergy and laity, but it was itself soon inflicting damage upon the Church's position. The flavour of crypto-Catholicism which the Movement acquired, particularly when it became ritualistic, was divisive of the Church, damaged its relations with Wesleyanism, caused problems in some of the constituencies and made even Tory politicians more chary of backing the Church unreservedly. Though opponents of the party still viewed it as assertively pro-establishmentarian, its leading figures were learning that religious issues were a minefield both in practice and in their theoretical implications. Peel's ministry of 1841–46 became embroiled in almost unmanageable problems of a religious character in all three countries. New enemies had been gained in Scotland, while in England and Ireland the zealots of the established churches once again felt betrayed by the leaders of their own party. Tory Anglican sensitivities rubbed raw by Maynooth helped to bring Bentinck down over the Jews Bill in 1847. Derby's ministry of 1852 saw the attractions of No Popery but burnt its fingers on the issue. Discretion was perhaps the better part of valour.

The divisions which were intensifying within the Church of England itself pointed to the same conclusion. Though the Oxford Movement had initially tended to revive and organize a spirit of resistance to Whig policy, as ritualism and what some held to be covert Popery developed within it 'Puseyism' found itself at odds not only with an older High Church tradition of establishment but also with the Church's large and influential Evangelical wing and with its small but articulate rationalistic intelligentsia (the Broad Churchmen). These Church parties had divergent views of the nature of establishment and of relations with Catholics and Dissenters and they had different expectations of Tory leaders too. They also fought each other. The intensity of the battles, particularly those between Evangelicals and Puseyites, soon made it almost impossible for Tory leaders to unite the Church for political purposes. The divisions showed within Parliament itself where, though the members for the universities remained prominent in the 'Church party', no-one fully replaced Inglis as spokesman for the Church as a whole once he left the Commons in 1854. The conflicts also added to the difficulties of Tory reunion, for younger men like Herbert and Gladstone gave the Peelites a Puseyite tinge much disliked on the Tory backbenches, and it encouraged Derby (even more his son) and Disraeli in a wariness of, even contempt for, the Church zealots. If the archetypal Tory bishop was Henry Phillpotts of Exeter, it only illustrated the danger of old-fashioned and opinionated bishops to both the Church and the Conservative party. But the long periods of Whig government were producing a Whiggish episcopal bench and this was something the short-lived Conservative ministries had to live with. They did so more cheerfully than many of the Anglican clergy and gentry. Indeed the leadership continued to disappoint the Church Tories who suffered an almost chronic sense of neglect, even betrayal, by their leaders. The Evangelicals and 'Protestants', however, received most of the consideration that was going and, when Disraeli wrote to Derby in the early 1860s of a malcontent 'coterie who hate us and think they have a monopoly of Church championship', he was referring to the High Churchmen.

But the Conservative party and the established churches remained closely identified with each other. The interests of the establishments were always close to the heart of parliamentary Toryism and it was perhaps because those interests were not so clearly threatened during the years of Palmerston's ascendency as earlier or subsequently that Tory 'principles' became so blurred. But even during these years, however circumspect the leaders became, among the intellectuals and the provincial backwoodsmen Conservatism retained a distinctively Churchy flavour. Even outside the Barsetshire hinterland immortalized by Trollope, squires and parsons provided the nucleus of Tory influence in innumerable parishes. (Electorally the party was most successful in the parts of England where the Church was the dominant faith.) In urban areas too the Church was indirectly doing the work of the party by attracting sections of the business and professional classes, establishing itself in the new suburbs as well as the grander residential districts of the cities and helping to incorporate the more prosperous bourgeoisie into a traditional style of Toryism. The foundation of numbers of new 'public schools' designed to educate the middle classes within the established Church worked to the same ends. In its social impact the Church of England was more vigorous and competitive in mid-century than the Tory party and soon it would emerge again as a driving-force of political resistance and revival as it had been in earlier phases. Meanwhile the party in Lords and Commons remained almost entirely united in the defence of the remaining props and symbols of establishment, notably church rates and the denominational character of the ancient universities. Irish establishment remained a special shibboleth of Toryism. Only on the question of popular education did major cracks show within the leadership. But on issues beyond the basic cause of Church defence the establishments of the three countries continued to throw up problems and complications for their political patrons. They provided no consistent voice, doctrine or policy; at times they weakened and harrassed the party leaders. Almost certainly the problems would have been greater had Conservative governments survived longer. It was hardly surprising that Tory politicians so often supplemented their Anglican identity with a 'Protestant' one.

Social Reform

One other area of policy and principle merits exploration. There remains something of a historiographical mythology about the Tory contribution to 'social reform'. The argument goes that, while Liberals backed free-market economics, retrenchment and governmental non-intervention, Tory ideals of paternalism, social harmony, religious duty and strong government helped to create a climate of social interventionism and inspired much of the achievement in social regulation and improvement from the century's second quarter onwards. Certainly Tory theorists included a crop of romantic paternalists, Southey, Coleridge and Wordsworth being among those who articulated hostility to market economics. One can point too to the rhetoric of the Young England frôndeurs, the multifarious good causes of Ashley (later Earl of Shaftesbury) and those Tories who opposed the implementation of the 1834 Poor Law Act, supported factory legislation and lamented the dominance of national policy by Whigs and economists. But as these sentiments were most developed during the century's second quarter when many other, non-Tory forces and pressure-groups were working for similar ends, it is difficult to assess the distinctively Tory contribution. None of the main social legislation was specifically Tory in its conception, political support or implementation. Nor did the enthusiasts dominate in their own party. Many Tories opposed the reforms demanded by the zealots and often the balance of Conservative opinion and influence lay against, not for, the more controversial measures. Many Tories anyway concerned themselves little with these issues and gave priority to more basic concerns like social order, political stability and party fortunes. To these people the enthusiasts for social measures often seemed cranky and disruptive, as Ashley came to sense his party and its leaders regarded him.

Admittedly one aspect of early nineteenth-century fears about domestic disorder and subversion had been an increased interest in social amelioration in contradistinction to political reform. Some conservatives argued that a modicum of social reform – or at least a show of social concern by the propertied classes – was the best way to ward off political change. Amelioration patronized from above might confirm rather than subvert a hierarchic society. But there were limits to these sentiments. Social improvement was never a coherent programme, more a rag-bag of causes and enthusiasms. Even Ashley, who starting in the late 1820s accumulated the most impressive record of good causes among his contemporaries, was not an omnibus reformer and on political and constitutional questions he was a hardline Tory. The causes that philanthropists espoused, moreover, were often shaped by concern for social control and religious indoctrination. Frightened conservatives usually managed to qualify their social conscience by prudence. This concern often took the form of religious teaching, the moralization of the poor and private philanthropy rather than legislation, administrative action or welfare measures. Indeed philanthropy was heavily influenced by two assumptions. One was that destitution and suffering were natural and inevitable, so that human agency could do little beyond their marginal alleviation; the other was that the poor should be encouraged to make efforts for their own betterment. Even the more romantic kinds of Tory paternalism usually incorporated these attitudes.

Religious commitment also played a part. Much of the philanthropic concern felt by Tories was channelled through the established churches which they held to carry the main duty of reconciling classes, teaching the poor and maintaining social harmony. The churches themselves were being challenged both by rival denominations and by radical critics, so philanthropic endeavour had the character of a self-protective reaction by the establishments as well as an attempt to serve secular authority by maintaining social order. Here were additional considerations pushing some Tories towards social action: not only did they have much to lose from turmoil, distrust and fear the lower orders and have no faith in or desire for political reform, but they also wished to render the established churches indispensible and secure by giving them social purpose and centrality. More generally too, the established order was to be saved by identifying it with moral purpose.

Some of these concerns rubbed off onto the governments of order early in the century. Measures to improve the endowments of Anglican livings, to build new churches and to extend the parochial system were influenced by concern for social conditions as well as for the weakness of the established Church. Peel's creation of the Metropolitan Police in 1829 reflected the government's perennial concern for the social and political state of the capital. Measures with any direct welfare content were much rarer. Significantly 1817, a year of repression, produced one of the most notable, the Poor Employment Act which was intended to stimulate public works and hence employment with government-backed loans. But the intense political pressure for retrenchment and tax reductions left government with little scope for measures involving expenditure. Despite the exhortation to good works proceeding from many supporters of government, there was little legislation to show for it. Issues like agricultural protection, religion and the constitution stirred Parliament from the 1820s to the 1840s as issues of social amelioration rarely did and this reflected the priorities of the parliamentary classes. Though opponents of Toryism labelled it financially profligate, the bulk of public expenditure went on servicing the National Debt, the armed forces, diplomacy and the machinery of justice, not on the material welfare of the lower orders. The one great exception was the poor-law system which bore much of the burden of dislocation and depression in the agricultural districts and of the periodic slumps in the industrial areas. The rising tide of grumbling about the poor rates by the 1820s showed that the limits of statutory generosity were being strained.

Even the current ideas did not point all in the same direction. Burke, considering the 'social economy' in the *Reflections*, had declined to try to improve the lot of the destitute as it was 'generally pernicious to disturb the natural order of things'. Few thinkers who followed him evinced much enthusiasm for any redistribution of wealth. Castlereagh had put the point firmly in 1819:

> Upon what principles could government act, if in seasons of difficulty they were to ... take from one class merely for the purpose of giving to another? Such a policy was equally inconsistent with all the rules of sound policy, and with the very nature of property in general.

Southey, however, was soon propounding a more interventionist line. Nervous about the potential for a lower-class rebellion, he argued in the *Quarterly* and in *Sir Thomas More: Colloquies on the Progress and Prospects of Society* (1829) for an active, high-spending government which would intervene to keep society, particularly the cities which the author feared so much, tranquil and stable. These appeals went largely unanswered, however, except by echoes in the writings of other paternalists over the next two decades. The Tory loss of office in 1830 meant that the Whigs were left to deal with poor law and factory reform in the 1830s. The Tories had no distinctive view on these issues, but the desire to undermine Whig government pushed numbers of Tories in and out of Parliament towards criticism (and in some cases a full theoretical critique) of Whig policy and of the free market theory which seemed to be finding a home on the Reform benches. The New Poor Law, which in 1834 had won broad support from the opposition both frontbench and backbench, became the target of the ire of some provincial Tories when magistrates found they had lost control of poor relief, clergy found their parishes unionized, ratepayers felt the cost of the new workhouses and the Poor Law Commissioners in London began to apply the system to the northern industrial districts during the trade depression of 1837, the year when the poor-law issue first made an electoral mark. Soon the Anti-Corn Law League's deployment of free trade theory against the Corn Laws and the aristocratic constitution encouraged some Tories further towards a rejection of the free market and its works. Some of the philanthropists who preached the virtues of a supposedly traditional paternalism went on to assert the moral legitimacy of parliamentary regulation of and intervention in the economy. In some of the industrial districts strange kinds of Tory Radicalism flourished, uniting elements among the textile operatives with Tory squires and parsons against Whig policy. Romantics like Manners and Beresford Hope were to go on dreaming for decades of what paternalistic philanthropy, high-minded legislation and a different kind of Conservative leadership might have done to turn back the progress of religious liberalism, political reform and middle-class radicalism. But Peel's ministry of 1841 was as non-interventionist in most areas as the Whigs, maintained the 1834 poor law and permitted only modest factory measures that fell well short of what Ashley and the operatives wanted. In the 1841 Parliament some fifty Conservative members were generally sympathetic to factory and poor-law reform, though measures like Ashley's bills on child labour in mines encountered much of the sternest opposition from Tories too. Graham was nervous of the influence of 'Oastler-Humanity Mongers' on his party's benches, but the committed rebels against the poor law were a handful in each House.[13] Social legislation attracted only modest support among Tory members compared to more traditional concerns and never gave the party the seismic shocks it experienced from Maynooth and corn. Peel's view, one probably shared by most protectionists too, was that the best social panacea was economic prosperity. Even agricultural and commercial protectionists

---

[13] Richard Oastler, sometime candidate for Huddersfield, was an angular Tory radical (motto 'The Altar, the Throne and the Cottage') who railed against the New Poor Law and against the 'Yorkshire slavery' of the textile factories.

doubted whether government intervention within the domestic economy was conducive to this end.

The collapse of the established leadership and of party discipline in 1846 unleashed the pressure-groups on the backbenches. There was a mood for revenge on free-trading manufacturers and for a blow against *laisser faire*. The strong Protectionist support for the 1847 Ten Hours Bill, all the stronger because Peel opposed it, owed something to these sentiments. But the 1848 Public Health Bill met with patchier enthusiasm among Tory members and frenetic opposition from some, notably two eccentrics, Urquhart ('un-English and unconstitutional, corrupt in its tendency') and Sibthorp ('he hated commissions, he hated jobs and he distrusted all governments'), who fought 'centralization' in the name of 'local self-government'. It was much the same story outside Parliament. No social measures attracted the broad support for Tory candidates that anti-Catholicism and, more ephemerally, protection did. As an issue social reform was no cure for the ills of the Conservative party. Stanley, scenting an election in March 1851, agreed with *The Times* that 'Protestantism, Protection and Down with the Income Tax' would be the right slogan for his party. It was hardly the cloth from which a social programme could be cut.

The mid-century years of opposition gave Tory politicians the leisure to indulge any predilections for philanthropy and social theory. Their enthusiasms were usually religious, educational (often the same thing) or extensions of the concerns of Quarter Sessions. A vogue for juvenile reformatories which united humanitarian squeamishness about children, concern for souls and alarm at crime rates enlisted several aspiring Tory politicians. The protectionist Charles Adderley, a Warwickshire landowner and a future minister, established a reformatory, a Church training college and a model town at Saltley, introduced a reformatory schools bill in 1852 and was responsible for the Young Offenders Act of 1854. Ashley, though he refused office in Tory administrations, remained active in a range of causes. Derby himself, though scarcely of Ashley's sympathies, played a distinguished part in the response to working-class distress during the Lancashire 'Cotton Famine' caused by the American Civil War and in the early 1860s he raised in the Lords the question of the displacement of the poor by railway developments in London. Though the party was not without its genuine social consciences and responded to the humanitarian tendencies of the times, a show of social responsibility also came in useful to opposition politicians keen to prove their fitness for office. But the enthusiasms remained those of individuals or of small pressure-groups. The party as a whole and the leadership as a group had no clear vision of or ambition for a social programme. The emphasis was always more on private philanthropy than on public action. Some of the fiercest opponents of legislative interference in the economy, like Lord Londonderry, the coalowner who persuaded his friend Disraeli to attack mines bills, were Tory parliamentarians. The laird who ranted to Croker in 1851 about the poor law in Scotland

doing the work of the revolutionists, by demoralizing the minds of the poor and crippling the means of the wealthy . . . Philanthropy seems to have gone mad everywhere, and to vent all its insane venom upon the unhappy proprietor.

was probably as typical a Tory as Adderley or Ashley.

If opposition gave the leisure for good works, it also encouraged a distrust of central government even among Tories less hyperbolic than Urquhart and Sibthorp. One influence was certainly the growing dominance of free market economics in intellectual life generally. *Laisser faire* made steady conversions among Tory politicians and ideologues once the fate of the Corn Laws and the Navigation Acts was clearly settled. But other aspects were more specifically Tory. Reflection upon the potential of future governments more democratic and radical than the Whigs for interference with property worried farsighted Conservatives like Robert Cecil. Tories who despaired of Westminster majorities also came to see the localities where often they still ruled as bastions to be defended against 'centralization'. Tory MPs played leading rôles in the destruction of the interventionist civil servant Edwin Chadwick in the early 1850s and trumpeted the virtues of 'local self-government'. A central concern of many of the gentry was to protect the influence of the magistracy in Quarter Sessions and to prevent anything like the ratepayer democracy of the municipalities from ever reaching the counties. The 'due influence' of property in general and landed property in particular was a shibboleth of the Tory benches. Nearly all the squirearchy extolled the virtue of low rates and taxes and the freeholders and tenant farmers of the counties agreed with them. So, on the whole, did the ratepayers and electors of the boroughs. Except when epidemics created temporary local panics, there was little demand for increased municipal or national expenditure on urban amelioration. Certain cities where Toryism was strong, Liverpool for example, displayed some civic pride and energy, but borough Conservatives were often conspicuous in 'economy parties' calling for municipal retrenchment and they never produced anything that could be called a civic gospel. Except where expenditure on the army and navy and on denominational education was concerned, cheap government was as popular a cry among mid-Victorian Conservatives as among their Liberal opponents.

Fashions in philanthropy came and went, but these basic attitudes endured and they were reinforced among the party's parliamentarians and theorists in the 1850s when the 'condition of England question' faded. The sensible course for leaders and managers weary of party splits was to avoid major social issues and to leave them to private individuals and lobbies. The post-1846 Disraeli soon left *Sybil* far behind. Tory cohesion, as earlier in the century, could hardly have been achieved without this sensible restraint. The poor law, factory regulation, public health and education had all stirred controversy in Parliament, the country and the press. Why set Tory against Tory and interest-groups against the party for causes of doubtful legitimacy and outcome? Even the question of popular education, which united most Conservatives behind the Church of England, could turn difficult and divisive. Pakington's zeal for educational extension rattled his colleagues, angered the Church, the National Society and sections of the party and in 1857 nearly precipitated a frontbench split between liberals and hardliners. Except on uncontroversial issues that permitted politicians to use the language of social responsibility without danger to themselves, it was more sensible to lie low and say little.

The conclusion must be that, though there was never a party orthodoxy on either social theory or legislative purpose, so that enthusiasts for

particular philanthropic causes enjoyed some latitude, and though Tories
were sometimes more openminded about social measures than about major
political reforms, the party as a whole was never clearly or enthusiastically
committed to social amelioration, to legislative paternalism or to social
interventionism. Most of its supporters remained more exercised about
expense, rates and taxes, the encroachments of central and local bureau-
cracies, the rights of property and the 'due influence' of the landowning
classes. These largely negative attitudes had sometimes wavered in reaction
against the more aggressive displays of *laisser faire* polemic by the Reformers or when the interests of the Church were concerned, but even
paternalistic and religious zeal looked more to the action of private
philanthropy and of the established churches than to legislation and public
administration. The men of theories and visions concerning the 'condition
of England question' had had little practical influence upon their party and
it was clear by the 1850s that their moment, if it had ever arrived, had
passed with the troubles of the previous decade.

5

Leaps in the Dark 1866–81

Parliamentary Reform

Two features of the confused events of 1866–67 were the apparent radicalism of the measure of parliamentary reform passed under a Conservative ministry and the refusal of the party to fracture under the strain of the proceedings as it had in 1830 and 1846. The painful remembrance of those occasions may have contributed both to the initial decision to permit a measure of reform and to the party's disinclination to come apart at the seams. Most men of sense seem to have concluded that Tories who chose to die in the last ditch and, worse, fought each other for the privilege would condemn themselves to another eternity of opposition. That and the belief that electoral reform was almost inevitable, so it was better to have a relatively safe measure passed by his own party than a more damaging version inflicted by the Liberals, seem to have been Derby's understanding of the lessons of past and present in the autumn of 1866. Nor was his decision to pursue reform altogether out of character. His two earlier ministries had shown a willingness to avoid Ultra rigidity and to make a show of contemporaneity, even to the extent of introducing a reform bill in 1859.

But a reasonable expectation as Derby gathered his ministry in July was that the Conservatives would block reform. They had just brought down Russell on the issue with the aid of the Adullamite Whigs and had anathematized any move towards 'democracy'. Yet the fact of a Conservative ministry, even one weightier in talent than the last two efforts, was itself a problem. The preceding months had seen moves towards a reconstruction or 'fusion' of parties to create a broad-based conservative coalition led, most probably, by a Whig peer and by Stanley in the Commons.[1] The schemes had failed, largely because the crucial figures of Derby and Disraeli had declined to be shouldered aside. The only coalition

---

[1] See M. Cowling, 'Disraeli, Derby and Fusion, October 1865 to July 1866', *Historical Journal*, VIII, 1965, pp. 31–71.

they considered once the prospect of office beckoned was a Tory-dominated one under their own management, an outcome unacceptable to those Whigs whose support they needed to command a Commons majority. Yet a Tory minority administration was vulnerable to repeated defeats in the Commons which would soon force either its resignation or a general election which it could hardly hope to win. Though the Liberal majority at whose mercy the new ministry lay had been divided by recent events, the precedents of 1852 and 1858/59 suggested that a taste of Tory government would soon reunite it. One worrying prospect was a general election like that of 1831 with reform enthusiasm in the country decimating Tory MPs and ensuring a reform measure more radical than any the old Parliament would have passed. All these considerations suggested that a minority Conservative party by itself could hardly uphold the existing electoral system against change.

The Queen, concerned with the stability of government and of the constitution rather than with a measure's detail, wanted to have the reform issue treated '*not* as a mere Party one, but with a view of settling it'. By September Derby, after cogitation, was

> not in favour of resisting all Reform, for which I believe there is a genuine demand *now*, however it may have been excited, but in favour of the acceptance of a moderate & Conservative measure.

Over the next three months Disraeli (initially opposed to reform), the Cabinet and most of the parliamentary party swung around to the idea of a Conservative initiative. There was no single explanation of this relatively painless transformation, any more than there would be for the twists and turns of events over the following months. One factor was the firm determination of Derby, Disraeli and most of their colleagues to retain office for as long as possible and to use the opportunity it offered for reversing Tory fortunes. The rigours of two decades of permanent minority and near-permanent opposition had hardened the party's resolve. For Derby himself, visibly failing in health, it was the last chance. The pleasure he found in office and patronage after seven lean years was soon heightened by the evident division and discomfort on the Liberal benches as the Tories emerged as contenders in the reform game. His rivalry with and antipathy towards Russell in the Lords contributed to the government's determination to humiliate the Liberals, as did Disraeli's similar relationship with Gladstone in the Commons. For many Tory MPs the undermining of Gladstone's authority and influence was the main sport. But there was a more serious purpose too. A Liberal return to power while the reform issue was unsettled was something most Tories dreaded. As Hardy put it, 'The fatal thing will be if ... the old lot come back triumphant, as dictators ...'. The party did not relish the idea of Gladstone in office again, whether in control of his troops or not, and there was also the menacing figure of John Bright mobilizing reform feeling out of Parliament and focusing radical aspirations within it. A new Liberal bill would hardly be tender to Tory interests and it was unlikely that the Conservatives could block a bill a second time. The political credibility and self-interest of the party dictated that it should cling to office, exploit Liberal disunity and try to settle the reform issue as far as possible on its own terms, even though initially it was not clear how.

But there were strategic as well as tactical arguments for a Tory measure. Though most Conservatives probably opposed any significant modification of the electoral system, others, like their leaders in 1859, showed a degree of open-mindedness. For years pragmatic Tories had argued the need to recapture some of the centre ground of politics and to combine a firm resistance to radicalism with a temperate, considered reformism within the bounds of the constitution. In 1866 electoral reform was not the only area in which ministers were anxious not to appear as 'obstructives'. This approach, it was hoped, would strengthen, not weaken, the aristocratic constitution and the interests it served, keep radicalism and 'democracy' at bay and identify the Conservative party with a broad enough swathe of opinion, including conservative Whigs and moderate Liberals, for it to become a party of government again. Though the context had changed, the approach was not very different from those pursued at various points by Liverpool and by Peel, though no-one this time wished for anything as strenuous and intemperate as Peel's performance after 1841. Survivors from the 1830s like Derby, Malmesbury and Disraeli were not unfamiliar with this apparently centrist style of politics, Edward Stanley was liberal enough to find it second nature and other young men like Hardy and Northcote, though they were to have reservations as the plot unfolded, relished their first taste of high office and had no intention of blighting promising careers by being labelled as 'obstructives'. Northcote would have preferred 'absolute inaction' on electoral reform but he recognized that to obstruct all constitutional change would have been, in his biographer's later phrase, to 'divorce the Conservative party from the current of affairs'. If one assumed, like Derby, that an instalment of electoral reform was now inevitable, then the best antidote to its dangers was to have the Tories settle it on their own terms and secure whatever credit was going from voters old and new. If this hope swayed more of the parliamentary party than might have been anticipated, the explanation lay largely with the immense prestige of Derby himself, with the discipline and solidarity which prolonged opposition had bred into the party and with the detestation of Gladstone and the fear of a Liberal government and of radical reform which was widespread among the party faithful.

By December Derby's instincts – a sportsman's instincts perhaps – were for a bold measure, as he told Disraeli: '. . . of all possible Hares to start, I do not know of a better than the extension to Household Suffrage, *coupled with plurality of voting*'. This device – lowering the borough franchise below the £7 householder figure proposed by the recent Liberal bill and balancing it with increased votes for the propertied and prosperous – was attractive as a settlement of the question, not least because it concentrated change on the borough franchise while reserving features like the constituency distribution and the county franchise for more circumspect treatment. Boldness on the borough franchise also seemed to be best calculated to quieten the largely urban agitations being stirred by Bright and by a series of large pro-reform demonstrations organized by the Reform League in London, though the latter proved to be more dangerous to the royal parks than to the government. Even Northcote had come to believe

> that we shall find no standpoint short of Household Suffrage . . . and, if we go boldly down to this point . . . shall have a fair chance of coupling [it] . . . with conditions which would make it safe.

But the Cabinet itself was divided and, to prevent resignations, its meetings in November and December decided to buy time by presenting resolutions to the Commons in February and then appointing a commission on whose recommendations a bill would be based. But pressure from a House under no firm control and feeling in his own party more positive than had been anticipated caused Disraeli to backtrack during February when the government now committed itself to an early bill. Despite internal wrangling, the Cabinet, taking its lead from Derby and Disraeli, decided to go for household suffrage in the boroughs tempered by a tough residence qualification and plural votes ('fancy franchises' and duality for direct taxpayers and for £10 householders). Cranborne, Carnarvon and General Peel (at the mention of household suffrage 'his eye lights up with insanity', Disraeli wrote) resigned from the Cabinet, but the rest stood firm despite their misgivings. 'The political situation is horrible but can we retrace our steps?' asked Hardy rhetorically. There were fears of a Tory 'cave' rallying around Cranborne and Peel, but a meeting of some 150 MPs at the Carlton at the end of February had supported Derby and the Cabinet majority by backing household suffrage and now only some 40 Conservatives offered regular opposition to reform in the debates and divisions that followed. Even the county members gave little resistance to ministerial proposals, perhaps tempted, like their predecessors in 1831, by the prospect of extra seats at the expense of the small boroughs, and there was support at the critical moment from within the small group of Tory members for large borough constituencies, notably from Graves of Liverpool and Laird of Birkenhead. In the Lancashire towns the local Tory leaders had to show some reformist inclinations to compete with the Liberals and now also sensed that anti-Irish and anti-Catholic feeling was swinging the working-class vote their way. Here there was greater empathy between the lower classes and the Tory sections of the business plutocracy than most other areas showed.

The party's conversion, however, was not a matter of constituency pressure. The issue was settled almost entirely among the parliamentarians with minimal reference to their support outside Westminster. The Conservative course was a tactical one dictated by the current balance of opinion in the Commons and latterly by the determination of Disraeli, who had effective charge of the bill in the Commons as the pace quickened and as Derby's illness removed him from much of the action, not to lose office by affronting that opinion. Precisely what the Tory leaders thought they were doing to the electoral and political balance between classes was far from clear. Indeed there were arguments and confusions within the party on this count all through the months of the bill's progress. Some argued that the Liberals could be undercut in the boroughs by the enfranchisement of a lower class of ratepayer than the £10 householder and Dudley Baxter, one of the party's electoral specialists, had promised increased 'Beer-barrel influence' from household suffrage. The rated franchise that had operated in municipal government since 1835 had shown itself capable of returning Conservative councillors and perhaps there was also, so Cranborne suggested later, 'an indistinct application to English politics of Napoleon's (then) supposed success in taming revolution by universal suffrage'. Certainly Lancashire Tories inclined to an optimistic view of class relations. Other Conservatives, however, still saw household suffrage as an evil in itself but argued that the rating and residence requirements would limit it and the plural votes and 'fancy franchises' balance it so much that its sting would be drawn. Both sides of this argument contributed to what Cranborne jeeringly called the 'phantom of a Conservative democracy' which figured in much of the rhetoric of the confused debates and divisions in the Commons.

The eventual Act differed substantially from the measure which Disraeli had introduced into the Commons in March. Showing the hand of the Liberal majority in the House, the Act omitted the limitation upon 'compounding' ratepayers which the bill had included, enfranchised £10 lodgers, reduced the residence qualification from two years to one and omitted the fancy franchises and duality of votes. In the counties the occupation qualification had been lowered from £15 to £12 and the vote had been given to £5 copyholders. The cross-voting which produced many of these changes was something the government had had to live with. Many amendments were accepted, though none of Gladstone's, and when the government was defeated on others it declined to resign or to request a dissolution. Disraeli's pliability alarmed, even disgusted, some of his colleagues. Hardy, who found the concessions 'odious work', asked himself whether he 'could ... again serve under so unscrupulous a man' and judged that 'All his thought is what Parliament will take & what will secure the Govt.'. But Disraeli's command of detail, procedure and tactics and his repeated defeats of Gladstone gave him a standing in the Commons which the years of leadership in opposition had never done. The popularity of the government's performance in the Carlton, where Gladstone was much detested, was beyond doubt. Despite the extensive cross-voting in the Commons, rebellion had been confined to a minority and the party had not fractured permanently.

The Lords also presented no insurmountable obstacle, though at one point an alliance between Tory hardliners led by Carnarvon and Rutland and conservative Whigs around Grey seemed to threaten the bill. But the ailing Derby exerted himself – he intended, he assured Conservative peers, 'to place the Tory party permanently in power' – and Russell declined to back his own right wing. Though the Tory peers imposed some amendments, most of which were subsequently quashed in the Commons, the government also accepted Russell's amendment to reduce the qualification for the lodger vote. Once again the ministry had avoided being caught in an anti-reforming posture. Derby's speech on the third reading, however, signalled his continuing conservative concerns:

> No doubt we are making a great experiment and 'taking a leap in the dark', but I ... entertain a strong hope that the extended franchise ... will be the means of placing the institutions of this country on a firmer basis, and that the passing of this measure will tend to increase the contentment of a great portion of Her Majesty's subjects.

Hardy, in the privacy of his diary, put his worries more clearly:

> What an unknown world we are to enter, but I believe more safely, or at least as safely, and more permanently than a £5 franchise would enable us to do. If the gentry will take their part they will be adopted as leaders. If we are left to demagogues, God help us.

This implied contrast between county and borough politics summed up the measure's implications as well as Tory preferences. Of about 1.1 million new voters in the United Kingdom about three-quarters were in the boroughs. There, if anywhere, was the 'unknown world'.

The Redistribution Act which followed in 1868 was shaped more clearly than the franchise measure to protect Tory interests. Though the Act was again much modified from the original bill, it still disfranchised completely only four small boroughs in England while depriving 38 of one member. Of these seats about half went to the English counties. The constituencies which the Conservatives feared most gained little. London, which on a weighting for its electorate might have expected some 60 extra members, received only a handful. Not only had redistribution been kept down to a level acceptable to party interests; the often crucial question of boundaries had been entrusted to a Tory-weighted commission which worked in collaboration with a Cabinet sub-committee and with the party's electoral specialists. Though their excesses were modified by a select committee of the Commons, the Conservatives had not lost on the intricacies of the measure. The complications of constituency revision had, however, still caused considerable feeling within the party, particularly between the central and the local agents and between the small borough, large borough and county interests. Inevitably the small boroughs had borne the brunt of reform, though Whig as well as Tory seats had suffered. The friction generated by this measure, despite the exhaustion of the Commons after its long labours on the franchise, showed how a more extensive redistribution would have divided and demoralized the party. A crucial trick in 1867 had been to keep the franchise and redistribution questions as separate as possible and to confine the most extensive change in the old system to the borough franchise. The measures of 1867–68 were notable not only for their apparent radicalism in this one respect but also for how little they changed the old pattern of constituencies and the social balance of county politics. The established interests among which the Conservatives were so strongly represented had escaped relatively unscathed.[2]

During the months after the passage of the main measure most Tories put a brave face on it. They could hardly afford to affront new voters by reminding them that the party had not originally wanted their enfranchisement. Conservatives vied with each other to profess, however improbably, their long-standing faith in the sort of 'democracy' the Act had ushered in. But there were also men who spoke of a betrayal of principle born of a discreditable preference for office over both consistency and prudence. Some of the conservative Whigs claimed that the balance of the constitution had been destroyed. In private and in the *Quarterly* Cranborne vented his bile against 'the Conservative surrender'. These attacks were the more demoralizing because in the remaining months of 1868 the government visibly lost its influence over the Commons. Gladstone, redirecting his party's energies towards religious questions, backed moves to end compulsory church rates. The Conservatives, who had resisted this change for decades, now acknowledged the unpopularity of compulsory rates with the

---

[2] The Scottish and Irish Acts had also passed in 1868. The Liberal benches had called the tune for Scotland and dictated a measure that damaged Tory interests. In Ireland's case the lack of general agreement and the pressure of time ensured that the Act changed little.

urban electorate and, with the general election looming, offered little resistance. Gladstone then announced his intention to take up the question of the Irish Church and pressed a Suspensory Bill to prevent appointments and dispositions of revenues and property in the Irish establishment until Parliament had settled its future. Again the Conservatives in the Commons offered only weak resistance, Stanley signalling his distaste for the Irish establishment and disheartening his backbenchers, while Cranborne's vindictiveness was directed at his party's front bench. Disraeli's personal preference for concurrent endowment (to include the Roman Catholics) was anathema to his own Low Churchmen and only the Tory High Churchmen led by Hardy fought fiercely for the Irish Church. It was left to Derby and the Whig Grey to block the bill in the Lords. Disraeli, who had succeeded as premier in late February when ill health forced Derby's retirement, scarcely rallied his party for the November general election. He made no speaking tour and his published address made little of either electoral reform or the modest achievement in social legislation since the Conservative return to office.

1868 was the most strongly contested election since the first after the Reform Act of 1832. Only 140 out of 420 constituencies were uncontested against a figure of 194 out of 401 in 1865. (The trend towards more contests was to continue until 1885.) As the results were coming in, Malmesbury, now leader in the Lords and once an enthusiast for electoral reform, began to shift the blame: 'Everything proves what a Radical bill Lord Derby and Disraeli have brought in ... The elections are going as badly as possible all over the country...' When it was clear that they had twenty seats fewer than in 1865, the Cabinet made the unprecedented decision to resign without waiting to meet Parliament. The results were scarcely surprising. The Liberals had not disintegrated as much or as permanently as Derby and Disraeli had hoped, the Tories were divided and uncertain in purpose after the Reform Acts and the Scottish measure in particular had done them practical damage. Disraeli lacked the standing within and beyond his party that Derby had commanded and the Irish Church was not an issue to rally centrist opinion. The post-1846 mould had not been broken. But the results were not uniformly disastrous for the Conservatives. Hardly any seats had been lost in England in net terms and the counties had performed hearteningly well. In Ireland, however, ten seats had been lost to the Liberals and the Tory total of forty was their lowest since 1837; in Scotland there had been a near-annihilation of Tory members, only seven being returned against 53 Liberals. In the longer term the radicalization of the 'Celtic fringe' would bring some benefits to the Conservatives, but for the moment the decline of landlord influence there was hitting them hard. Against a generally gloomy picture in the large towns, there were gains in England's industrial North West where the Tories took 21 of the 34 Lancashire seats and Gladstone lost his. There anti-Irish and 'Protestant' feeling, heightened by the Irish Church question and by recent Fenian outrages, had made its mark, not least among working-class voters. These results strengthened the 'Protestant' forces on the Tory benches in the Commons and seem to have confirmed Disraeli in his view that anti-Catholicism would be one of the most effective lines with the enlarged electorate. But only 25 of the 114 seats in all boroughs with over 50,000 inhabitants had been won and, despite victories in Middlesex and Westminster and a better performance than usual to take one of the four City of London seats, the Conservatives had only four of the 25 metropolitan members. The traditional Liberal strongholds outside the North West had remained Liberal and there was not much sign of 'Tory Democracy' or of, in Cranborne's sneering phrase, 'the eternal gratitude of the artisans'. If there was any significant movement of opinion the Conservative way apart from the 'Protestant' backlash, it was a just perceptible hint of reaction among the business and suburban pluto-cracy.

One lesson perhaps was that the party's best long-term course was to remain a clearly conservative party and not to mix it with the Liberals by seeking to outbid their Whig leaders in radical or mock-radical measures. So long as the political left in Britain and Ireland showed itself radical enough to scare established interests, the centre ground of parliamentary politics could be won by a stance of conservative consistency without the need for any doubtfully genuine displays of progressive zeal. Cranborne, who succeeded as Marquess of Salisbury in 1869, argued this case tren-chantly. In a savagely anti-Disraelian article in the *Quarterly* he accused his former frontbench colleagues of having sought to hold on to office at all costs, particularly the cost of those interests the party existed to serve, namely 'the power of the middle and upper classes'. Instead of admiring the tricks of 'the mere political gamester', the party, he argued, should reconcile itself to pure and principled opposition and to assisting the Whigs in their resistance to radical change in a re-run of the Derby/Palmerston co-operation of 1859–65.

Opposition Again

The strategy Salisbury recommended was now scarcely feasible. Gladstone had become more radical than Palmerston and Disraeli was weaker as leader than Derby had been; the political balance had changed within the Liberal party as well as in Ireland, Scotland and Wales. The Irish Church would meet the fate the general election had ordained. The Conservatives in the Commons could hardly mount effective opposition. The constituen-cies outside Lancashire had declined to rally to the defence of the Irish Church and the party had no prospect of winning a general election on this issue. Only in the Lords was there resolute and hopeful opposition to a measure which many Tories regarded as unconstitutional, a despoliation of property and a harbinger of similar moves in England and Scotland. Derby made his last stand on an issue which had helped to draw him to the Conservatives in the 1830s. His intransigence at the head of a phalanx of hardline peers endangered the bill and threatened a major conflict between the two Houses. But the Queen encouraged a compromise and the official Tory leaders were similarly inclined. The former Tory Lord Chancellor Cairns negotiated a compromise with the government which allowed the measure through while the Irish Church retained a larger proportion of its property. A group of peers switched their votes to let the measure pass and Derby was left, with 55 others, to sign a protest against the bill that questioned Parliament's right to confiscate ecclesiastical prop-erty. His death at the end of 1869 weakened the traditionalists, left Salisbury as the effective leader of the Tory right-wing in the Lords and put the house of Stanley under the more liberal management of the former premier's son, the fifteenth Earl, whom many saw as a potential leader of the party.

The period of opposition from late 1868 to February 1874 divided into two contrasting phases with the break in 1871–72. The first was characterized by weakness and even by demoralization. The Conservatives faced a government with Gladstone at its head and Bright in the Cabinet, a Commons with a large Liberal majority including an enhanced representation of Dissenters and an Ireland, itself being radicalized by Fenianism, which Gladstone held it was his 'mission' to attempt to 'pacify' by measures of concession. The 'democracy' which the Tory leadership had helped to concoct in 1867–68 now appeared as a threat to established interests rather than a reassurance, an intensification of pressures for radical change rather than a settlement. Many men began to look back with nostalgia to the security of Palmerston's ascendency.

Even after Irish disestablishment had been settled, Ireland and the other two established churches remained among the central issues. Gladstone's Irish Land Bill of 1870, designed to give tenants the right to compensation for unexpired improvements, was a modest measure in itself but deeply disturbing to the landowning classes both in Ireland and elsewhere as a legislative interference with the rights of property and freedom of contract. The Conservative leaders were cautious and selective in their opposition, focusing on technical points while avoiding an undiscriminating solidarity with landlords against tenants. There were seats at stake in Ireland itself and Irish landlordism was not the most popular cause in Britain. The leadership did not oppose the second reading in the Commons or divide the Lords, though many of the parliamentary party were angered by this temporization. Party emotion and party strategy pointed in different directions. The leaders and managers feared the potential of the land measure, with its 'tenant right' implications, for driving a wedge between landlords and tenants in Tory-held constituencies; they also wished to avoid a display of intransigence that would stem any drift of Whigs their way. In 1871 the government's University Tests Act ended the religious tests at the universities and colleges of Oxford and Cambridge. Many Anglicans, not least the clergy, took it as a major blow and the Church interest in the party fought the measure hard, Salisbury taking a foremost part in the Lords. Another measure that provoked a sharp reaction was the abolition of the purchase of army commissions and promotions proposed by the former Peelite Cardwell. Its meritocratic or 'middle-class' implications and its depiction by many Liberals as a blow against 'privilege' inflamed the opposition of the greater part of the officer corps among whom the Tories were so well represented. A group of MPs known as 'the colonels' mounted a filibustering opposition in the Commons, despite friction with Disraeli and his front bench, and the Conservative majority in the Lords blocked the Army Regulation Bill. The government responded by abolishing purchase by royal warrant, a device that gave a flavour of unconstitutionality to proceedings despite the subsequent passage of the bill. Though the measure had been intended by Cardwell and his advisers to increase military efficiency, the controversy had generated a flavour of class warfare and the Tory defeat left not only bitterness in sections of the party but also a permanent strain in relations between the

Liberals and the officer corps which henceforth looked to the Tories as its protectors.

The 1870 Education Act also had constructive and nonpartisan provenance. Its architect, the Liberal minister W. E. Forster, sought to promote popular education on a non-sectarian basis, as many Liberals wanted, while protecting the existing denominational system to which many Liberal Anglicans, nearly all Catholics and some Nonconformists were attached. His negotiations with the Tory leaders and with the Anglican bishops influenced details of the bill significantly. Backbenchers on both sides were, however, much less enthusiastic than the men in front of them. The Church lobby feared the proposed Board schools as a threat to the Church of England's dominant position in the denominational system, while the gentry and farmers of the country districts feared the intrusion of the elective Boards into their preserves and the imposition of education rates. One result of the Act was a spate of foundations of new Church schools to fill the gaps in existing provision and so to prevent School Boards from being established. In the rural districts many influential Tories strove to exclude the Boards, while in the towns and cities they entered into the fierce party rivalry which the annual School Board elections generated. The 1870 Act was to be a major contribution to Liberal disunity and Tory revival, but its initial impact was to alarm the interests that looked to the Conservatives for protection and to convince many that adequate protection had not been provided. The sense of 'the Church in danger' which fed the frustrations and resentments of squires and parsons was further heightened by the increased strength of the Liberation Society, the pressure group for the disestablishment of the 'state church', on the Liberal benches in the Commons and in many constituencies.

The Licensing bills introduced by the Liberal Home Secretary, H. A. Bruce, in 1871 and 1872 had a non-partisan intention. The milder of the two, which became the 1872 Act, was only a quarter-step towards the panacea of local option which the main lobby against the drink trade, the United Kingdom Alliance, wanted – it complained that the measure had been 'compromised by an official coalition' – but any Liberal move in this direction was enough to antagonize 'the trade' and to shift much of its electoral support the Tory way. A highly influential interest and pressure-group was thus attached to the Conservatives and the turning of by-elections their way dated from the controversy over the 1871 bill. The issue, which had religious and social implications, had caused the Commons leaders some embarrassment and some of them had looked for a compromise measure, but the weight of the outraged interests moving behind them would determine the Tory stance for the future. The most strenuous resistance had again come from the Tory peers, led this time by Richmond and Salisbury, the latter putting emphasis on economic freedom and opposing social engineering through legislation.

Down to 1871 the party had lost on most of the controversial issues, the outnumbered Commons party taking the brunt of the defeats. The leadership was criticized on its own back benches, by a body of Tory peers and by various interests in the country for its tendency to temporize and to seek compromise with the government. Though this approach had helped the Church over popular education, many Tories declined to recognize the achievement and called for firmer and more 'principled' opposition to the government and all its works. The strongest resistance had been from unofficial groups like 'the colonels', from the Church lobby, from Tory peers pursuing an independent line and from various interest groups outside Parliament. Disenchantment with the leadership, particularly with Disraeli, communicated itself to his colleagues among the ex-Cabinet ministers and discussion of his future culminated at a meeting at Burghley House in January 1872 when only Manners and Northcote spoke for him. Derby's refusal to seek the leadership ensured Disraeli's survival. But the latter's ill health, apathy and attention to other concerns (his novel *Lothair* was published in 1870) were only part of the reason for what appeared to be supine leadership. The men around him were divided in opinions and immediate aims – on religious matters beyond the basic defence of the English and Scottish establishments they were not a harmonious crew – and there were still scars from 1867–68 unhealed. After the electoral defeat of 1868 and while the recalcitrants of 1867 were still unreconciled, it was hardly possible to blow the trumpet of 'Tory democracy', but neither was it possible to disown what had been done over electoral reform or to ignore its implications. That course was not only incompatible with the positions of Disraeli and Derby in the collective leadership, it was also likely to inflame the new borough voters about whom thinking Tories already worried so much and to check any drift of conservative Whigs towards the party. Nor was the parliamentary party quite so homogeneous as it had once been. The Ballot Bill of 1872 had met with hostility from the Tory county members but the much less numerous but often articulate Conservatives from the large boroughs had been sympathetic to a measure they thought helpful to them. It was hardly surprising that Disraeli and his colleagues were pursuing a Micawberish policy of waiting for something to turn up. This attitude and the post-1867 worries about 'the working class' helped to account for the bizarre episode of the 'New Social Movement' in 1871 when half the ex-Cabinet negotiated on various social questions with a group of labour leaders under the auspices of J. Scott Russell, an engineer and a protegé of Pakington. Once the talks became public, the Tory participants played down their involvement and denied any commitment to a legislative programme. Matters ended amidst embarrassment and recrimination. The episode showed the nervousness and uncertainty of prominent Conservatives towards working-class opinion, but also their sensitivity towards existing interests and attitudes in the party. There were always hardliners like Salisbury on the look-out for new betrayals. For the moment the main worry for the leaders was the grumbling discontent, admittedly nothing new, of agricultural and Church interests with the party's direction and performance.

Revival

The turn-around in party fortunes in the second half of 1871 had more causes than simply the recent Licensing Bill. The measures of the Liberal government, far from settling questions, had tended to provoke antagonisms and to inspire unrealistic expectations, leaving supporters dissatisfied and divided and generating resentment among the interests that had suffered. Concessions to Irish discontent and to Catholicism (the unpopularity of which had been intensified by the Vatican Council of 1870), the perceived threats to the landowning classes and to the officer corps, the alienation of militant Nonconformity by the Education Act, all left doubts and resentments among former supporters of the government. There was also a vague but pervasive sense of Britain's international weakness following from Russia's renunciation in 1870 of the Black Sea clauses of the Treaty of Paris, the controversy over the Alabama arbitration involving the United States and the government's cautious and hesitant attitude towards colonial difficulties. Gladstone, characterized as one of the 'peace party' of the Crimean years, was already under press attack for his supposed diplomatic weakness. In 1870 the Tory *Standard* had harped on his 'singular and proved unfitness for the position of a War Minister' and the Palmerstonian *Morning Post* had accused him of seeming to 'court peace at any price' when 'a manly policy . . . an English policy' was called for. There was also alarm over the creation and growth of a Home Rule party in Ireland, over the apparent vogue for republicanism when the monarchy seemed to hit a trough of unpopularity in 1871 and, among landowners and farmers, over the spasm of agricultural trade unionism in the early 1870s. While the Liberals suffered from the disaffection of many of their constituency activists, the Tories began to benefit from a move of conservative, centrist opinion away from a government that had lost the image of Palmerstonian success and assurance.

Disraeli claimed to notice the change of public mood first when he and Gladstone met with sharply contrasting receptions from the London crowd after the thanksgiving service for the Prince of Wales's recovery in February 1872. But even before this he had decided to seize the opportunity to visit Lancashire to address a major Conservative rally, a visit which he had been warned off previously because of local hostility towards his conduct in 1867–68 and his leadership. In Manchester's Free Trade Hall in April 1872 he used his speech to a great gathering of the county's Conservative associations to answer Liberal criticisms that the Tories were bereft of policies. Condemning the government for unleashing a radicalism it could not control, he depicted the Liberal party as a threat to Crown, House of Lords, Church and national honour and security. More briefly he touched on the Conservative contribution to sanitary reform ('Sanitas sanitatum, omnia sanitas'). Heartened by positive press and party reactions to this effort, he returned to some of the themes at the Crystal Palace in July. He asserted the essential Conservatism of the working classes, made more of Empire (self-government for colonies should have been 'accompanied by an Imperial tariff' and 'some representative council in the metropolis') and hinted at the need to co-ordinate national and colonial defence, decked out his earlier reference to social reform ('air, light and water') and advised the electorate that 'the time had arrived when social and not political improvement is the object which they ought to pursue'. The reception of these performances put Disraeli's leadership beyond challenge in his party. Their rhetorical flourishes had come, however, when Liberal disintegration, measured by continuing by-election reverses, was already well advanced.

Gladstone's troubles were compounded when, trying to conciliate the Catholic bishops, he sought to secure agreement to the creation of a Catholic university in Dublin. The outcome was that nobody was satisfied: negotiations with the Catholic hierarchy broke down in acrimony, Anglican opinion contrasted the initiative with the removal of Anglican tests in English universities, 'Protestant' opinion resented further truckling to Catholic interests, Liberal Nonconformity was confused and distressed. In March 1873 a combination of the Tories and the Irish, aided by Liberal abstentions, inflicted a defeat on the government in the Commons and Gladstone resigned. Disraeli, backed by half his prospective Cabinet, declined to take office. Not only did he hope for further demoralization among the Liberals, he did not wish to expose divisions on his own side and to provoke Salisbury, the main critic of the 'office without power' performance of 1866–68, by forming another minority government. Gladstone resumed office and further Tory by-election successes followed, one at Bath permitting Disraeli the opportunity to define his stance more circumspectly than the previous year. Now the conservative emphasis was clear. His open letter to the candidate charged that the Liberal government had 'harassed every trade, worried every profession, and assailed or menaced every class, institution and species of property in this country'. More than a 'career of plundering and blundering', it amounted to 'civil warfare'. Gladstone's unexpected dissolution in January 1874 was on a platform of the abolition of the income tax. Disraeli's address harped on the 'incessant and harassing legislation' the government had inflicted upon the country and claimed that the radicals who were pressing Gladstone on were enemies of the constitution, particularly of the Crown, the Church, the Lords and the Union with Ireland. Little was said of empire or social reform. The message was a Conservative version of Palmerston: stability and order at home, patriotism abroad – 'a little more energy in foreign policy and a little less in our domestic legislation'.

The Conservative majority returned in 1874 was the first since 1841 and it surprised contemporaries by its decisiveness. It was achieved, moreover, without any 'reconstruction' or 'fusion' of parties of the kind which many had seen as the most likely way to end the near-permanent Liberal majority. The Tories gained over 80 seats, 65 of them in England, the largest gains coming in the English counties (14) and the larger boroughs (38). The party's overwhelming predominance in the English counties – 129 out of 154 seats – was reminiscent of 1841 and marked the end of the hold on a sizeable bloc of county representation which the Liberals had established under Palmerston. The gains in the larger boroughs were crucial, though here the party, gathering 72 of the 159 seats in English boroughs with more than 20,000 inhabitants, remained in a minority. A significant improvement in Scotland after the disaster of 1868 was, however, almost cancelled out by further losses in Ireland, though the Liberals were the major sufferers from the return of over fifty Home Rulers, a sharp divergence by Ireland from the pattern of British politics which portended trouble. Though the Conservatives made only modest gains in the small boroughs, which were less susceptible to movements of opinion than the large ones, they stood out in parliamentary terms very much as the party of England and it was more of a cross-section of English constituencies than for decades. Once again anti-Irish and anti-Catholic feeling had worked for the party, above all in Lancashire which now appeared as a Tory stronghold. Despite the caution of some of its leaders on the issue, 'Protestantism' was a trade which paid the party well.

Though some Disraelians rhapsodized about 'Tory democracy' and claimed a delayed action for the 1867 Act, there was little in the results outside the North West to link them with the franchise extension. The dominant mood in 1874 was a widespread desire for stability and normality after the strains and stresses of Liberal rule. Liberal disintegration was more in evidence than Tory resurgence and in many constituencies it was the fall or division of the Liberal vote since 1868, not any surge of the Tory vote, that led to seats changing hands. The security of Palmerston's days, not the heady excitements of 'democracy', Tory or otherwise, was the desire the results suggested. So far as Disraeli had done much (in fact much less than Gladstone) to produce those results, it was the resolutely conservative Disraeli of 1873–74, purveying a familiar and reassuring style of aristocratic centrism, not the breathtaking opportunism of 1867. The pre-1867 electoral system would have produced much the same result and there was little sign that the newly enfranchised voters were a particular source of strength to the Conservatives. The clearest shifts of sentiment in the boroughs seem, indeed, to have occurred among the business and professional classes. Some features, admittedly, had changed since Palmerston's death. Ireland was now more radicalized, the issue of relations with Catholicism was more fraught, the Church of England was more fearful and offended, the drink trade had moved significantly the Tory way (though not so decisively as to warrant Gladstone's sanctimonious claim that his party had been 'borne down in a torrent of gin and beer'), landowners were more nervous. But most of this only confirmed the predominantly conservative mood. When Disraeli formed his ministry, the first with assured longevity since Peel's, it included the anti-reformers of 1867 and its conservative credentials were obvious. Salisbury and Carnarvon joined Richmond, Derby and Cairns on the Lords front bench, while the weight alongside Disraeli in the Commons was provided by Hardy and Northcote, two loyalists who had not relished the 'democratic' tactics of 1867–68.

One other aspect of the 1874 victory merits comment. It has sometimes been depicted as an organizational triumph for a modernized party which, through the creation of the National Union in 1867 and of Central Office in 1870, had geared itself specifically and successfully to the post-1867 electorate. The ambitious lawyer John Gorst, who combined the post of national agent, to which Disraeli had appointed him, with the secretaryship of the National Union, certainly claimed much of the credit for the 1874 results for himself and his organizations. The innovations though, had been inspired less by purposeful strategy than by a sense of threatening circumstances. Many figures in the party had been nervous of the boroughs and of 'the working men' after 1867 and the election defeat of 1868 had only confirmed their worries. An attempt to improve organization both in the constituencies, particularly those most transformed by the recent legislation, and at the centre was anyway a natural response for a defeated party unsettled by major electoral reform. Initially the National Union was only one among several bodies seeking to draw constituency associations into some central union and it survived and succeeded largely because of Gorst's connection with it. Disraeli's appointment of a national agent with an office of his own was a break with the previous reliance upon solicitors' firms and upon the whips for all electoral management.[3] The rôle of the former had been diminished by a measure of 1868 which had removed the hearing of election petitions from the Commons and the creation of a counterbalance to the whips may have reflected Disraeli's sense of insecurity within the parliamentary party of 1870 and his uneasy relations with the chief whip, Colonel Taylor. Gorst, however, proved to be an inspired choice, even if he was not the only influential figure in the improvement of Conservative organization. He had a mission – to integrate the business and professional men who led borough Toryism fully into a party which was still overwhelmingly aristocratic and rural in its concerns and its leadership – and his appointment nearly coincided with the movement of prosperous urban opinion towards the Conservatives in the early 1870s. Gorst's personal empathy with these reinforcements was important, but he was swimming with the tide of sentiment. If the Tories were better organized, financed and co-ordinated in the boroughs in 1874 than in 1868, particularly in the large boroughs where organization counted most, it owed something to Gorst's willing labours but more to an independent shift in the balance of certain kinds of opinion the Tory way, to the alarm and urgency felt within the party in reaction against Liberal measures and to the simultaneous disorganization of the Liberals. There were obvious similarities to what had happened in the late 1830s when central organization had been only factor among many in the party's revival: in 1874, as in 1841, the party enjoyed a triumph in the counties where the new kinds of organization were scarcely in evidence. How far and where improved organization operated as an autonomous factor in Tory success is difficult to say, just as it is how Gorst would have fared in the more difficult circumstances of 1868.

Government with a Majority

The ministry of 1874 did not represent a single style of Conservatism, though it may have been significant that Salisbury and Carnarvon, the resigners of 1867, were kept away from domestic ministries. It was by no means clear what politics would be pursued on the issues of the day. Disraeli's preference for a quiet life ('We came in on the principle of not harassing the country') had to be set against the views and enthusiasms of his colleagues in a highly departmentalized structure of government, against the pressures put upon ministers by civil service or press opinion, against the demands of noisy and assertive pressure groups and against the attitudes and expectations to be found on the swollen Tory benches. If 1874–76 witnessed a notable concentration of domestic legislation, another reason was the surplus of £5½ million which Gladstone had bequeathed reluctantly to Northcote at the Exchequer. It meant that the Treasury could, for the moment, be relaxed about measures which made demands on central expenditure. In 1874 Northcote reduced income tax, abolished sugar duties and extended grants in aid of local authority expenditure on police and asylums; in 1875 he established a Sinking Fund to reduce the National Debt. If the last gratified the City, the extension of local grants did something for the county ratepayers and for the powerful backbench lobby

---

[3] On the organizational developments see E. J. Feuchtwanger, *Disraeli, Democracy and the Tory Party* (Oxford, 1968), ch. 5, and H. J. Hanham, *Elections and Party Management* (1959), especially pp. 356–68.

that made 'the relief of local burdens' its cry. (The Local Taxation Committee of the Central Chamber of Agriculture apparently included some 62 Tory MPs.) Agriculturalists remained dissatisfied, though, with the failure to repeal the malt tax. By 1876 mounting budgetary difficulties were among the reasons why enthusiasm for domestic legislation petered out. But finance was not the only factor in the legislation of the ministry's early years. Though the government as a whole showed little commitment to a social programme, some individual ministers were at least open-minded on some of the current legislative questions. Though not the first choice for the office, the Home Secretary R. A. Cross, a protégé of the Stanleys and the only genuine Northerner in the Cabinet (perhaps Disraeli's thanks-offering to Lancashire), had more grasp of urban conditions and issues than most Tory politicians. He was also sensitive to the importance of the larger boroughs to the party's electoral fortunes. His Artisans' Dwellings Act of 1875 was a product of the concern which lower-class housing in the cities had inspired among the informed and the squeamish since the 1850s. In giving urban authorities powers of compulsory purchase and clearance, however, it only enlarged the scope permitted to local initiative; its permissive character indicated how far the government was from compelling local authority action and from anything like a national crusade on working-class accommodation. Indeed caution in anything that might change the relationship between central and local authority to the latter's detriment was a hallmark of the government's approach. That was true of the 1875 Public Health Act, largely a consolidation of existing legislation and the work of George Sclater-Booth, the President of the Local Government Board, whose exclusion from the Cabinet showed the low priority Disraeli gave to one of the most important domestic departments.

Similar caution was apparent in the handling of the regulation of merchant shipping, an issue publicized by the Liberal Samuel Plimsoll. Northcote alerted Disraeli to the political dangers of the compromise bill being introduced by Adderley, the President of the Board of Trade (and also outside the Cabinet), in 1875:

> The bill is one of a most critical character, politically speaking, and there are dangers on every side. Our shipowners hate it ... Plimsoll and his followers mean to trip us up if possible; and he has a great many friends in our own ranks ...

MacIver, Laird's successor at Birkenhead and one of the MPs for ports with working-class electors to consider, warned that the government 'cannot equally please those interested in inferior shipping property and those who desire to stop needless waste of life at sea'. When the shipping interests assaulted the bill, Disraeli and Northcote retreated, the former proclaiming that 'the maintenance of freedom of contract is one of the necessary conditions of the commercial and manufacturing greatness of the country'. When the government withdrew the measure to give priority to the Agricultural Holdings Bill, a significant indication of its priorities, Plimsoll raised Cain in the Commons and agitation mounted in the country. With MacIver warning that continued obstruction would '"keep going" a general growl against the Conservative party in every port in the kingdom', the government panicked, introduced a temporary measure, under pressure conceded the point of a load line (Disraeli complained that some Tory members were 'Plimsollized *too* much') and then in 1876 brought forward a permanent measure. When it was amended in Plimsoll's direction in the Commons, the government used its majority in the Lords to weaken its provisions again. The resulting Act fell short of what the reformers had demanded but it bought off the worst of the political agitation.[4] The episode showed how far the government was from a firm commitment to working-class welfare or to a 'Tory Democracy' programme but also how far it could be pushed by determined pressure-groups, particularly when the seats of Conservative members seemed to be at stake.

Perhaps the most remarkable step was the labour legislation of 1875. Previously the Conservatives had not shown themselves to be tender towards trades unions and their demands. Tory lawyers, given a lead by Cairns, had been hostile on points of legal interpretation and the generality of gentry and farmers had been alarmed and affronted by the agricultural trade unionism of the early 1870s. Tory votes had helped to ensure that the Liberals' Criminal Law Amendment Act of 1871 fell short of being acceptable to the unions. Yet in 1874, when a *Quarterly Review* article condemned the 'dangerous and encroaching despotism' of trade unionism, Tory candidates in many industrial constituencies met with demands from working-class electors for changes to the recent Act. W. R. Callender, the leading Manchester Conservative and himself a new borough member, reported that 'every candidate for a borough constituency has had to promise compliance'. Cross, backed by Disraeli but with no other positive support in the Cabinet, now replaced the old Master and Servant law by an Employers and Workmen Act which decriminalized most breaches of contract and, after some hesitation, he repealed the 1871 statute and substituted the Conspiracy and Protection of Property Act which legalized the organization and practice of peaceful picketing. The few grumbles on the Tory benches came from county members, though there was more criticism from employers outside Parliament. The considerations which persuaded Cross and Disraeli to take a major step in the reform of labour law seem to have been largely ones of electoral expediency, though there may also have been some gratitude to those sections of the enfranchised working classes which had voted Tory in 1874. If so, it was another part of the Lancashire dimension of contemporary politics. More generally, though, it reflected the persistent unease among leading Conservatives about the political attitudes and potential of 'the working man' – worry about the implications and consequences of 1867 had not been entirely calmed by 1874 – and a desire to forestall a bid for trade-union favour which was gathering support on the Liberal benches. As yet the influence of major employers and their trade organizations in party councils was weak and the party's sense of its electoral interests could comfortably outweigh them. It was a moment when Disraeli's inconstant taste for gesture and rhetoric towards the working-class electorate had the opportunity to take a concrete form, but the episode only delayed the identification of the party with hostility to trade-union interests which was soon to become apparent.

---

[4] See Paul Smith, *Disraelian Conservatism and Social Reform* (1967), pp. 230–42, for this episode. The work is the outstanding study of the party in relation to social issues from 1866 to 1880.

It was not only working-class trade unionists who inspired nervousness about electoral prospects. Despite the electoral triumph in the English counties in 1874, the mounting difficulties of agriculture and the continuing grumbles about rural rates and burdens made the party's strategists uneasy, all the more so because of Gladstone's Irish Land Act and the worsening relations between the landlord and tenant classes in Ireland. The party stood to lose a great deal if comparable discontents developed in the English counties. The Agricultural Holdings Bill of 1875, a measure dear to Disraeli's heart, was intended to extend to farmers something of the security of compensation for unexpired improvements which Gladstone had given to Ireland and to appease those Conservative politicians who made themselves spokesmen for the tenant farmers. But landowners were not to be affronted or undermined. The Act was only permissive in character and merely established a statutory framework which landlord and tenant could agree to adopt if they chose. Freedom of contract and landlord's rights were thus preserved.

Indeed in the discussions of most social and economic questions ministers and backbenchers made clear their commitment to property rights and to freedom of contract. Far from representing a theoretical, even romantic, rejection of free-market economics of the kind some of the fringe Tory writers had preached earlier in the century, the measures promoted by Disraeli's ministry were conceived and argued in terms of a careful balancing of economic, legalistic, humanitarian and political considerations. Northcote, who so often argued for economic orthodoxy in the House, could argue in private that 'the true policy of the *laissez faire* school' was to 'endeavour to enforce the shipowners' responsibility' through an element of statutory regulation:

> ... we must insist that you shall not evade your responsibilities under the specious plea of freedom of contract, which is (or may be) a good enough plea as between the contracting parties, but is one to be very jealously scrutinized when it affects the lives of other persons.

This reasonable balancing of humanity and economic freedom operated even with issues less influenced by electoral considerations than merchant shipping. It showed in the persistent if tentative interest of various Conservative politicians (but not only Conservatives) in the question of working-class housing, though here arguments that squalid accommodation handicapped the missionary efforts of the Christian denominations and encouraged incest among the poor added to the concern of the pious and the moral. But where such considerations did not exist and particularly where public expenditure was concerned, the verities of free-market orthodoxy, of the sanctity of property rights and of freedom of contract were asserted strenuously on the Tory benches and in the Tory press. Indeed the legislative endeavours of 1874–76 were sandwiched by periods when most Conservative politicians sought to depress expectations of legislative interference in social and economic processes. The party, after all, was one of tax and rate payers, as the economy-minded gentry on the back benches were ever ready to remind ministers.

These apparently contradictory positions were not in fact irreconcilable. Most Tory parliamentarians came from the landed classes of the counties, where they wished to appear as responsible and honourable in their social relationships. They usually accepted that property had its responsibilities as well as its rights. An orthodox commitment to freedom of contract and to property rights coexisted with a sense of social duty and a modicum of moral paternalism. Attitudes of this kind could colour the consideration even of legislative questions. Northcote became persuaded of the need for some statutory enforcement of ship-owners' responsibilities towards their dependants; Beach, a responsible, sympathetic landlord when his own tenants suffered during agricultural depression, could readily accept some aspects of Liberal land legislation in Ireland – it required all landlords to do what the good ones were doing anyway. 'Responsibility' was a word and a concept prominent in discussions of many social questions. It was a view of society from the bench of Quarter Sessions. Politicians who served as magistrates in their own localities understood the pathology of society and they tended to prefer goals like stability, order and social harmony to abstract dogmas. Their sense of responsibility was also reinforced by prudence. As a Devon knight of the shire put it in 1874, 'if cottages were not built in which labourers could live in decency and comfort, it was natural they would become members of Agricultural Labourers Unions and listen to agitators'. Attitudes were conditioned by a mixture of concerns: for social and political stability, for the security of property and privilege, for a style of social leadership and for the interests of the party. They helped to ensure that the party never presented an adamantine front against social legislation, as it often did against constitutional change. Inevitably, however, the distaste for increased public expenditure, for central intervention in the localities and for interference with property rights ensured that the outcome was often more cosmetic than substantive. Politicians were well aware of the potential for gesture and rhetoric. Derby thought working-class housing 'a good subject to take up, but [one] which will require cautious handling if we are not to carry State interference beyond its legitimate limits'. In 1868 Disraeli had wanted popular education discussed by the peers to forestall a Liberal initiative in the Commons: 'it must be kept in the Lords now; at any rate we want education discussed by Dukes and Bishops. It will have a beneficial effect on all'. A show of concern and responsibility by society's leaders was both morally elevating and politically stabilizing. The party's image could be improved more easily and painlessly than social realities.

Behind this mixture of endeavour and non-endeavour lay a desire for consensus. In the aftermath of the 1874 victory most responsible Conservatives sought to heal the wounds they believed had been inflicted on the polity by Liberal government and radical agitation and to settle issues on a basis which reasonable men could accept. To this end they were willing to restrain some of their own more atavistic supporters. Agitation might stir them into action because agitation was dangerous, but not so as to encourage further agitation or to create serious counter-grievance. Much of what was done in the social field had broad support across the parties and was not a matter of party conflict. Although subsequent mythology has made much of the special social reform commitment of Disraelian Toryism, there was very little distinctively Tory about most of what was done and nearly all of the (usually modest) measures could have been passed just as well under a Liberal government. Many of them passed with the aid of

Liberal votes and in many cases the content of the bills reflected the approaches of largely non-partisan civil servants. Only perhaps in their hostility to major constitutional legislation, which left parliamentary time available for the less controversial social questions, were the Conservatives a particular help. On the rare occasions when Disraeli made himself felt on questions of domestic legislation, electoral considerations rather than a considered policy or theoretical approach were his concern. Here outbidding the Liberals and the establishment of a social and political consensus were nicely mixed motives.

But there were areas of legislative activity where different considerations applied and partisanship was sharper. Church questions were one and popular education, itself largely a religious issue, was another. Only a few Anglican zealots believed Forster's Act of 1870 could be unscrambled, but a large body of Church opinion was dissatisfied with its operation. Tories varied widely in their interest in popular education. Some, like Smith and Sandon who served on the London School Board, believed in its potential for social good, others saw it as a painful necessity, others still as a positive menace. But virtually all agreed that as large a part of popular schooling as possible should be controlled by the Church of England and that it was the party's duty and interest to sustain and promote denominational education, which meant largely Anglican education. By 1874 many Church schools in rural districts were short of both pupils and income as they faced the competition of new Board schools or the threat of the creation of a local School Board. The remedy seemed to lie with an element of compulsory attendance which would increase both pupils and income. The Bill introduced in 1876 by Sandon, the Vice-President of the Privy Council, provided this by restricting child labour. Though backbenchers recognized its intentions, there was disappointment at the measure's mildness and Albert Pell, one of the 'farmers' friends', introduced an amendment to eliminate superfluous School Boards, so gratifying county ratepayers and the Church interest together. Sandon grasped at the opportunity: it was 'one of our most important moves, which is immensely popular with all our party in the House of Commons, and will be most acceptable to all the country except the big towns'. Disraeli, ever distrustful of the High Church dominance of the National Society, which backed Pell, and convinced of the dangers of identifying the Conservatives with 'the Sacerdotal party', tried to have the amendment killed, but the Cabinet majority forced the clause's acceptance. The 1876 Education Act still fell short of what the Church interest wanted, particularly in not making religious teaching compulsory in Board schools. The Church of England, in fact, received less from six years of Conservative government than it might have expected. Most of its recent defeats – over church rates, Irish disestablishment and university tests – were beyond redemption, but even on other issues the government was unwilling to attempt much beyond protecting the Church from further depredations by its opponents. Nothing was so likely to 'unsettle' the consensus the ministry sought than religious controversy.

Another problem was the continuing party division within the Church itself which disrupted Tory unity on a range of issues. Disraeli's own preferences, tangibly expressed through ecclesiastical patronage, antagonized the High Church wing. The outburst of Sir William Heathcote,

former member for Oxford University, to Salisbury in 1876 on 'the
incubus of your present Chief' showed the frustrations: 'Cold and lukewarm in all that might serve the Church or religious Education and thus . . .
real conservatism, he is earnest only in sensational claptrap'. High Churchmen particularly resented Disraeli's indifference to Anglican exclusiveness
and his emphasis on the 'Protestant' character of the constitution. In turn
the premier, influenced perhaps by Lancashire, warned ministers of 'the
temper of the Time. At present, the national spirit is full of alarm about
Popery & Sacerdotalism . . .' In 1874 the Queen and Archbishop Tait had
concocted a measure to control the excesses of the ritualist clergy in the
Church. Though it was not a government bill, Disraeli gave it his personal
support in the Commons, braving the resentment of Salisbury and several
other Cabinet colleagues. The acrimony which the Public Worship Regulation Act caused within the Church rubbed off on the Conservatives,
damaging both the government and the party's relations with the Church.
The bitterness of the High Churchmen was to contribute to the divisions over the Eastern Question and to make the Church in 1880 less united
as a political force and less committed to the party than it had been in
1874.

Disraeli's 'Protestantism' was peddled more cautiously in relation to
Ireland, where his preference for quiet times was clearly displayed. The
tough-minded Chief Secretary, Hicks Beach, had the advantage of inherit-
ing a Coercion Act from the Liberals. His firm, dispassionate administration of the laws and his refusal to be panicked into concessions helped to
settle Ireland in the mid-1870s. Soon he was starting to think constructively
and, like others before him, to woo the Catholic bishops and influential
laity. He managed to obtain general consent to an Intermediate Education
Act in 1877, but Disraeli's reluctance to stir the Irish brew and the palpable
difficulties of extending the area of consensus prevented further legislative
endeavour. When Beach moved to the Colonial Office in 1878, Ireland
counted as a success for Conservative government. Greater order and
stability had been achieved and no controversial concessions had been
made. Over the next two years, however, the obstruction in the Commons by the Home Rulers, agricultural depression and the agrarian discontent exploited by the Land League combined to dissipate this sense of
success.

More flamboyant, superficially at least, was the administration's handling
of colonial and imperial questions. The Act to make Victoria Empress of
India in 1876 was more the Queen's inspiration than the government's,
though Disraeli took a leading part in the Commons proceedings and in
providing the rhetorical window-dressing for a measure that left many
politicians uneasy. Though there had been little to prepare opinion for the
Queen's oriental fantasy, the Conservatives had recently been making
much of their traditional loyalty to the Crown, in contrast to the attitudes
they claimed existed on the Liberal side, and Liberal criticism in Parliament
of the new title emphasized the contrast between the parties. In fact the
ministry changed little in the government of India, the main changes
having come after the Mutiny. Disraeli's purchase of a major holding of
Suez Canal shares for the government in 1875, though doubtfully constitutional, had at least a political purpose in securing Britain's position in the
eastern Mediterranean, in Egypt and on the route to India. No British

government was less than committed to India, but maybe the Indian situation where the British minority ruled alien masses apparently by a combination of military might and moral ascendency had a fascination for Tory politicians who sometimes felt themselves to be attempting something similar at home. For Disraeli the Asiatic empire certainly had a romantic appeal, but most of his government's moves were responses to circumstances rather than a coherent and deliberate policy. Indeed, despite earlier Tory criticism of Gladstone's ministry for weakness and vacillation in colonial policy, the new ministry had designed no 'forward policy' for the colonies. The influence of figures like Derby and Northcote helped to ensure that, even if Carnarvon at the Colonial Office was less negative and cautious. The wars in which the country found itself embroiled in Afghanistan and southern Africa by 1879 were the doing more of the pro-consuls Lytton and Frere than of the Cabinet or the responsible ministers. The Cabinet itself, giving priority to European matters and alarmed at the likely demands on military and financial resources, tended towards caution and procrastination. During 1879 both Afghans and Zulus inflicted military defeats and compounded the problems which were accumulating for the government. Though it had continued the work of claiming the mantle of patriotism and national assertion from the once-Palmerstonian Liberal party, its colonial achievement by 1880 looked uncertain and accident-prone rather than a tale of vision and resource.

From 1875 the main preoccupation of the Cabinet and especially of Disraeli had been European diplomacy, notably the revived confrontation between Ottoman Turkey and Russia. British interests, as traditionally defined, were at stake and opportunity offered for a replay of the Palmerstonism of the Crimean War. Disraeli saw British interests as requiring a firm commitment to Turkey's control of Constantinople, the Straits and the Dardanelles, though his Cabinet was divided on both aims and means. The initial impact on public opinion was affected by the Turkish massacres of Bulgarian Christians in 1875–76 and the outcry was increased when Gladstone returned to public controversy with a best-selling pamphlet *The Bulgarian Horrors and the Question of the East*. The former Liberal leader (he had resigned in 1875 and been succeeded in the Commons by Hartington) condemned the morality of support for a non-Christian power that repressed Christian subjects by barbaric means and this translation of national interest into the language of religious morality stirred not only Nonconformity, which had well-developed qualms about despotism, militarism and the immorality of governments, but also sections of Anglican opinion, particularly those High Churchmen who identified with the Orthodox communion. Though the Queen, Disraeli and several of his colleagues regarded Gladstone's behaviour as close to treachery, most Conservative opinion was uncertain and defensive as Gladstone's campaign rolled on during 1876 and most of 1877. Inevitably, though, it set an example which government supporters could try to emulate. Though Cabinet opinion remained badly divided, by late 1877 there were party activists working to organize a patriotic, pro-government response to the hostile agitation. Early in 1878, when the diplomacy was entering a new and sensitive phase, a wave of 'jingoism' swept sections of public opinion, notably in the public meetings, music halls and press of the cities.[5] The nature and extent of this phenomenon remain unclear, but its political impact strengthened the government's confidence and helped to tilt opinion in the Cabinet towards the hard-liners. The two most pacific ministers, Carnarvon at the Colonial Office and Derby at the Foreign Office, resigned; others who had qualms like Northcote and Salisbury toed the line; and Salisbury soon emerged as a Foreign Secretary of skill and weight who was prepared to work closely with Disraeli. The government, backed by Austria–Hungary, rejected the treaty which Russia had imposed on Turkey and from the resulting Congress of Berlin Disraeli and Salisbury emerged with 'peace with honour' – a Balkan settlement slanted less Russia's way and the cession of Cyprus by Turkey to Britain. Here indeed was a Palmerstonian climax for Disraeli: achievement as a European statesman and patriotic acclamation. It ensured that the 'peace party' within the Conservative leadership remained diminished and discredited, above all by the departure of Derby.

Though not a straightforward victory of the hard-line right over the liberal wing of Conservative opinion, the Eastern crisis left its mark on the party. Salisbury, Beach and Cranbrook had emerged as the strong figures close to Disraeli, while of those who might have resisted the drift of the party towards a patriotic, even bellicose identity, Derby was gone (he supported the Liberals in 1880 and joined Gladstone's Cabinet formed that year) while Northcote was left more isolated and vulnerable. More generally the polarization of party politics had tended to strengthen the more belligerently anti-Liberal elements at the expense of the instinctive centrists. It had also prepared the way for a further radicalization of the Liberal party which would generate a reaction within the Conservative opposition in the 1880s. But all this was the outcome rather than anybody's design. Circumstances and the way the Cabinet, after initial uncertainties, found itself responding to them had helped the Tories to appreciate the patriotic stance and to pin more firmly upon the Liberals the moralistic, internationalist and 'Little Englander' identity which had begun to emerge during Gladstone's first ministry. Perhaps this development was inevitable as British politics recovered from the impact of Palmerston. The weight of Protestant Nonconformity served to incline the Liberals that way – 'the Nonconformist conscience' was a phrase coined in these years – while the Tories had no corresponding interest or body of opinion to hold them back from a more jingoistic identity. Indeed their connections with the military officer corps made them more naturally the party of the militaristic response. Disraeli's own instincts and ambitions worked in the same direction once the crisis and the opportunity developed, but it was hardly an outcome he had planned in 1874 when Derby, Northcote and Carnarvon had gone to crucial ministries or even in 1876 when Northcote was given the lead in the Commons.

[5] See H. Cunningham, 'Jingoism in 1877–78', *Victorian Studies*, 14/4, 1971, pp. 429–53. Though 'jingoism' was largely a feature of the large boroughs, its incidence was uneven. Cities with major industries that expected to benefit from military expenditure, for example Sheffield, were more pro-government than others where local industries feared the disruption of their trade by war.

Down and Out Again

In 1876 Disraeli's health had forced him to leave the Commons and move to the Lords as Earl of Beaconsfield. Northcote rather than the more truculent and acerbic Hardy, who had been at odds with the leader on religious questions, was chosen to lead the Commons. As Hardy soon opted for the Lords too, the Commons front bench was left thin on major talent, a factor which told when it took the brunt of Gladstone's comeback and of the controversies over foreign policy. By the end of the Parliament Irish obstruction and the discontents of the industrial and agricultural constituencies were unsettling the Conservatives in the Lower House and supporters outside it. Disraeli himself, with little time or energy for matters outside foreign affairs, contributed to the sagging of morale and performance. Diplomacy apart, his greatest enthusiasms were his relentless working upon the Queen's favour and opinions ('laying it on with a trowel', in his phrase) and his equally relentless exploitation of patronage for party and personal purposes. (His notably partisan use of patronage, particularly his pulling various categories of public service appointments back into the political domain, attracted hostile comment from his opponents. He was like the elder Derby in not only maximizing the exploitation of patronage for party purposes but also rewarding personal friends and supporters within the party.) The keeping of the Queen and of large sections of the party happy were among the reasons why Disraeli's leadership remained secure until his death, even though complaints about the direction of government and the management of the party were multiplying well before 1880. Gorst, who resigned as national agent in 1877 and embarked on a career as a critic of the leadership, complained of Disraeli's lack of interest in organization and in the cultivation of borough opinion. The leaders of borough Toryism resented his indifference to their opinions and constituencies. Even after 1874 the leading members for the large urban constituencies had rarely been conceded a more prominent rôle in the House than the seconding of the Address at the start of the session. Though two members for city seats, Sandon and Smith, sat in the Cabinet by 1880, they were hardly typical borough members (Sandon was heir to an earldom) and they were equalled in number by dukes. Disraeli's unwillingness to change either the style of government or the social character of the party's ministerial élite was self-evident. During his ministry the balance of leadership had shifted back to the Lords from the Commons.

The lack of purpose and creativity – even Disraeli's rhetoric was flagging by 1880 – was shown in other areas too. After the 1876 session most of his domestic ministers had exhausted whatever modest legislative programmes they had once had. Though legislative quiescence was hardly a failure for a Conservative ministry – indeed it was something the electorate had been promised before the 1874 victory – arguably the urban electorate relished some show of creativity and some spectacle from a government. The government's credibility in financial management petered out too. Northcote now found himself presiding over deficits as military expenditure mounted and as tax yields fell with the onset of economic depression. He had to raid his own Sinking Fund and to raise income tax again. There were no further resources available for relieving the burdens of county rates, despite the grumbles of the squirearchy, or for social legislation that required central finance. Far from demanding further social reforms, Tory opinion during the last years of the government was critical of the burdens of central and local expenditure on taxpayers and ratepayers. The old cry of cheap government had outlasted any limited social mission that individual ministers may have conceived for themselves in the heady days after 1874.

Adding to the political problems was the sharp economic depression which set in in 1879–80 and which affected agriculture, manufacturing and trade. Agricultural depression during the late 1870s, when bad harvests at home coincided with falling prices as imports flooded in, meant that the counties were never again to be as settled for the Tories as they had been in 1874. Discontents multiplied among the farmers and the gentry, tensions grew between tenants and landlords, bankruptcies escalated and calls for some protection of domestic production grew in number and volume. Some of the prominent county members came under severe pressure in their constituencies. Ironically C. S. Read, a Norfolk MP and one of the leading spokesmen for the farming lobby, was to be among those who lost their seats in 1880. (An implication of the now accelerated rate of rural depopulation was that any future redistribution of seats would reduce county representation in favour of the cities and so diminish the Conservative's main electoral asset.) Ireland suffered perhaps even more from the vicissitudes of agriculture. The mounting of arrears of rent and a spate of evictions worsened the strained relations between the Irish landlord and tenant classes. The 1870 Land Act proved inadequate to stabilize the situation and by 1880 the new Land League of Davitt and Parnell was becoming a threatening spokesman and organizer of the struggling tenant farmer.

The commercial depression was an electoral problem for the Tories who had some of their most vulnerable seats in the larger boroughs. Many of the constituencies where they had made gains in 1874 now turned sour. The spokesmen of business worried and complained. Many blamed the tariffs of rival trading nations; some began to demand protection, at least in the modified form of reciprocity. But though 'Fair Trade' became a familiar call of aggrieved manufacturers and merchants and in some cities had links with the Jingoism of 1878, the government remained unsympathetic, Disraeli himself firmly ruling out the possibility. Few leading parliamentarians believed that a move towards protection would be other than disastrous electorally and for party cohesion. Free trade and *laisser-faire* doctrine, moreover, had sunk deep into most Tory politicians and intellectuals since the 1840s. But rising bankruptcies and unemployment, falling profits and business confidence, formed an unhappy backcloth for the general election the government was contemplating.

The dissolution of early 1880 was recommended by the party's electoral specialists, advice which may have reflected the poor feel of Gorst's successors for borough opinion, though Disraeli said subsequently that he had hastened the election to forestall 'an insurrection of our old and natural friends, the farmers'. Never an enthusiastic electioneer, he was now precluded by his peerage from active campaigning. He and Northcote put their main emphasis on the government's foreign policy success and resistance to Home Rule. The outcome of a fiercely contested election (there were only 70 uncontested seats, the lowest total yet and about half that of 1874) was a chilly awakening for a party not expecting so sharp a reversal of 1874 and for a government appreciative of its own achievements in office and incredulous that Gladstone's conduct since 1876 could reap such reward. To Disraeli it was 'a discomfiture vast and without an adequate cause'. Few Tories had recognized the full weight of Gladstone's attacks on 'Beaconsfieldism' (the supposedly assertive and risky foreign policy) in his Midlothian campaigns of 1879 and 1880, orchestrated though they had been for maximum press impact. The economic situation, however, had certainly hit the government hard in both counties and cities. '"Hard Times" . . . has been our foe,' concluded Disraeli, though Salisbury heard tales that the Anglican clergy had failed them, 'either by actively voting against or at least by skulking'.

Most of the seats newly won in 1874 had been lost. Indeed the last election now appeared as no final fracture of the mid-century mould but only a temporary Liberal setback. Net Tory losses had occurred in all types of constituency in all parts of the United Kingdom. Even Lancashire had moved away from the party, despite Disraeli's customary appeal to anti-Irish 'Protestantism'. (The switch of Derby's influence to the Liberals may have compounded the impact of the economic downturn on the county.) Overall the party had won more than one hundred seats fewer than in 1874 and the total of 235 was worse even than in 1868. Now a minority even in the English seats again, the Tories had dropped to 110 out of the 154 county seats and to 36 out of 159 in the boroughs of more than 20,000 inhabitants. Only in Ireland, where the Home Rulers had improved their tally to 61, was the pattern very different from that of 1868. But in the largest boroughs the Tory performance was rather better than in 1868; not all the new support had been lost and it was a straw in the wind that three of the four City of London seats were won by overwhelming majorities, easily the best performance there since 1832. But in the generality of boroughs Conservative organization had performed less effectively than that of its rivals and it had conceded some notable triumphs to city Liberal associations now linked with the National Liberal Federation, a body of radical purpose spawned by Birmingham and Joseph Chamberlain. The success enjoyed by a radicalized Liberal party seemed to portend further electoral reform to equalise the county and borough franchises, a change expected to hit the Tories hard; the Home Rulers and the Land League were growing in strength in Ireland at the expense of both Conservatives and Liberals; Gladstone was again Prime Minister and Chamberlain now in the Cabinet. Conservatives committed to the interests of landownership, Church and constitution could hardly look forward to another period of Liberal government with any confidence.

Disraeli continued as party leader, Northcote as his coadjutor in the Commons. Relations had been less close between them since the Eastern crisis and possible successors were positioning themselves even while Disraeli lived. During the 1880 session the main scope for successful resistance to a resurgent Liberal party lay in the Lords where Disraeli and the Tory majority sat in judgement upon the government's legislative programme. He let the Ground Game Bill pass (though most landlords disliked it, the farmers and those Tory politicians who cultivated them were in favour), amended the Burials Bill (a concession to Dissenters that irritated many parsons) and rejected the Compensation for Disturbances

Bill which, seeking to strengthen the 1870 Land Act, picked at the sore of landlord/tenant relations in Ireland. It was already clear that Ireland would be a crucial area of party hostilities and the question how to use their strength in the Lords a critical one for the Conservatives.

The Disraelian Legacy

The death of Disraeli in April 1881 removed a figure who, despite his ambiguities, had attained a stature by his seniority and by the triumphs of 1874 and 1878 which no-one else in the party could rival. The significance of his contribution is made harder to assess by posterity's tendency to cultivate Disraelian myths, but the truth turns out to be much more prosaic than the fiction. His main commitment was always to the interests of his party and to its basic conservative purposes. This loyalty had been displayed in the long haul on the opposition front bench and it had eventually won him the leadership of the party and the grudging respect of most of its parliamentarians. His premiership after 1874 had displayed a similarly narrow partisanship and by 1880 even Salisbury was convinced that Disraeli was loyal and safe. Inevitably this devotion to recognized interests left little room for originality except on the margins of rhetoric and gesture. Disraeli, like other Conservatives, had seized the plentiful opportunities offered by Gladstone's first ministry, but he did little to reshape Conservatism significantly in either thought or policy. At one point Crown, empire and social reform had been useful additions to the slogans of a leadership anxious about Tory fortunes in the boroughs, nervous of the enfranchised working man and keen to exploit divisions among the Liberals, but they were opportunistic responses and even before the 1874 victory the emphases had changed. In office afterwards Disraeli and his colleagues did little to direct government and party towards those ideals, if genuine ideals they had ever been. The government kept with some consistency to its promises not to 'harass' the country with 'unnecessary' legislation and its stance in the 1880 election – a strong policy abroad and negativity at home – showed how far it was from any determined creativity of the 'Tory democracy' kind. The politics of the early 1880s were to be dominated by familiar issues – Ireland, land, religion and parliamentary reform – not by an agenda set by Disraeli's set-piece speeches of 1872.

Like many other party strategists, Disraeli had seen the need to give the Tories a broader appeal and to win much-needed borough votes by supplementing their identification with the still powerful interests of landownership and the established churches. But this endeavour was inspired and shaped by his commitment to that 'aristocratic constitution' which he had accused Peel of tending to subvert in the 1840s. A phrase from a speech in 1868 – 'when the people are led by their natural leaders . . . the Tory party is triumphant' – shows the traditionalism underlying the show of 'Tory democracy'. His public performance had always flourished on the tension between rhetoric and reality. The element of myth and gesture had been given more scope once he began to escape from Derby's shadow early in 1867 and then, as on some other occasions, it took a form concrete enough to amend the statute book. Quite apart from his relish for the colour of phrase and idea, he could also be diverted from his conservative purpose of stabilizing the constitution by a well-developed appetite for office. Short-term calculation of how to obtain or prolong office had often played a part in Disraeli's politics. As with his predecessor Derby, opportunism sometimes overcame consistency. That was an influence in 1867–68; another was sheer mischief-making to discomfit the Liberal leadership opposite. Unrestrained by more conventional figures like Derby, Northcote or Salisbury, Disraeli was quite capable of succumbing to the temptation to play the maverick. Many men, some in his own party, always saw him as 'unprincipled'. Until the last years Salisbury saw him as the personification of the sacrifice of permanent interests to short-term personal and party advantage. Disraeli encouraged the distrust some men felt for adversarial politics.

Yet by 1880 nearly everyone in the party except the more bitter High Churchmen had come to recognize his conservative instincts and achievement. Disraeli, like Derby, had seen and rarely forgot the error of Peel in the 1840s. The nature of the Tory party did not lend itself to a consistent outbidding or undercutting of the Whigs. Strenuous legislative endeavour was not in its character and certainly it did not exist to play the radical. Derby and Disraeli knew that its instincts were to block or at least to delay and dilute the changes which threatened the privilege and property embodied in the aristocratic constitution. This simple and natural stance had become complicated latterly because Palmerston, exploiting the Conservatives' post-1846 divisions, had captured for his own brand of Whiggery the conservative, patriotic identity which had formerly been theirs. His stance of a patriotic assertiveness in foreign policy and a conservative quiescence in domestic affairs was one which many Tories, like a good deal of centrist opinion, admired and supported, but its success denied the Conservatives themselves any prolonged tenure of office. When Palmerston's death gave them the opportunity, Derby and Disraeli sought to break the mould of mid-century politics and to undermine the Liberal leadership by outbidding them on the borough franchise while still warding off the kind of parliamentary reform that would have damaged the Tories permanently. In 1871 the New Social Movement showed the front bench to be still ready for stunts and novelties, but by then it was becoming apparent that the better course was simply to wait for Gladstone's Liberal party to fall apart under the pressure of its own reforming momentum and internal contradictions. Palmerstonian opinion was moving towards the Conservatives – the *Morning Post* was a straw in the wind – and the leadership now had only to assert its conservative credentials, criticize the government for weakness abroad and for reckless hyper-activity at home and wait to reap the benefits of Liberal difficulties. In 1874 this fundamentally conservative line was evident in the official campaign (though a minority of Conservative candidates did otherwise) and it was even more so in 1880. Instead of Palmerston's conservatism in Liberal clothing, Disraeli and his colleagues now offered conservatism in Conservative clothing. Circumstances had permitted the party to assert its true nature again and, as the Liberals became more radical, to present itself as a conservative party of order, stability and safety at home and abroad. Though not a posture that guaranteed success, it worked in 1874 and again in 1886. But arguably Disraeli, though he worked with the grain of this development, was unable or unwilling to exploit it to its fullest extent by encouraging permanent schisms on the Liberal side. His record of partisanship and adversarial confrontation had made him anathema to the Whigs. His tendency to polarize issues, an effect at odds with his underlying desire for a consensus style of aristocratic conservatism, held back the disintegration of the Liberal right after Palmerston's death and helped to delay a major reconstruction of parties. His loyalty to a narrow and partisan conception of the Conservative party and his indifference, even hostility, to the construction of a more broadly-based coalition was a limiting factor. Without a reconstruction of the kind Derby and Disraeli had rejected in 1865–66, the Conservatives could only wait for the Liberals to accomplish the task in their own time and it turned out that the disintegration of the early 1870s had been no permanent Liberal collapse. Through the travails and delights of six years of office after 1874 Disraeli seems never to have considered seriously the idea of a major reconstruction, as Northcote did subsequently. If such possibilities existed at all, his willing rupture with the younger Derby in 1878 was a final rejection of them. Yet the Tory defeats of 1880 and 1885 showed the limitations of the Tory position without some combination of Liberal schism and of 'fusion' in the centre-ground of party politics of the kind Disraeli had set himself against.

More than most politicians Disraeli kept rhetoric and purpose at some distance from each other. Subsequent myths have tended to feed on his words and ignore much of what he did and did not do. In fact, if one ignores the window-dressing, he stuck very close to the mood and requirements of his party. Other men, admittedly, might have led it in rather different directions and certainly with a different style: the centrist utilitarianism of the fifteenth Earl of Derby, the aristocratic consensus politics which Northcote sought, the highminded negativism offered by overly self-conscious conservatives like Salisbury. Disraeli brought a flavour of his own, even an exoticism, to the leadership, but his claims to any fundamental creativity and originality are dubious, particularly for the years after 1868. Though the extent to which he sought consciously to emulate Palmerston is uncertain, what he was offering by the early 1870s was a Tory equivalent. It was pre-Peelite in character rather than Peelite, for Disraeli did not woo the business plutocracy energetically as Peel had done nor did he have any taste for the dominant rôle in political change and modernization which Peel had attempted to seize for Conservative government. He was ready, however, to give conservatism a contemporary, even populist flavour and he felt contempt for diehards like Redesdale who could not respond sensitively to changing circumstances. He led with an eye to 'the temper of the Time' and to 'what is going on in the country, its wishes, opinions and feelings', as he put it, but this capacity for adaptation produced more novelty in presentation than in substance. On social legislation, for example, he had abandoned by 1874 even the vague and limited rhetoric of 1872 and soon his ministry, by settling most of the outstanding issues on a non-partisan and fairly pragmatic basis, had exhausted most of the interest of his ministers and supporters. In 1880 the Tories were not a social reform party and indeed they had never been one. The exaltation of the monarchy, an opportunistic response to supposed republicanism among Liberals, had little practical content beyond the Indian title (the Queen's idea and a political embarrassment), though it confirmed the party's identification with tradition, inheritance, the aristocracy and the constitution. The emphasis on empire certainly entailed a critique of the Gladstone ministry's performance and a more bullish approach to colonial questions but no new scheme or vision of Britain's imperial commitments and opportunities, despite the unusually positive enthusiasms of Carnarvon in this area. By 1880 the ministry was conspicuous for its inability to control its proconsuls and for the priority it accorded to European policy rather than for any determined and coherent imperialism. Derby's fall had, however, removed an obstacle to a strong, traditional style of foreign policy and to a reasonably positive attitude towards colonial acquisitions which accorded with the drift of opinion in the party. (On various occasions party feeling in and out of Parliament had been much less cautious than the Cabinet's on both European and colonial questions.) As for religious issues, still a staple of politics, the defence of the English and Scottish establishments remained a central purpose of the party, though Disraeli followed many other Tories in subsuming much of this commitment in a 'Protestantism' which antagonized many High Churchmen and which was clearly anti-Irish as well as anti-Catholic in its bearing. This had a populist dimension, particularly in Lancashire, but Disraeli was largely indifferent to the opportunities for 'Tory democracy'. There was no systematic encouragement by the leadership either of the large borough associations or of the recently enfranchised electorate. Despite the modest interest Disraeli had taken in organizational improvement (in fact most of the enthusiasm had come from others), the momentum had been lost soon after 1874 and the influential figures in borough Toryism were feeling neglected and slighted. Gorst resigned in dudgeon and the front bench, once the controversies over domestic legislation had died down, paid little attention to the borough associations, to their MPs in the House or to their opinions. It took the Eastern crisis and Gladstone's agitation to make them look to the popular Jingoism of the cities for help and encouragement. Much the strongest influence within the parliamentary party remained the gentry of the county constituencies for whom 1874 had been as much of a triumph as it had been for the much less numerous Tory members for the larger boroughs. Disraeli never sought to balance the influence of the gentry by throwing greater weight behind the urban and business elements in the party and the perceptible movement of business opinion towards the Conservatives since Palmerston's death was not the result of a deliberately 'Peelite' policy of cultivating the urban plutocracy by the leadership. Indeed Disraeli left a legacy of strained relations between the parliamentary leadership and the big borough associations which boded ill for his successors. As for 'the working man', Disraeli had felt the same nervousness about the working-class enfranchisement of 1867 as most Tories and it influenced his handling of several issues, notably labour law. His support of Cross in working to conciliate trade-union opinion was a rare instance of the premier overruling a Cabinet majority. But this line was spasmodic and soon exhausted. Long before 1880 the government, sensitive to the hostility of much of the party to trade unionism, was confining its cultivation of the working-class electorate to the patriotism and 'Protestantism' that were its staple appeals anyway. Perhaps the greatest novelty of the Conservative position in the 1870s was its rôle as the protector of the drink interest and this had been determined by developments on the Liberal side rather than chosen by

Disraeli and his strategists.

In so many respects it is the continuity and traditionalism of the Disraeli ministry that stands out, not any new departure. Certainly the party had become more self-consciously patriotic in its appeal by 1880 than at the time of Palmerston's death, but this was a reversion to an earlier rôle, was entirely compatible with the party's existing composition and instinct and was supporting a firmly conservative line of domestic policy. The experience of office with a majority had confirmed the essential conservatism of the still predominantly aristocratic parliamentary party with which Disraeli instinctively identified. The party at large was not inclined to the radical or the exotic and the triumph of 1874 – a victory for a largely traditional Conservatism in a largely unchanged electoral system, despite the Second Reform Act – had shown that its own brand of conservatism was after all capable of winning a majority. Disraeli did not struggle against this conclusion. For him, as for his leading colleagues, leaps in the dark were out of fashion. There were limits to how far his occasional idiosyncracies could reshape either the government or the party. The Cabinet was always a broad-based one and included influential figures who were not Disraeli's puppets. Derby departed in 1878 because he was at odds with the Cabinet majority and not simply with Disraeli. The ministry attempted little that might put it at odds with opinion on its backbenches and in the Carlton. Disraeli could afford to affront sections of opinion that lacked more general sympathy, like the High Churchmen, but not the party as a whole. The unconventionality of Disraeli's proceedings was often exaggerated by the hostile reactions of his enemies. In foreign policy 'Beaconsfieldism' was nothing like as novel and reckless as Liberal propaganda claimed. It was the Liberal party, particularly its militant Nonconformists, and the Home Rulers who were forcing on the post-Palmerstonian polarization of national politics. What they represented was profoundly unwelcome to Disraeli and most Conservatives, who set themselves to resist, but ironically this process helped them by restoring their traditional mission after years when the Whigs had appropriated the cause of patriotic conservatism. The polarization of politics which the rhetoric of Conservatives conventionally deplored was in fact their opportunity. A Tory ministry would no longer have to pose as the champion of modernity as in 1859 and 1867 but instead present itself as the embodiment of resistance, stability and safety. It was significant that the one figure in the collective leadership who might have steered it in more progressive directions, Derby, was squeezed out in 1878. The centrist, rather liberal dimension which he had brought to the front bench and which had once been seen as vital to its prospects was now dispensable.

This conclusion will disappoint romantics who wish to find profound creativity in Disraeli's leadership. If there is anything which can properly be called Disraelian Conservatism (and it is doubtful), then the emphasis should be on the second word. The party was simply adjusting naturally to the post-Palmerstonian situation and reasserting its traditional commitment to stability and security both at home and abroad in contradistinction to what the Liberals and the Home Rulers seemed to offer. In essentials Disraeli left his party much as he had inherited it from the elder Derby; the changes had come mainly in the circumstances in which it operated. Disraeli had prevented it from shifting to either a significantly more progressive or a more rigidly diehard position and, with the support of the majority of Tory parliamentarians, he had maintained Tory politics on a broad base of interest and sentiment. The party would thus be in a position to pick up the pieces of Liberal disintegration in the years after Disraeli's death. But when the major reconstruction of party politics came, it would not be of his making.

6

Towards 1886 and After: Salisbury's Party

Lost Leaders

1881 was not a good year to succeed Disraeli. He was replaced in the Lords by Salisbury, neither an automatic nor a widely acclaimed choice, who, with Northcote in the Commons, provided a dual leadership for the party, though Northcote was regarded by the Queen as the senior figure and likely to head a future Conservative administration. Both men were under pressure in their Houses – Salisbury from the former leaders Cairns and Richmond, Northcote from the coterie known as the 'Fourth Party' which from the start of the 1880 session had set out to embarrass him – and the problems of controlling their followers made tactical decisions more difficult. The standing and influence of the collective leadership had suffered from the 1880 defeat. Much of the party was fearful and resentful: the squirearchy and the farmers, the borough Tories who had suffered such a haemorrhage of seats, Irish landlords, the Church interests. Short of emulating the obstruction practised by the Home Rulers, there were limits to what the mangled Commons party could do to Liberal measures other than set a style of opposition and await Liberal disintegration. The Lords, however, had a normal Tory majority and there was scope, as Disraeli had shown, for purposeful selectivity towards government bills. But few senior Tories relished the prospect of major constitutional conflict between Lords and Commons, there were fears of an early general election fought on the obstruction of the peers and the Queen made known her objections to an Upper House bent on persistent and partisan obstruction of business.

There were strategic as well as tactical considerations. Resignations from the ministry seemed like portents of a larger Liberal schism. How far, then, should the Conservatives seek 'reconstruction' and on what terms? Northcote's strategy was to work for a major Whig secession by holding to the centre ground of responsible conservatism and avoiding extremes of reaction or provocation. The Tories would show themselves to be a party fit for Whigs to join or at least to collaborate with. Salisbury's more combative instincts spurned the consensus and collaboration that Northcote's game required. He believed that a Whig secession would not happen quickly and

that meanwhile the party would be demoralized by the apparent supineness of their leaders. The Tory leadership would, he feared, resist the drift
of Liberal legislation only so far as Whig susceptibilities permitted and
would, in effect, be collaborating in further radicalization. Salisbury also
stood to lose personally if Northcote's strategy succeeded. His image of
diehard rigidity was unappealing to the Whigs and they were unlikely to
find him as acceptable a partner as Northcote. Rather like Derby and
Disraeli in 1865–66, Salisbury could afford reconstruction only on his own
or at least the Conservatives' terms. Yet his view of the Whigs, though less
welcoming than Northcote's, was more deterministic. He believed that they
would not need winning over and that sooner or later the radicalism of
Liberal policy would force them into the Conservatives' arms. Meanwhile
the party should resist radicalism firmly, maintain its conservative credentials and not hesitate to confront or polarize when the demerits of Liberal
measures warranted.

Neither strategy worked well. Northcote's sweet reasonableness was
dispiriting to his backbenchers and even to some frontbench colleagues. No
significant Whig secession materialized. Granville was personally too close
to Gladstone, Hartington ('in his heart a Conservative, a gentleman,'
Disraeli had assured the Queen) too interested in the apparently imminent
succession to Gladstone. Northcote, lacking the rhetorical and tactical skills
of Disraeli, was unable to put fire into the bellies of his supporters and
constantly muffed opportunities to embarrass the government. Sensible,
experienced and respectable, he was a civil servant's politician, good with
an official brief but unsuited to the rougher trade of opposition. His earlier
closeness to Gladstone, whose private secretary he had once been, left him
at a disadvantage in dealing with the Liberal leader and this rankled with
Tories whose fear and detestation of Gladstone had not eased. In his last
months Disraeli had made known his reservations about Northcote and
had hardly discouraged the insubordination displayed by the Fourth Party.
Many Tory MPs, particularly ambitious men like Gorst and Churchill,
disliked the idea of alliance with the Whigs and the revolt over Bradlaugh
in 1880, which spread from the Fourth Party to the majority of Tory
members, was intended to undermine Northcote and the other Disraelian
veterans.[1] But Salisbury too had problems. Cairns and Richmond were
unresponsive to his lead and seemed set on compromises with the government. Tory landlords in the Upper House and in Ireland itself were not as
resolute as Salisbury had hoped. Like Northcote, Salisbury had little
personal support in the country at large and few major interests looked to
him as a natural patron and protector. Nor perhaps were his political
instincts yet attuned to the party's problems.

The early engagements over Ireland underlined the predicament. The
Liberals' Land Bill of 1881 proposed judicial commissions to revise Irish
rents and went some way to establish the fixity of tenure and free sale
(virtual co-ownership) demanded by the Land League. This interference
with property rights and freedom of contract was anathema to most Tories
both in itself and as a precedent for Britain, but resistance to the measure

---

[1] For the long and largely Tory campaign to prevent Charles Bradlaugh, freethinker,
republican and Liberal MP for Northampton, from taking his seat, see W. L. Arnstein, *The
Bradlaugh Case* (Oxford, 1965).

proved to be far from solid. Richmond had already committed himself to the arbitration of rents in Ireland, rejection of the Compensation for Disturbances Bill had provoked a rents boycott and a large part of the Irish landlord class, fearing for its rents and lives, was already caving in and acquiescing in arrangements similar to those in the new bill. Conservative attempts to arrange a compromise amendment of the bill in the Lords foundered upon the intractability of Salisbury who now found himself at odds with Northcote and his senior colleagues. Eventually, on the advice of the leading Irish Tory, Edward Gibson, the bill was allowed through largely intact. The only consolation from a debâcle which had divided the Tory leadership more than the Liberal was the simultaneous passage of a severe Coercion Act.

Similar problems occurred over the 1882 Arrears Bill which Conservatives denounced both as a subsidy to indebted tenants from public funds and as part of a deal they suspected had been made with Parnell upon his release from Kilmainham gaol where he had been held under the Coercion Act. (The Land League had been suppressed too.) The Tory mood hardened further when the new Irish Secretary Cavendish, appointed upon Forster's resignation over the 'Kilmainham Treaty', was assassinated in Dublin by Fenians. Salisbury and his fellow peers pledged themselves to impose two major amendments on the bill, but again Conservative unity dissolved. Gladstone threatened resignation, the Queen appealed for compromise, Irish landlords, desperate for peace, again showed themselves ready to accept what the government offered and Cairns and Richmond reneged on the agreed arrangement, though Salisbury and Cranbrook held out to the bitter end against the majority of their colleagues. Again the peers, divided in will and leadership, had shown themselves incapable of either blocking or substantially modifying a government measure for Ireland. Gorst had advised that the party was in no shape in the constituencies to fight a general election if Gladstone threatened a dissolution. Altogether by the end of 1882 the Conservatives, now perhaps less tolerant of opposition status than in earlier years, were revealing their own weakness and division more than exploiting those on the Liberal side. Yet the bent of the government's policies on land and Ireland and the threat which radicals and militant Nonconformists posed to the church establishments worried many Tories deeply. As yet even foreign policy gave them little scope for effective opposition. The damage done to the government by the defeat by the Boers at Majuba Hill was repaired by a rallying of patriotic opinion produced by the bombardment of Alexandria and the occupation of Egypt in 1882.

Down to the end of 1883 both Conservative leaders were struggling, but 1884 was to ensure Salisbury's survival and supremacy. This outcome followed from the struggle over parliamentary reform and from Randolph Churchill's assault upon the party leadership. During 1884 the government introduced its long-awaited measure to equalize the county and the borough franchises and so to enfranchise the majority of rural householders, among them large numbers of agricultural labourers. Chamberlain viewed it as a master-stroke against the Whigs in his own party as well as against the Tories. Conservatives had long feared franchise equalization as likely to undermine both the influence of the landlord class and their own party's hold on the county seats. The leadership, however, was again divided. Some, like Beach, acquiesced in the standardization of the existing lop-sided franchise, while others joined Salisbury in seeking ways to check a further lurch towards 'democracy'. The Commons party could merely delay the measure and even then with trepidation, for the danger of a determined but unsuccessful resistance was that large numbers of new electors would then resent the party's opposition to their enfranchisement. Though the party was better placed to resist in the Lords, the worry was that the government would call a general election, one it would almost inevitably win, either to force the bill through the Upper House or, if the measure passed, immediately the new franchise was operative and without waiting for the major redistribution of seats which some Tories hoped would limit the impact of franchise reform. Eventually, as a compromise between different approaches within the party, the Conservatives agreed to block franchise reform until redistribution was linked to it. Some genuinely wished for redistribution, others hoped that a stand on the issue would block reform altogether and force the government into an election in circumstances of disarray. So the bill was held up in the Lords and negotiations started on a redistribution measure which the government would agree to bring forward before a general election. Conservatives differed on the likely effects of redistribution itself, but most party managers held that it would be acceptable, perhaps even helpful, so long as boundaries were fixed by a neutral commission and the borough constituencies were separated as far as possible from the rural ones. Surprisingly perhaps in view of their record, the Tories emerged as advocates of a larger rather than a smaller redistribution and pressed for the elimination of most of the small boroughs and for the replacement of the old double-member constituencies by a single-member system. The idea was 'minority representation'. Although almost no Tories felt they could gain from reform, many felt that in smaller constituencies more MPs would be elected by pockets of Tory support, while in large constituencies Tory minorities would be swamped by Liberal majorities. A single-member system, they were coming to believe, would save the party from a worse fate in the counties, where their previous dominance was bound to suffer, and also benefit it in the cities and their suburbs where the perceptible growth of Conservative sentiment over recent years might well now win additional seats. Though the party failed in some endeavours – for example in seeking to reduce the representation of Ireland, which was now over-represented in terms of population – its gamble on giving priority to redistribution at least helped to save it from appearing entirely negative during the reform debates and negotiations.

It also gave Salisbury the chance to emerge as the strong man of the party. The bill was being held up in his House and he was the man with whom, above all, the Liberals had to deal. Though Northcote attended most of the crucial negotiations, his command of tactics and detail contrasted poorly with Salisbury's. Soon Northcote was labouring to steer through the Commons a Redistribution Bill which many of his own side did not entirely like and contending with Churchill's attempts to sabotage his leadership by exploiting these discontents. He found himself damaged beyond repair. In August the Liberal Dilke noted the success of 'the game of Salisbury' and concluded 'He has made himself the undisputed master of his party'.

Churchill's endeavours served this end, whether he intended it or not. His rebelliousness in the early stages of the Parliament, in collaboration with his small group of friends, Drummond-Wolff, Gorst, restored in 1880 as party agent, and Balfour, Salisbury's nephew, had elicited amused sympathy from the backbenches. By 1883 it had given way to a more serious and calculated attack on the leadership. Churchill, a highly theatrical politician conscious of his own abilities and intensely ambitious, saw the vulnerability of the dual leadership, particularly of Northcote, and sensed the potential of the discontents of the borough Tories associated with the National Union, a body with which Gorst had close links. Two articles in the *Fortnightly Review* in November 1882 and May 1883, probably written jointly by Gorst and Churchill, were bitterly hostile to the official leadership and speculated about where 'Elijah's Mantle', the supposedly Disraelian garb of 'Tory Democracy', might alight. They attracted considerable attention in the party and prepared the way for Churchill's bid to mobilize borough opinion in 1884. Elected to the National Union's Council in 1883, Churchill now became its chairman. His sights were trained on Northcote, on the Central Committee, a body of managers and whips which had been entrusted in 1880 with the supervision of party organization, and on the traditional style of Tory politics associated with Northcote, Salisbury and the 'Old Gang'. In the *Fortnightly* he had deplored their indifference to the National Union and their vision of a party run 'by orders sent down from the Carlton':

> Unfortunately for Conservatism, its leaders belong solely to one class; they are a clique composed of members of the aristocracy, landowners and adherents whose chief merit is subserviency. The party chiefs live in an atmosphere in which a sense of their own importance and the importance of their class interests and privileges is exaggerated, and which the opinions of the common people can scarcely penetrate.

Presenting demands for the abolition of the Central Committee, for the financial independence of the National Union and for the allocation to it of a more influential place in party management and policy-making, Churchill wrote a letter of threatening import to Salisbury in March 1884:

> In a struggle between a popular body [the National Union] and a close corporation [the Central Committee], the latter, I am happy to say, in these days goes to the wall: for the popular body have this great advantage – that . . . they can at any moment they think proper appeal fully (and in some measure recklessly) to a favourable and sympathizing public, and . . . in such a course as this the National Union will find that I may be of some little assistance to them.

Another letter sent to Salisbury by Churchill as chairman of the National Union Council not only asserted its 'dissatisfaction with the conditions of the organization of the party' but also commended the example of the National Liberal Federation, 'a name of evil sound and omen in the ears of aristocratic and privileged classes'. The culmination came in a speech at Birmingham in which Churchill declared his intention to stand as a parliamentary candidate for the city: 'Trust the people . . . trust the people and they will trust you. . . . I have no fear of democracy'. Northcote warned Salisbury that 'Randolph is going in boldly and will ride "Tory Democracy"' pretty hard'. Yet a bitterly fought annual conference of the National Union at Sheffield in July left both sides exhausted and worried enough for Salisbury to be able to conclude a concordat with Churchill. By this deal Churchill agreed to work with the party leaders in return for their recognition and consideration, Beach became a compromise chairman of the National Union Council in place of Churchill, the Primrose League was recognized by the party and Bartley, the new party agent, took charge of the National Union's finances. Gorst was aghast at this 'Great Surrender' which marked Churchill's abandonment of the Fourth Party frôndeurs and his acceptance into the party's collective leadership. Northcote suffered more: he took no part in the deal between Salisbury and Churchill and was unable to influence its conditions. His concurrent problems in the Commons over tactics on parliamentary reform only underlined his virtual downgrading within the dual leadership. Even with the 'Old Gang' Northcote's hesitancy in dealing with Churchill, in contrast to Salisbury's initially firm stand, had weakened the Commons leader's standing.

One has to distinguish between the phenomenon of Churchill himself and the conditions which he exploited. Churchill, who combined the urgent ambition and audacity of a political adventurer with the social prestige and advantage of a ducal family, probably had no firm standpoint of principle. At times, particularly in 1882–84, he seemed to represent a radically-inclined 'Tory Democracy', cultivating the mythology of Disraeli's contribution to that cause, playing to the non-aristocratic Toryism of the large boroughs and apparently threatening the privilege and influence of his own class. There were personal circumstances which may have inclined him to the rôle of class traitor.[2] Yet at other times he assumed a more traditional style of aristocratic conservatism, one which sought to bolster privilege and property and to resist 'destructive' radicalism. Even the grounds of his persistent hostility to Northcote varied from the latter's supposedly Whiggish liberalism that failed to protect his own party's causes to an inert conservatism which failed to exploit the dynamic potential of the political situation. Churchill later described himself as motivated simply by ambition. But his own motivation was only part of the explanation. Opportunistic as he was, Churchill caught something of the contradictions and difficulties of contemporary Conservatism and the sharply opposed reactions to him within his own party show how divided it was in complexion and approach. By accident more than design, the party found itself in a situation with some potential for populist politics. Churchill cultivated the mythology of Disraelian Tory Democracy but he did not have to invent it. However little Disraeli and his generation of Tory leaders had intended to create a new and broader political culture, the reform episode of 1867–68, the Tory gains in the cities in 1874, the slow shift of the prosperous bourgeoisie towards the party, the Jingoism and the patriotic triumph of 1878, the cultivation of popular 'Protestantism' and of anti-Irish nativism, the attachment of the drink interest with its considerable urban support, even the party's commitment (admittedly *pis aller*) in 1884 to a future based more upon the city constituencies – all gave a new

---

[2] For these personal circumstances and for Churchill's political career as a whole, see R. Rhodes James, *Lord Randolph Churchill* (1959), and particularly R. F. Foster, *Lord Randolph Churchill. A Political Life* (1981).

dimension to the Conservative image and a potential for a more populist (or at least non-aristocratic) Toryism. Most people of Churchill's background regarded it all with unease and uncertainty. The relations between borough Conservatism and the parliamentarianism of the landed classes were difficult and rather distant, as even the usually plutocratic borough Tories who reached the House of Commons found. Often they experienced in official Conservatism the frigidity embodied in Northcote's comment to another patrician politician in 1883: 'we cannot go in for Democratic Toryism'. For the most part it was only the political press that bridged the gap between these two cultures effectively and mediated their relationship, though Gorst had set out to do something comparable with the party machine. Churchill leapt the gap and cultivated borough Toryism in the early 1880s on a scale no previous Conservative of substance had attempted, though by 1883 Salisbury was submitting himself to speaking tours of the cities. Speechifying of this kind was a trend of the 1880s, but few entered into it with Churchill's exuberance. Much of the party was unhappy with this style. As Northcote understood, it was not a party of 'democracy' and men became resentful and fearful when they heard their familiar world of the country houses, Parliament, the London clubs and 'Society' denigrated by Churchill and his provincial collaborators. In an antithesis then fashionable, much of the party saw itself as representing 'the classes' against 'the masses'. Churchill understood this attitude even when he chose to mock and affront it and with the settlement of 1884 he retreated smartly from the embrace of a radically-tinged populism that might endanger his own prospects. Yet he had already made enemies, including Henry Chaplin, the influential backbench squire, and sections of opinion at the Carlton, who were to dog him in the years ahead.

Openness towards the possibilities of demotic politics was only one course available to Conservative leaders. In different ways Northcote and Salisbury stood for a more traditional and more parliamentary style of conservatism. The former strove to identify and develop a centrist consensus in which cooperation with disillusioned Whigs would become possible; the latter emphasized the distinctiveness and integrity of the Conservative party as the uncompromising defender of established interests. Each approach had supporters among the patrician classes, yet neither quite answered the dilemma the party faced in these years, a dilemma in which fear of Liberal policies and of the developments in Irish and foreign affairs compounded the frustration felt at the defeat of 1880. Many Tories felt that the familiar political system was facing a breakdown ('Disintegration', as Salisbury's last article in the *Quarterly* called it) and that the barrier against radical change that threatened property, privilege and the constitution had become inadequate. Impotent rage fed into the hatred which so many felt for the *bêtes noires* Gladstone, Chamberlain and Parnell. It seemed that the Disraelian attempt to revive or at least imitate the Palmerstonian equipoise had failed catastrophically. In the counties forebodings about the future of landed property and nervousness about the impending extension of the county franchise were intensified by the impact of agricultural depression which was hitting the gentry and the farmers hard. In consequence Northcote lacked the secure political base that contentment among men of his own kind might have given him. Economic difficulties affected the large boroughs too and helped to increase the interest in 'Fair Trade', a cause to which several of the party's celebrities gave a passing nod without serious intent. More important in the short-lived revolt of the National Union was the discontent of the Tory borough associations after the 1880 election had halved their parliamentary representation and reduced their influence with the leadership. Neither Northcote nor Salisbury showed much interest in remedying a sense of neglect and rejection which had started to develop during Disraeli's ministry. The National Union, once Churchill and Gorst began to stir it, became an alternative vehicle for borough interests frustrated in Westminster politics and Churchill's readiness to play a leading rôle helped to dramatize a brief confrontation between the traditionalism of the front bench and the largely bourgeois politics of the large boroughs.

Yet the interests represented in the National Union, flattered though they were by Churchill's attentions, were fundamentally loyal to the party and its leadership, as they were to prove once they received their share of attention. Parliamentary seats in more abundance, honours now extending to baronetcies and even to the occasional peerage, the activities of the Primrose League, all would assist the integration of a growing body of urban and suburban support into the party in the years ahead. Despite the charges of social and family exclusiveness later levelled against him, Salisbury was ready enough to accept the urban plutocracy into the parliamentary party and to exploit its political value, even though, like most of his kind, he had little detailed grasp of borough politics and of its social bases. Churchill, whose snobbishness towards the 'Marshall and Snelgrove' element in the government once broke out in the House in sneers at 'the Lords of suburban villas ... the owners of vineries and pineries', probably underestimated the importance of the business plu-tocracy to the party's prospects. If the party leaders had to 'trust the people', it was not the undifferentiated masses or even the working-class tail of the Tory vote but rather the urban business, professional and employer classes who had the wealth and influence to run and finance the local Conservative associations. The 'lords of suburban villas' would display much the same conservatism as the patrician classes once they were granted access to Parliament, party positions and patronage. Salisbury came to recognize the interest of these classes in social order, constitutional stability and the defence of property rights and he was willing to cultivate their support for the largely traditional political order with which he was identified.

Salisbury and Minority Government

If the dilemma of party strategy remained, at least one problem had been resolved by the end of 1884. Salisbury was now in firmer control of the party and Northcote's eclipse meant that tendencies to confrontational politics were less restrained. Though Salisbury's reliance on the Lords to block or mangle Liberal measures had shown its limitations, it had succeeded in exacting the early redistribution measure from Gladstone. During 1885 the focus of attention shifted back to the Commons where Beach, a brusque and combative figure, and Churchill relished supplying some of Northcote's deficiencies. Salisbury, who had so often preached the virtue of a principled and obstructive negativism as the means of thwarting

Liberal government, now toyed with the option of opportunistic tactics which he had formerly condemned as both futile and reprehensible. Meanwhile the vacillation and apparent incompetence of Liberal policy abroad had been highlighted by the Sudan problem, which came to a head when the news of Gordon's death at Khartoum reached England early in 1885. The reaction in the press and among the wider public encouraged the Conservatives to press the government towards either resignation or a dissolution once redistribution was completed. Salisbury, anxious to resume his own grip on foreign policy, now qualified his conviction that an early resumption of office would only damage the Conservatives and reunite the Liberals: he reflected that 'it is the duty of the opposition to do all it can to turn out the Government, however disagreeable, & injurious to us as a party, such a result might be'. It was the dilemma of 1873 with the opposite answer. Beach and Churchill were crucial to this answer: since their experience of the government of Ireland in the 1870s, they had maintained their contacts and developed what were, by Tory standards, sympathetic attitudes to that country's problems. A vote of censure over the Sudan failed, but help from the Home Rulers enabled the Conservatives to inflict a defeat on the government in June, though the scale of Liberal abstentions suggested that the ministry itself was not averse to resignation. For the Irish party there was an understanding that an incoming Tory government would not renew a Coercion Act soon due to expire.

Salisbury now formed a minority government to await the election that would follow the completion of the electoral changes. He took the Foreign Office together with the premiership, Northcote was kicked upstairs with an earldom and the largely honorific title of First Lord of the Treasury, Beach took the lead in the Commons and Churchill went to the India Office, though most of the veterans of Disraeli's Cabinet remained. Though few Conservatives understood the significance of the links with the Home Rulers, it was Ireland that was about to break the mould of party politics. But for the moment the new ministry provided a show of competence and decent activity to contrast with what they presented as the flaccidity and disintegration of Liberal government. Salisbury displayed calm competence in confronting Russia over India and Churchill took the initiative in the annexation of Burmah. Patriotism and resolution made up the image they sought to project in overseas policy. Two Liberal bills, one on working-class housing and the other to establish the Secretaryship for Scotland, were ushered onto the statute book. Some Tories supported these measures and there was no electoral advantage for the party in opposing them. More controversial was the appointment under Northcote's chairmanship of a Royal Commission on the Depression in Trade and Industry, a gesture towards the Fair Traders. More significantly an Irish Land Act, known as Ashbourne's Act, helped to give reality to earlier statutory provisions for land transfer in Ireland. This encouragement of the sale of land to tenants by the provision of cheap loans from public funds served the interests both of Irish landlords, many of whom were ready to sell now that rents and the land market were depressed, and of those tenants who wanted to own their farms. In this way the tenant farmers might be weaned from supporting agitations like the banned Land League. Despite their qualms about this use of public revenue, the idea of creating a conservative class of small proprietors was attractive to Tories who were anxious to preserve the Union and make Ireland governable. The measure also served as a counter to the 1881 Land Act and its distressing imposition of 'dual ownership', a feature which most Tories viewed as detrimental to landlords' interests, property rights and free contract. Land purchase facilitated by Ashbourne's Act would at least re-establish single ownership and this was welcome to Conservatives worried about the theoretical implications and political precedent of the 1881 Act.

At another level Ireland was central to the Cabinet's thinking. The implications of the franchise reforms, which had trebled the Irish electorate, had alarmed many Conservatives and there was a distinct possibility that the Home Rulers would win enough seats to hold the balance in the new House. As Tories were also concerned about their own performance in Britain after the 1884 measure, it made sense to cultivate whatever support was available to bolster their representation, particularly as Chamberlain's Radical or Unauthorized Programme was expected to enhance the Liberal appeal to the newly-enfranchised labourers and to hit the Conservatives hard in the counties. The issues raised by Chamberlain were the main concern of most Conservative supporters. Disestablishment of the churches in England and Scotland was made a central issue by Chamberlain and by the Liberation Society and the Conservative leaders were happy to fight on this ground. Disestablishment was a question that divided Liberals badly in both Parliament and the constituencies, whereas it served to rally and unite Tories. Home Rule was not a major issue in the campaign because as yet neither Liberal nor Conservative leaders wanted it to be, but the possibility of some form of Irish self-government was a pressing topic of private discussion among them. A hint of a willingness to think in this direction was essential to the Conservatives' tacit pact with the Home Rulers. Gladstone, who knew a poisoned chalice when he saw one, preferred to leave the Tories to deal with the issue and tried to encourage them to repeat the concessionary performances of 1829, 1845–46 and 1867. For Salisbury, though the vision of settling Ireland had certain attractions, there was no serious flirting with the idea; he predicted his party would 'devour' him if he proposed Irish self-government. But Carnarvon became a convert to the idea and met Parnell clandestinely to discuss the possibilities; Beach and Churchill were convinced of the need to explore Irish options with an open mind and with tactical freedom. Their decision not to renew the Coercion Act had provided the basis for cooperation with the Parnellites and both sides, despite their different standpoints, were convinced of the Liberals' mismanagement of Ireland. A debate on Parnell's appeal for a review of convictions arising from a murderous atrocity at Maamtrasna, Co. Galway, gave an opportunity for a display of sympathy with the Irish party. Though the Cabinet had decided to reject the motion, Beach, Churchill and Gorst joined in accepting the request for review, braving the antagonism of their backbenchers who were further inflamed by Gorst's reference to 'reactionary Ulster members'. The limited tolerance on the Tory backbenches of fellow-travelling with the Parnellites was evident. But for the wider public their common commitment to denominational education was adduced as grounds for collaboration between the Tories and the Home Rulers. Though there was no formal deal – indeed studied ambiguity was essential for Salisbury as he strove to hold his Cabinet together and to keep his following in the country blissfully ignorant – Parnell advised Irish voters in Britain to support Conservative candidates, a move reckoned to be significant in some twenty borough constituencies.

The results of the 1885 election, the only one fought after the 1884–85 reforms and before the Home Rule crisis, were a mixture of the predictable and the surprising. The Liberal majority of 86 over the Conservatives amazed nobody, though perhaps its size was less than earlier predictions of the impact of the recent changes. There had been a net Tory gain of ten seats over 1880. The pattern of party strengths across the constituencies had changed dramatically, the Liberals now winning many county seats while the Conservatives considerably increased their strength in the large boroughs. The predominance of smaller, single-member constituencies was bound to help the minority parties in the old constituencies. There were now, however, signs of a shift of urban opinion, not just the Irish voters, the Conservative way to balance the Liberal enthusiasm of the agricultural labourers in the counties. During the campaign the radical wing of the Liberals had become disturbed by the dominant attitudes among the city electorates, particularly in London.[3] Dilke, fighting Chelsea, noted the unpopularity of the Chamberlainite policies of disestablishment and free education. Mundella concluded 'Our Philistines [the urban bourgeoisie] are dead against increased rates' and noted the unpopularity of the London School Board with ratepayers hostile to the idea of free schooling. Chamberlain's own post-mortem verdict was that 'the boroughs do not care for our present programme'. Whatever the contrary swing in the counties, the ratepayer democracy of the growing cities, faced with a Liberal party increasingly inclined to social interventionism, seemed to have moved towards the Conservatives as the party of property and cheap government. If 'Villa Toryism' continued to develop as a political force, the party's reluctant gamble on redistribution in 1884 might yet pay off.

For the moment, however, a Liberal majority remained, though the lead over the Tories was exactly cancelled out by the 86 seats of the Home Rulers, 'now undeniably the Irish party', as Gladstone put it, a party more disciplined as a voting bloc than in 1880. The 'Hawarden Kite', a press leak in mid-December, revealed that Gladstone's thinking was moving towards Home Rule, though he still hoped that the Conservatives would propose it. The revelation pushed the party at large into an overwhelming rejection of the idea and the Cabinet turned down Gladstone's proposal that they remain in office and settle Home Rule with his personal support. ('His hypocrisy makes me sick', wrote Salisbury.) All but Carnarvon were agreed. Iddesleigh, remembering 1867, rejected any re-enactment of 'gradual surrender of position after position at the bidding of our opponents' and even Churchill condemned the opportunism displayed in the 'Disraeli

---

[3] London, the greatest gainer from the 1885 redistribution, now had 85 seats. With the adjacent county and borough seats included, Greater London now accounted for over one-tenth of the Commons. The Conservative swing was more marked in London than in most cities because Nonconformity was weak in the capital and because London had most experience of what Hamilton, the victor in Middlesex in 1868, called 'the outpouring of professional men, tradesmen and clerical employees into the rural outskirts ... [which] had steadily changed the tone and politics of the constituency'.

epoch of constant metamorphoses of principle and party'. Once Salisbury had decided not to resign before meeting Parliament, he sought to convey the appearance of a united Cabinet (Carnarvon's resignation was kept secret) and to keep his government's policy low-key. But the ambiguities were now over; the Conservatives had become a consciously and overtly Unionist party. When Parliament met in January Beach and Churchill had to abandon their pose of ambiguity in face of the passionate Unionism of their party. Though the government could hardly hope to avoid defeat on a vote of confidence, they announced a policy for Ireland consisting not of self-government but of a Coercion Bill and a Land Bill to extend the scope of Ashbourne's Act, policies which were to be the twin pillars of Unionist policy for the next two decades.

Gladstone returned to office, though without Hartington's adherence, and in April introduced a Home Rule Bill which produced Chamberlain's resignation from the Cabinet and the dissent of nearly 100 Liberal MPs, mostly on the party's conservative wing and looking to Hartington as their leader but also including a body of Chamberlainites. The Bill's tenor was more radical than most of the ideas of self-government current among party leaders in 1885 and, though short of a complete repeal of the Union, it appeared to be close to the Parnellite definition of Home Rule. Already the fury of Ulster Tories had helped to polarize opinion and Churchill willingly made contact with Major Saunderson, the most prominent figure in Ulster's resistance to Home Rule. Churchill's visit to the province in February was thick with hints of armed resistance to the Liberal measure and it gave him the opportunity to bury his previous sympathies with the concept of self-government. 'Ulster will fight and Ulster will be right' was hardly a novel idea but its expression by a former Cabinet minister showed how far the leadership had moved from the uncertain ambiguities of 1885, though Churchill himself tended to denounce 'repeal of the Union' rather than the actual Liberal bill. The people he had once dismissed as 'foul Ulster Tories' welcomed the readiness of prominent parliamentarians to play to the 'Protestant' sentiment which had served the party so well in earlier years. More than most frontbenchers Churchill used the language of Protestantism rather than of Unionism or loyalism. Repeal, he claimed, would entail 'the most bitter and terrible oppression of Protestant by Catholics'.

This language denoted political calculation rather than emotion run out of control. Both Churchill and Salisbury were seeking to block the possibility of a government led by Hartington, whether a Liberal ministry without Gladstone or a centrist coalition in which the Conservatives might find themselves junior partners. Though Salisbury appeared on a Unionist platform with Hartington in April, he then deliberately polarized the politics of the issue by a speech to the National Union in mid-May which compared the Irish to Hottentots in their incapacity for self-government, recommended emigration to Manitoba as the solution to Ireland's agrarian problems and offered the country twenty years of unyielding government to restore social order and to depress political expectations. The speech, characterized by the Liberal Morley as 'manacles and Manitoba', was an affront to Whig traditions of reformism, a denial of the possibilities of consensus government on the Irish issue and a casting of the Conservatives as the only true Unionists. Centrist schemes came to a halt. Fear of

Hartington's succession as Liberal premier also explained Salisbury's urgent desire for a general election while Gladstone still held office. Though his colleagues mostly wished to avoid an early election, Salisbury encouraged the Queen to seek one. When it came, Gladstonians and Liberal Unionists would fight each other into irreconcilability and the split in the Liberal ranks would more likely be permanent. The electoral pact which Salisbury offered to the Liberal rebels (and which his party managers arranged in detail and sold to the constituency associations) similarly accentuated Liberal divisions and made Liberal Unionist seats conditional upon Conservative support, as well as making a Gladstonian victory less feasible. This strategy, one of destruction rather than reconstruction, amounted to an isolation of the Liberal Unionists – confirming their separation from the Gladstonian Liberal party but distancing them from a coalition or alliance with the Conservatives which they might dominate at Cabinet level. (Though the premiership was to be offered twice to Hartington in the following months, it was done in circumstances in which he could hardly accept.) The interests of most leading Tories required another exclusively Conservative ministry, not a fusion which would reduce them all in place and influence. Chamberlain, menacing to Salisbury as a potential ally though damaging to Gladstone as an actual opponent, only confirmed shrewder Conservatives in their distrust of ties with the Liberal dissidents.

The defeat of the Home Rule bill in the Commons by 30 votes – 93 Liberals joined the Conservatives in the majority – precipitated the general election Salisbury had wanted. The electoral pact operated with remarkable smoothness and 316 Tories and 79 Liberals supporting either Hartington or Chamberlain were returned on the Unionist side, giving a majority of about 120 over the Liberals and Home Rulers. Though not an overall majority for the Conservatives themselves, it was to prove sufficient for a Tory ministry draped in the flag of Unionism to survive for six years. Iddesleigh took the Foreign Office, Beach, relinquishing the Commons lead which had suited neither his temper nor that of his party, took the critical post of Irish Secretary, and Churchill, at the age of 37, assumed both the Exchequer and the leadership of the Lower House, a remarkable culmination to an exhilaratingly rapid ascent. But otherwise the composition and tone of the ministry were largely conventional; most of the 'Old Gang' remained in place, as Churchill's former allies complained. Since the general election was now past and since there was no further tactical requirement for ambiguity on Ireland, the colouring was less centrist than that of the caretaker ministry of 1885. Yet uncertainties remained. Though the ministry's survival depended on its now unequivocal Unionist identity, its day-to-day fortunes would depend once Parliament met on the relationship with Liberal Unionists whose own posture was uncertain. Some of them were drawn to the idea of a reconciliation with the main Liberal body if Gladstone stood down and Home Rule was dropped. Their leading men, Hartington and Chamberlain, were ill-assorted and perhaps incompatible. Nor, on the Tory side, were Salisbury and Churchill naturally compatible and there would be policy areas – foreign policy, budgetary dispositions and relations with Liberal Unionism – where they would pull apart in the months ahead.

It was apparent that the 'reconstruction' of parties anticipated since

Palmerston's death had occurred at last, but its permanance was not assured. Nor was its character settled, beyond the common Unionism and anti-Gladstonianism. Would it lead to a formal alliance, to coalition or even to 'fusion', or would the Liberal Unionists operate largely independently of the Conservatives? Would they still opt for Conservative government if a post-Gladstonian Liberal party beckoned? If they continued to support Tory administration, what would be their terms? It was far from settled how conservative in character the new relationship would be. These questions were of considerable significance for the Conservative party itself. If the Liberal Unionists called the tune as the price of their support, then something different from the traditional style of Conservatism might have to emerge. Chamberlain added to this uncertainty. His career and political base marked him as much more radical than Hartington and much less inclined to sink his differences with the Conservative party. The junior leaders of their respective parties, Churchill and Chamberlain, shared uneasy relations with their seniors, unorthodox inclinations at odds with the style of aristocratic centrism that had dominated parliamentary politics for so long and a fast-developing political friendship. Salisbury dealt only with Hartington, but Churchill cultivated Chamberlain to the extent of discussing confidential Cabinet business with him. Churchill seems to have calculated that collaboration of this kind would not only draw the Liberal Unionists closer to the government and away from Liberal reconciliation but would also establish his own ascendency within the ministry. Though he may not have intended to replace Salisbury in the premiership, he certainly aspired to greater influence within the government, over certain policy areas and over colleagues and appointments. His restlessness and a growing irritability, to which worsening health may have contributed, soon generated friction with colleagues and strained relations even with Beach, his main collaborator in the Cabinet.

During the short session of August–September 1886 Commons business and the task of nursing his party had kept Churchill comparatively quiet, though strains were already appearing within the ministry and between Tories and Liberal Unionists over questions of coercion and land reform in Ireland. But the autumn recess brought the start of Churchill's bid for ascendancy in policy-making when he made a much-publicized speech at Dartford in early October. The 'Dartford Programme' set out a menu of policies, some of them distinctly radical in flavour: free education, elective local government for the counties, a less confrontational policy towards Russia, reduced expenditure and taxation, land purchase in Ireland with no evictions and with coercion only as a last resort, modest agrarian legislation in Britain. Churchill advocated an alliance with the whole of Liberal Unionism, including Chamberlain, of whom he spoke warmly. Though Churchill claimed subsequently that he had cleared the speech with Salisbury and that its contents were little different from the latter's keynote speech at Newport before the 1885 campaign, this was disingenuous. Salisbury had never intended or commended programmatic politics of this sort, he had never set his sights on alliance with someone like Chamberlain, nor did he believe in permitting the parties to outbid each other for popular support. The general party reaction was also discouraging. Though there was support from old enthusiasts for Tory Democracy, Chaplin was fiercely hostile and there were rumblings among his confreres in the Carlton, *The Times* began to distance itself from Churchill, hitherto a favourite son – Buckle's editorial commended his break with 'the obsolete traditions of high and dry Toryism' but condemned him for being 'exceedingly temperate' with Ireland when he should have been 'exceedingly firm' – and the Cabinet was at best tepid towards the Dartford ideas. Salisbury, writing to Cranbrook who was lobbying against Churchill's latest initiatives, described his Cabinet as 'an orchestra in which the first fiddle plays one tune and everybody else another'. Its resistance stiffened, the 'Old Gang' creaked into action or at least complaint. Distrust of Churchill deepened: the *Daily News* predicted a few days after Dartford that a Conservative bill for Irish self-government involving extended local government and provincial assemblies would be prepared. Churchill was indeed lobbying for such ideas, which Salisbury curtly condemned as 'too much like real Home Rule'. With Chamberlain's encouragement, Churchill began to press the issues of county government in England and called for a measure to establish county councils elected by ratepayers and with wide powers which would include control of the Poor Law. Salisbury was violently hostile to the last idea which was, he argued, 'like leaving the cat in charge of the cream jug'. Even those Conservatives who favoured county councils usually wished to limit the 'democratic' character of their powers and their mode of election. Beach, for example, wished to give additional electoral weighting to property owners.

Soon the reactions in the party persuaded Churchill to write complainingly to Salisbury:

> I am afraid it is an idle schoolboy's dream to suppose that Tories can legislate
> ... They can govern and make war and increase taxation and expenditure *à merveille*, but legislation is not their province in a democratic constitution ...

He suggested that Henry Chaplin was 'the natural leader of the Tories in the House of Commons, suited to their intellects and their class prejudices' and concluded with a hint of a resignation threat: 'I certainly have not the courage and energy to go on struggling against cliques, as poor Dizzy did all his life'. Salisbury's reply was both a warning shot across Churchill's bows and a master-class in party strategy.

> The Tory party is composed of very varying elements ... the 'classes and the dependents of class' are the strongest ingredients in our composition, but we have so to conduct our legislation that we shall give some satisfaction to both classes and masses. This is specially difficult with the classes – because all legislation is rather unwelcome to them, as tending to disturb a state of things with which they are satisfied. It is evident, therefore, that we must work at less speed and at a lower temperature than our opponents. Our bills must be tentative and cautious, not sweeping and dramatic. ... The opposite course is to produce drastic, symmetrical measures, hitting the 'classes' hard, and consequently dispensing with their support, but trusting to public meetings and the democratic forces generally to carry you through. I think such a policy will fail. I do not mean that the 'classes' will join issue with you on one of the measures which hits them hard, and beat you on that. That is not the way they fight. They will select some other matter on which they can appeal to prejudice, and on which they think the masses will be indifferent; and on that they will upset you ...

Meanwhile Churchill was upsetting the services ministers, Hamilton and Smith, by trying to cut their estimates. Both Chamberlain's support and the promptings of his own Treasury advisers were encouraging him to push lower taxation, retrenchment on the army and navy and, by implication, a cautious foreign policy. But the services had many friends in the Conservative ranks and, as Russia's pressure in the Balkans raised international tension again, the predominant feeling within the party was that the forces had already suffered dangerously from Liberal underspending in the early 1880s. By mid-December Churchill was facing an alliance of Smith, Salisbury and the Queen over the army estimates. The budget proposals which he unveiled to the Cabinet had already been discussed with Chamberlain. Their gist was a reduction of expenditure, lower income tax, though with an additional gradation introduced, and a sharp increase in a now consolidated and sharply graduated succession duty. Later labelled a 'democratic budget' by Churchill's son and biographer, it provided for the reduction of duties on items of general consumption and for sharply higher taxes on various luxury items, including horses. The death duties were likely to be particularly controversial; Churchill had been warned that every estate in the House of Lords stood to suffer. Initially numbed, the Cabinet soon turned to questioning and criticism. Salisbury complained that 'your local taxation proposals will relieve the towns more than the rural districts' and spoke up for the landowning interests still so prominently represented on the Tory benches. Extra burdens would fall on 'the ordinary country gentleman', a figure much worried about by Salisbury and widely regarded in the party as ill-used by the times. Churchill's uncompromising reply – 'the country gentlemen, like the farmers, always think they are being plundered and ruined' – was followed by an offer of his resignation. He had decided to stand and fight for a line of policy and, perhaps even more, for his own determination of that policy. He challenged his Cabinet colleagues to face up to the alternative, which he claimed was not just his own departure but also the loss of Liberal Unionist support. Salisbury was ready to settle scores with Churchill and, perhaps calculating that the latter would soon repeat his familiar tactic of offering or threatening resignation, he had prepared his ground with the crucial figures, Hartington, Beach and the Queen. Now he accepted Churchill's profferred resignation as a *fait accompli*. Perhaps not anticipating this response, Churchill had failed to prepare his allies Beach and Chamberlain. Salisbury's determination was beyond doubt. When mediation was offered, Salisbury replied that Churchill's 'opinions on several subjects were not those of his colleagues' and that 'his friendship with Chamberlain ... made him insist that we should accept that statesman as our guide in internal politics'. His nephew Balfour put it more succinctly: 'we cannot turn Radical even to preserve the Tory party'.

Salisbury emerged from the crisis of New Year 1887 with a government more to his liking and closer to the instincts of most of his parliamentary party. The dangers within the party had been minimized by Churchill's miscalculation and unpreparedness. The apparent issue – a Chancellor resigning out of frustrated antipathy to military expenditure – was unlikely to win much Tory sympathy and Churchill carried virtually no significant support with him. More problematical was the reaction of the Liberal Unionists. Chamberlain had been unable or unwilling to influence events.

The crucial man was Hartington who now had the premiership and the possibility of 'reconstruction' offered to him, though in circumstances in which he could hardly accept. Salisbury and the Queen, however, persuaded Goschen, a former Liberal minister and publicly regarded as close to Hartington, to take Churchill's place at the Exchequer. Viewed as a token of Hartington's support for the government's continuation, it was also a considerable accession of financial expertise. The ministry's stock now rose in the City of London for which Goschen had once been MP. Of all the senior Whig Unionists Goschen, a financier and former banker, was the one best fitted to confirm the ministry's conservatism over a range of political and social issues. He had opposed Gladstone's Irish land legislation of the early 1880s as an attack on property and capital and he had been the only Liberal MP to vote against the 1884 franchise bill. As the historian Acton wrote, 'he dreads the Radicals . . . He is moved by the fears to which City men are prone'.[4] His commitment to property rights and to free enterprise was almost unequalled among political contemporaries. His friend the Queen had long seen him as central to the possible formation of 'a strong Whig party which the Conservatives would support and which might lead ultimately to an amalgamation or rather juncture of Conservatives and Whigs'. In early 1886 she had urged him that 'the object to be *obtained* for the safety of the Country is a *union* with the *Conservatives* to put a check on *revolutionary* changes' and had suggested 'Loyalists' or 'Constitutionalists' as the title for the new party: 'it is the *only chance* the Country has of a *strong government* able to resist Democracy and Socialism as well as separation (as regards Ireland)'. But the royal dreams had now found a rather different realization with Salisbury and his Conservatives dictating most of the terms. Though Salisbury enjoyed elements of luck during the Cabinet crisis – Iddesleigh's sudden death enabled the loyalist press to redouble its condemnation of Churchill, his former baiter – there was no doubt of his strategic purpose. It was to maintain a Conservative government in a firmly Unionist and defensive stance and to establish his ministry's broadly conservative purpose and credentials with the minimum of damage and disruption. The Conservative party would be unmistakably the dominant component of the conservative forces in national political life. There had been no take-over by Whigs or Liberal Unionists as the Queen might have wished; Salisbury indeed had worked to prevent it. Hartington's support had been secured without the difficulties and dangers of Hartington himself. Only one Liberal Unionist had been brought into the ministry, which was as much as Tory opinion showed itself ready to tolerate, and he was a highly conservative figure who had expressed his profound distaste for the 'Tory Democracy' of Churchill and his kind. Above all, Chamberlain had been rebuffed and the Tories had been saved from an influence which had threatened to force the nostrums of Birmingham radicalism upon them. Few, if any, Conservatives could yet envisage Chamberlain as the close collaborator he later became, particularly on imperial questions; his political identity had been formed by domestic issues and here he appeared as among the most threatening of the radical critics of established institutions. Salisbury probably hoped to drive a

---

[4] T. J. Spinner, *George Joachim Goschen. The Transformation of a Victorian Liberal* (1973), is a helpful modern study.

wedge between Hartington and Chamberlain and so ensure that the Conservatives would have to deal only with the former's relatively conservative attitudes. Now Chamberlain, rebuffed, spent the early months of 1887 in a 'Round Table Conference' to discuss his reunion with the Liberal party.

The personal drama of Churchill's fall should not obscure the larger issues of party identity and political strategy which were involved. Salisbury's coup suited the tastes and instincts of most of his party, particularly of the men who populated the parliamentary benches. Neither the gentry nor the business plutocracy had more than a limited enthusiasm for the political excitements Churchill offered. They did not want progressive, 'democratic' politics if it entailed steeply graduated taxation, interference with property rights, a foreign policy that seemed to neglect national interests abroad, competitive bidding between the parties for lower-class support and a consequent politicization of agricultural labourers and urban workingmen. That price was too great to pay even for successful resistance to Home Rule. The strains of the period since Palmerston's death had confirmed a taste for stability, order and quiet times. Though Salisbury had worried initially about the support Churchill might carry with him, no major section of the party rallied to him. His departure caused little regret in the Cabinet where only Beach, feeling he had been duped by Salisbury, tried to hold out for a larger reconstruction of the government and even advocated its resignation. (In March he resigned himself, ostensibly for health reasons.) Despite some regrets, mainly among the provincial papers and those with 'Fair Trade' enthusiasms, opinion in the party press backed Salisbury and the government over a resignation which editorial comment often depicted as capricious and disloyal. Buckle and *The Times* had deserted Churchill smartly and the *Standard*, the most important of the Tory London papers, was firmly loyalist. In the parliamentary party those who understood the issues at stake preferred the continuation of their own government to a sharing of power with Whig Unionists or, worse, with Chamberlain, which was what Churchill seemed to offer. Some saw Churchill simply as a traitor. He heard 'the Carlton would like to tear me limb from limb'.

The Problems of Unionist Government

The minor reconstruction of the New Year 1887 was far from being the end of difficulties. On anything other than resistance to Home Rule the government's tenure was precarious and its performance uncertain. Salisbury was denied the 'repose' which he had once defined as the end of true conservative government. The 1887 session was a troubled one. Churchill intrigued subversively on the fringes, by-elections went the Gladstonian way and the Liberal Unionists, themselves not united in purpose, helped to mangle several government bills in the Commons. Ireland remained a great problem in itself and a source of tensions within the Cabinet and party and between the Conservatives and their allies.

If Salisbury had expected to capture Hartington and his supporters for pure Conservative government, he was disappointed. Goschen proved to be a tower of strength, but Hartington's instincts were rather different from those of the Conservatives, certainly Conservatives of Salisbury's kind, and he had the Liberal credentials (and seats) of his supporters to worry about. This was the case with Chamberlain too. He did not return to the main Liberal party as Salisbury may have hoped and he did not break with Hartington and the main body of Liberal Unionists. Instead he worked to keep Birmingham and his West Midlands 'duchy' safe and this required the injection of a degree of radical purpose into Liberal Unionism and its relations with the government. He could not afford the appearance of a sell-out to Toryism. His support for the ministry in votes of confidence and over Home Rule had to be balanced by shows of dissent and contrariness. He made demands which the government managers in the Commons regularly found it hard to resist, despite Salisbury's irritation at the concessions. But the premier acknowledged that his minority ministry could not always have its own way as a majority administration might have done. He warned his supporters.

> you must not wonder, you must not blame us if to a certain extent ... the colour of the convictions of the Liberal Unionists joins with the colour of the convictions of the Conservative party in determining the hue of the measures that are presented to Parliament.

Ireland was one of the problems. Beach had argued that 'legislation must have two sides – one "kind" to the farmer, and the other, severe to the intimidator': in other words, generous measures on land combined with renewed coercion, though Beach's ideas on the latter were less draconian than those of Salisbury and his wing of the party. Land reform was likely to cause trouble among the landlord or pro-landlord Conservatives, coercion among the Liberal Unionists. Beach had wanted a new Land Act that provided for the revision (inevitably downwards) of the judicial rents fixed under the 1881 Act and this had been recommended by the Cowper Commission on Irish Agriculture. But the measure introduced by Balfour, Salisbury's nephew and Beach's successor as Chief Secretary, fell far short of this. When the Liberal Unionists in the Commons joined with the opposition to pass amendments to permit rent review, Smith, the Leader of the House, and Balfour capitulated. After prolonged resistance from Salisbury, Cranbrook and other hardliners, so did the Cabinet. Salisbury was contemptuous about the measure and about his own colleagues' lack of will to resist proposals 'inconsistent with the rights of property' when 'electoral purposes' were at stake. Less opportunity was offered to the Unionist allies over coercion, a policy dear to Tory hardliners. A Coercion Bill tougher than the one Beach had designed was pushed through by Balfour despite protests and even defections from Liberal Unionists and in August, without advance consultation with the government's allies, the National League was proclaimed unlawful. A controversy over an incident at Michelstown in which police had killed demonstrators showed that, over the coercive side of government policy, Balfour and Salisbury would make few concessions to the sensibilities of the Liberals, Unionist or otherwise. But already it was clear that areas of Irish policy were going to be shaped by a sometimes uncomfortable and unpredictable interaction of Conservatives and Liberal Unionists and that Salisbury's instincts could not always impose themselves. The existence of a broad-based, if informal, Unionist alliance was inevitably diluting the narrowly Tory and conservative style of government to which Salisbury had wanted to bend events.

Ireland was not the only area of domestic policy where Liberal Unionists had axes to grind, but the uncertainties of policy were compounded by the evident divisions among Conservatives themselves. The party's electoral base had been broadened and diversified by the sharp increase of its borough seats in 1885. The instincts and interests of 'the ordinary country gentleman' to which Salisbury paid such deference were no longer so dominant even with the parliamentary party, despite the prominence of agricultural spokesmen like Chaplin and Barttelot, let alone among the Conservative associations across the country as a whole. But urban Conservatism itself was divided. It included representatives of the tradition of Cross – the most prominent now was Ritchie, the President of the Local Government Board – who had experience of the problems and possibilities of urban government and who were ready to develop purposefully the legislative and administrative framework for local government activity. Yet legislation with a social purpose could affront vested interests, as Ritchie found when he tackled the drink question in 1888, and an improving spirit was not what most of the party wanted in its ministers, as Salisbury often reminded them. Spokesmen of the county ratepayers had long been familiar among Tory MPs; now there appeared spokesmen of their urban equivalents, among them a former national agent Bartley, whose idea of good local government was centred on low expenditure and low rates. Tories of this kind would soon find a *bête noire* in the London County Council. Whatever ministers with an itch to write their names in the statute book might think, the Conservatives in many of the city constituencies were becoming something of a ratepayers' party, fearful of active, interventionist government and of the high rates and taxes it entailed. Salisbury's administrations met this problem by stressing decentralization and by giving the maximum scope and discretion to local authorities (and so to local ratepayer electorates) in their dealings with Whitehall. Salisbury assured the National Union in 1887 that 'The object of local government is to diminish central government'. But fine phrases could not disguise the unease which many Tories felt about the trend of affairs. By the century's end Goschen would not be alone in feeling that a creeping socialism was arriving through extensions of local authority action and responsibility: 'In no direction have blows more serious been struck at the very foundations of private enterprise'. But most Conservatives had been more fearful of central government than of its local equivalent.

This mixture of pressure and opinion among both Conservatives and Liberal Unionists found expression in the 1888 Local Government Act. The measure's main purpose was the establishment of elective county councils, a step that many traditionalists had reluctantly conceded as inevitable after the 1884 extension of the parliamentary franchise in the counties. The measure was also advocated by many Liberal Unionists and had been demanded by Chamberlain. But most Tories, whose natural preference was the retention of the administrative functions of quarter sessions, were adamant that the threat posed by the new bodies should be countered and direct democracy should be checked by provisions for a substantial co-option of council members and by restrictions upon the councils' powers. Poor law responsibilities, which Churchill had talked heretically of vesting in the proposed councils, remained beyond their scope. Salisbury, though, regretted that the Tory squirearchy had done little to counter Liberal Unionist pressure and to water down the measure further. (In fact the county MPs had become more circumspect in their defence of landowners' interests now that their seats depended on the electorate enlarged in 1884.) He warned the gentry to mobilize to control and neutralize the new bodies. But the aspect of the measure which he resented most was the creation of the London County Council, a step for which the Liberal Unionists, including Goschen, had argued. As soon as the Progressive Party won control of the first LCC, Salisbury turned bitterly hostile and tried to prevent any Conservative co-operation with it. Many metropolitan Tories became fierce critics of the Council and its policies, as they had done earlier with the London School Board, and in 1897 Salisbury's third ministry would create a second tier of London government, the metropolitan boroughs, to counterbalance the LCC.

Though the surface pattern was confused, the trend within the party was towards a more deliberate and self-conscious assertion of free-market economics and a greater wariness of social reformism. The enfranchisement of large numbers of working-class electors had created at least the potential for welfare politics, for the promising by politicians hungry for votes of material benefits which would have to be financed from the pockets of the prosperous. The course of Liberal land legislation had also suggested more direct ways of hitting at property-owners. The vision of an expropriating democracy had always terrified Salisbury. So too had the readiness of some party colleagues to make concessions to 'agitation' when it suited the short-term interests of the party or themselves. He had disliked Disraeli's tendency to buy off trouble by conceding radical demands and he had seen in Churchill's Dartford Programme a deliberate bid for lower-class votes. Despite his soft spot for measures on working-class housing, Salisbury remained convinced that welfare legislation would promote an appetite among the poor which could never be sated short of the dispossession of the wealthy. His deterministic pessimism persuaded him that matters would come to that pass in the end. Meanwhile the task of the Conservative party was to keep the floodgates closed for as long as possible. Social peace in his time, the secure enjoyment of their own by men of property, was Salisbury's overriding aim in domestic politics. In 1892 he accused Gladstone of a 'revolutionary appeal to the jealousy of the poor' and in retrospect he criticized some of the legislation of his own ministry of 1886–92 as 'democratic' or 'socialistic' folly. His views inevitably had some influence on Cabinet policy decisions, though his absence from the Commons weakened his control of parliamentary tactics, and the ministry's commitment to the rights of property was now reinforced by Goschen's voice. (As a Liberal he had opposed the 1885 Artisans' Dwellings Bill which, ironically, Salisbury himself had supported.) The position of men like this in government ensured that social legislation would be scrutinized closely in its relationship to economic theory and to property rights. The hostility which Salisbury expressed publicly in 1889 to a bill to limit the working day to eight hours was not untypical of these attitudes:

> To make such a law would be an unpardonable interference with the freedom which Englishmen of all classes have established for many generations, would interfere with the natural relations of trade, would drive capital out . . . and would ultimately be ineffective because it would ultimately lead to a general redistribution of wages all round.

What might have been conceded as a paternalistic gesture by a self-assured patriciate formerly was less negotiable now that property felt itself to be under pressure from 'democratic' demands. If the Conservatives competed with the radicals for working-class votes, what real security was left for the interests that looked to the party to protect them? Better, Salisbury and his kind argued, to depress any expectations which the lower classes had of material benefits from political action and to focus their attention on safer issues like Home Rule. Better by far to stress the questions that united 'the classes' and 'the masses' and to avoid those that might set them against each other.

Though views like these were heard frequently, they were never the totality of Tory attitudes. Most men were not as coldly analytical as Salisbury. The argument that the worst consequences of 'democracy' could be prevented only by a vigilant and resolute resistance to 'socialism' suffered from the lack of an agreed definition of the latter. Did it include what Chamberlain in 1885 had listed as 'every kindly act of legislation . . . the elevation of the poor . . . levelling up'? (His call for an attack on 'excessive inequalities' and his advocacy of graduated taxation may, however, have confirmed some people's distrust of kindliness.) Many Conservatives both in and out of Parliament were less theoretical and paranoid about ideas of this sort than Salisbury, Goschen and the free-market theorists who were now clustering around the party. Balfour, who had to work with Chamberlain's capricious support in the Commons, accepted that Conservative government needed a flavouring of social purpose, if only to keep its new allies and various pressure-groups happy. He once depicted 'social legislation' as 'the direct opposite and . . . most effective antidote' to that socialism which entailed institutional radicalism, class conflict, expropriation and the restriction of free enterprise. Like some other thinking Tories, Churchill among them, he noted Bismarck's success in buttressing a conservative régime in Germany with a social insurance system. Among the less sophisticated there survived a feeling that a little social legislation would serve to keep much nastier things at bay and was a necessary part of the management and neutralization of 'democracy'. In 1895 even Salisbury, moved to welcome his Liberal Unionist coalition partners, depicted 'the improvement of the daily lives of struggling millions' as the task before the new Parliament. Many Tory MPs, particularly those with marginal seats, were disinclined to argue dogmatically against social interventionist measures that seemed likely to improve their electoral prospects. A large body of working-class constituents often encouraged at least a pose of 'Tory Democracy'. But the surviving Tory Democrats of the Churchill school were not popular in the parliamentary party. Gorst, though he continued in government offices, was distrusted as, in Balfour's phrase, 'rather publicly pledged to take the side of the wage-earners on every possible occasion' and he was denied promotion. There were always powerful voices against unduly generous legislation. In 1897 MPs were lectured by one of the Treasury ministers:

> We have done away with personal and individual bribery, but there is a still worse form of bribery, and that is when a man asks a candidate to buy his vote out of the public purse.

– and that year Chamberlain, now in the Cabinet, found his partners unenthusiastic about the full rigour of his Workmen's Compensation Bill.

Conservatives, strict for property rights and for freedom of contract, forced the inclusion of the 'contracting out' provisions which employers' organizations had demanded. The Tory mutiny against the measure included Middleton of the party organization, Londonderry, the spokesman of the coalowners in the Lords, and James Lowther, an influential Commons backbencher and a former minister. Lowther told the National Union Conference

> that there had been rather more than enough of far-reaching and subversive legislation, that they had had too much of ambitious departmental administration, and that what the country required was a much-needed repose. (Cheers) ... there should be anti-Radical administration, and non-Radical legislation. (Cheers)

The excision of the compulsory provisions that Chamberlain and the trades unions had wanted showed the limits of the radicalism he could inject into Unionist policy and underlined his wisdom in confining his main rôle in Salisbury's last administration to colonial questions.

The conflicting pressures exerted upon the legislative policy of the Salisbury administrations make it difficult to categorize neatly. There were divisions about both purpose and emphasis within the party and the Cabinet. The tactical situation in the Commons often decided the issue and many measures foundered there. The influence of the Liberal Unionists, who held the balance in the Commons, was not all in one direction. Goschen, the government's talisman of the support of the City, was almost obsessively concerned to defend free enterprise and property rights against socialism; Hartington was a conservative Whig who was sensitive about his Liberal credentials; Chamberlain had to nurse his power-base in the industrial West Midlands and he was still learning to discipline his instincts in order to work with Conservatives. Historians have differed about the impact of Liberal Unionism upon the Conservatives, some attributing the more progressive legislation passed under Salisbury to its influence, others arguing that it provided the bridge over which hardline free-market theory passed from the Liberal party to the Tories. The truth in both views suggests not only that Liberal Unionism was itself a divided force but also that intellectual currents did not always determine the political outcome. The Conservative party itself was being pulled in different directions by electoral calculation, by intellectual trends, by the pressures from interest groups and by parliamentary tactics. The party was adapting to changed circumstances even without the influence of the Liberal Unionists, who probably accelerated the changes more than they altered their direction. An important feature of these years, though one perceptible well before 1886, was the movement of propertied opinion, both aristocratic and bourgeois, away from a Liberal party being radicalized by Ireland, Nonconformity and mass enfranchisement. The mood of great property became more nervous and defensive, many business interests being particularly opposed to legislative regulation and to the growth of trade-union influence. A party with a leader like Salisbury, implacably opposed to 'socialism', offered a haven to such people. The main appeal of the Conservative party in this was its basic conservatism as the party of resistance to radical change. Some of the support moving its way was that of drifting centrists, often former Palmerstonians, who wanted not a Tory party of Ultra reactionaries but a decently conservative, conventional, even mildly progressive party which could carry enough national opinion with it to block the road down which Gladstone, the radicals and the Irish sought to move. Fortunately for the party Salisbury's strongly Anglican high Toryism and his intellectual negativism were always tempered by the softer-edged centrism of men like Northcote, a former Peelite, Smith, an ex-Palmerstonian, and the sceptical Balfour who between them led the party in the Commons for nearly all the late-Victorian period. Yet this drift of centrist opinion would have been a slow one if left to itself. The crisis of 1885–87 was a catalyst of Liberal disintegration and of the reconstruction of national politics and it gave the Conservatives the otherwise unlikely opportunity to spend most of the next two decades in office. In particular Home Rule accelerated the shift of middle-class support in parts of the country where it had been happening more slowly than in London and Lancashire.

One consequence was to make the Conservatives – even more the Unionist alliance – much more the party of industry, finance and commerce than they had been for most of the Victorian period. The brewers and distillers had special reasons for their attachment, but other business interests – bankers, shipowners, railway companies, manufacturers, coalowners – were now well represented on the Commons benches and in the leadership of the constituency associations and they looked to the party as a protector. As the growing weight of trade unionism ranged itself largely on the Liberal side, though some of the Lancashire cotton unions were pro-Conservative, the employers' organizations and the chambers of commerce tended to move the Conservative or Unionist way. By the 1890s, a decade of troubled labour relations, the Conservatives, with the legislative gestures of 1875 well behind them, had emerged clearly as the party of opposition to trade-union demands. The controversies over employers' liability underlined this, as did a series of appointments of judges strongly hostile to trade unionism and committed to freedom of contract by Salisbury's Lord Chancellor, Halsbury. Taff Vale and Osborne lay ahead. Equally striking was the warm relationship between Conservative governments and the City of London. Until 1868 the City's seats had been almost monopolized by the Liberals; from 1885 to the Great War the Tories took both City seats either without a contest or by overwhelming majorities. Commerce and finance were signalling their preference for conservatism and stability over the reform and progressivism which the Liberals seemed to offer. 'Democracy' of a kind had had to be accepted; now it was being replaced as the party's bugbear by 'socialism', a threat which seemed real enough to many beneficiaries of wealth and privilege. When the Labour party appeared on the scene with its socialist rhetoric and its trade-union links, it was to be a natural and ready-made opponent for the Conservatives.

Liberal Unionism neither created nor prevented that development. It caused problems, however, with one traditional and still crucial association of the Conservatives. The Church of England was not an obvious gainer from the Unionist alliance. Though in Scotland Liberal Unionism supported the established Church, in England it was much cooler towards the Anglican establishment. Though Goschen was a zealous Churchman, Hartington was Whiggishly tepid towards the Church's claims and privileges, while Chamberlain had long advocated disestablishment. The crisis of 1886 had also committed the Conservative party to the loyalist Presbyterians of Ulster, encouraged it to woo anti-Catholic Nonconformists like the Wesleyans and confirmed its 'Protestant' identity rather than a narrowly Anglican one. Yet the degree of identity between the party's following and that of the Church of England gave support to the contemporary jibe that the Church was 'the Conservative party at prayer'. The attacks of the Liberal party's militant Nonconformists upon the establishment had left little sympathy for that party among the Anglican clergy and the committed laity. How compatible, then, would the Tory dependence on Liberal Unionist votes be with the party's relationship with the Church? Tory managers in the Commons certainly had to moderate their commitment to Anglican interests in order to accommodate Liberal Unionist susceptibilities. Not for the first time, the 'Church party' on the Tory benches became restive at the apparent lukewarmness of their government. Salisbury fretted. He lamented the lack of zeal for the Church among many of his Commons supporters – the gentry were roused more by other causes and many MPs had to conciliate Nonconformist opinion in their constituencies – and he found both Smith and Balfour unresponsive to his ecclesiastical enthusiasms. His main concerns in this area were tithes and denominational education and he did not intend relations with the Liberal Unionists to compromise them. The premier pushed forward successive bills to enforce the levying of tithes under the 1836 Commutation Act, a process which had met with some resistance in the 1880s, particularly in Wales, but the measures were unpopular with the county members and the farmers' spokesmen as well as with the Liberal Unionists. After messy failures in 1887 and 1890, a Tithe Recovery Act was passed in 1891. Popular education was a more crucial issue, however, and one where Liberal Unionist sensitivities were clearly involved. The School Boards were still resented by many Tories – Salisbury, who objected to them on religious grounds, also denounced them as 'the most recklessly extravagant bodies in England' – and the Church feared that a future Liberal government would strengthen the Boards while reducing the financial subsidy to the denominational schools in order to undermine the Anglican system. A further problem was the coolness towards Church schools of the civil servants at the Privy Council Office for Education; Salisbury felt that his Lord President, Cranbrook, had been suborned by his officials. In 1891, braving friction between the Houses, Salisbury had a measure pushed through to establish virtually free elementary education, one of Chamberlain's longstanding demands, and to increase Exchequer funding of the schools to compensate for the loss of fees. Though presented as a generous, even radical, measure and as a gesture towards the Liberal Unionists, it was intended as a life-line to the Church schools. Salisbury's commitment to cheap government had wavered when the Church was involved and the Act was a masterstroke in combining its interests with the dictates of the Unionist alliance and of electoral advantage. This favour to the Church and Salisbury's notably partisan appointments to the episcopal bench helped to consolidate the almost solid support of the Anglican clergy for the Unionist case when the Liberal ministry introduced its Home Rule bill in 1893. But popular education was only one problem settled. Chamberlain's commitment to disestablishment survived – it inspired a serious clash with local Tories in his West Midlands duchy just before the 1892 general election – and subsequently he voted for the Liberal bill to disestablish the Church in Wales. The 'Church party' continued to distrust the Unionist allies and the Church might indeed have received scanter consideration from Conservative government after 1886 but for Salisbury's personal influence. Nonetheless Tory government was inevitably more sympathetic than Liberal government to the Church and the Liberal Unionists had done the established churches a considerable favour by keeping the Liberals out of office at a time when they posed a serious threat to the establishments.

After 1886 the Conservatives continued to cultivate the image which they had already done much to secure as the party of national strength and purpose in overseas policy. The potential of patriotism for binding the enfranchised populace to traditional Toryism was too clear to be neglected and the Liberals, when in office, continued to offer opportunities which their opponents could exploit. The Irish issue heightened this contrast between the parties. Home Rule was easily depicted by Conservatives as a recipe for damage to the national will, prestige, security and strength. Could a party committed to Home Rule really be entrusted, they asked, with the responsibility for British interests around the world? Salisbury's unquestioned proficiency in foreign affairs helped his governments and his party to project this image of national strength and assurance. Party opinion at large had little difficulty in assuming the Palmerstonian mantle. The party's close links with the officer corps, the instinctive patriotism of the gentry, the overseas interests of many Tory businessmen and financiers, only helped the development, while Ulster loyalism, now enhanced in its significance, added its own flavour of assertive patriotism. There was almost nothing that corresponded to the pacific and anti-militaristic influence that Nonconformity brought to bear on the Liberal party. Salisbury strove to limit any damage to his party's patriotic image, for example from Churchill's Gladstonian tendencies in foreign policy and in cheeseparing the services estimates. The 1889 Naval Defence Act, which committed Britain to the 'two-power standard' and to a five-year construction programme, was the outcome of one of the periodic naval scares, but it was also a considered riposte to Gladstonians whatever their party. The emergence of the Conservatives as the party of Britain, Empire and patriotism presented no difficulties with the Liberal Unionists either. Hartington and Chamberlain, the two most influential Liberal Unionist seceders, were instinctive supporters of a strong foreign and colonial policy and, once their informal understanding with the Conservatives was established, it was natural for the two sides to emphasize a line on which they could agree. In 1888 the government appointed Hartington to the patriotic task of chairing a royal commission on the state of the army. Though the main Liberal party also had its imperialists, notably among its parliamentary leaders, the 1890s saw the Conservatives strengthening their own identification with patriotism and empire. One feature was their public exaltation of the Crown as a symbol of constitutional stability, national unity and imperial greatness, a tendency encouraged by the opportune celebration of the two royal jubilees in 1887 and 1897, years of Tory government. The burgeoning activities of the Primrose League and its branches gave prominence to the associated themes of Crown, Empire and patriotism which, by the century's end, had become shibboleths of the party. The practice of government, however, was inevitably rather more restrained. Conservative Chancellors were never an easy touch for the service ministries and Salisbury was far more cautious as a diplomatic practitioner and more committed to the maintenance of peace than the touchy bellicosity of some of his followers suggested. But Salisbury was ready enough to drape his party in the Union Jack when political advantage required, as he was to show by calling a snap election during the Boer War. His third ministry, which saw the appointment of Chamberlain to the Colonial Office, the prominence of the Transvaal question, the outbreak of the Boer War and the manifestations of popular jingoism in London and other cities, and the 'khaki election' of 1900 when the Unionists exploited wartime patriotism and smeared the Liberals as Boer sympathizers, would extend to Unionism as a whole the image which the Conservatives had appropriated. It was a stance which enjoyed considerable support in the press, both metropolitan and provincial, and with elements in all classes. It helped to bind 'the classes and the masses' and widened the appeal of Conservative clubs and associations to the enfranchised working-classes of the boroughs, though the jingoism of the Boer War period seems to have been particularly strong among the white-collar lower-middle class. It was an appeal, though, which was strongest in cities with an economic interest in assertiveness overseas, for example places with major armaments industries, and it was spasmodic in its intensity. The Unionists could not guarantee that attention would always be diverted away from domestic issues as easily as in the 'khaki election'.

Of all the issues between the parties, Ireland was the one which gave Salisbury's governments the firmest base in majority sentiment, though it was a clear majority only in England, not in Scotland, Wales or, of course, Ireland itself. Conservative publicists emphasized the centrality of Home Rule as an issue. Whenever public attention was diverted elsewhere, Conservative support suffered, the Unionist alliance languished and the Gladstonian Liberals benefited. The trend of by-elections underlined this fact: during the Parliament of 1886–92 the government's normal majority dropped from over 100 to about 70 as the Irish issue proved itself to be a variable asset. The coercion policy of 1887, which had dismayed even Liberal Unionist opinion, had coincided with a series of articles on 'Parnellism and Crime' in *The Times*, a paper itself fervently Unionist. They suggested that Parnell had been implicated in the murder of Burke, the Irish Under-Secretary who had died alongside Cavendish in 1882, but, after an initial revulsion of opinion against the Nationalist leader, a commission of enquiry found the allegations to be based on forged documents. Feeling now swung sharply against the government, which had associated itself unequivocally with *The Times*'s charges. The consequent unsettlement of the two Unionist parties was a factor in the shambles of the 1890 session when the government found itself unable to control either the House or its legislative programme and Salisbury had similar problems with his Cabinet. Only the O'Shea divorce scandal and its consequences – the disenchantment of British Nonconformity with Parnell, his condemnation by the Irish Catholic bishops and the split in the Irish party – rescued the Conservatives from this trough.

In the 1892 election campaign the Tories would emphasize their resolute opposition to Home Rule, but both Unionist parties knew they had to fight on a broader front than this. Since 1887 the Tories had kept two other strands to their Irish policy. One was the advancement of the land-purchase scheme launched by Ashbourne's Act. Despite its call on Exchequer funds, it appealed to most Conservatives as well as to the Liberal Unionists (Chamberlain was enthusiastic for small proprietorship as a successor to old landlordism) and to Irish tenant opinion. Whatever their motives, at least the government could claim credit for contructiveness in this respect. The other plank in their Irish platform enjoyed narrower support. The strongly repressive policy which had triumphed in the Cabinet in 1887 continued, producing not only a firmer and more consistent backing for the forces of law and order than in recent administrations but also a permanent legislative framework for Irish coercion. Balfour, who made his reputation (as 'Bloody Balfour' to his Nationalist opponents) by the unrelenting vigour of his administration as Irish Secretary from 1887 to 1891, at least showed some sensitivity to Liberal Unionist opinion. Salisbury, less inclined to listen even to allies, evinced an appetite for coercion uncommon among leading politicians, at least in their public utterances. This approach, welcomed by the hardliners of the party's right wing, found much less regular scope or need in Britain, but it was clear that the Irish situation had reawoken a strain of repressiveness not seen among Tories since Chartist times. 'Firmness' towards Irish (and sometimes British) disorders was a favourite theme of Tory meetings and publications. Though the clash between armed troops and unemployed and socialist demonstrators in Trafalgar Square in November 1887 ('Bloody Sunday') owed more to the ineptitude of the Home Secretary, Henry Matthews, than to design, it confirmed the government's reputation for a heavy hand with agitation. Salisbury was determined to end liberal vacillation in such matters: 'Our national fault is that too much softness has crept into our national councils'. In 1887–88 cavalry were sent in to help enforce the distraint of goods during the Welsh 'tithe war'. It was reminiscent of early nineteenth-century Toryism rather than of its mid-century phase. The party was now abandoning the vigorous defence of civil and constitutional liberties (except those of private property, of course) to its Liberal opponents. Without the moderating influence of the Liberal Unionists the Conservatives might have gone further in meeting popular agitation with coercion. On the other hand it was the reliability of Liberal Unionist support in the last resort in the Commons that enabled Salisbury and his colleagues to rule Ireland with an iron hand for so long and so consistently.

The Commons remained, nonetheless, a bed of nails for the ministry. The apparent precariousness of its position as a minority government dependent on Liberal Unionists put a premium upon sophisticated and sensitive management which Salisbury's instincts did not always encourage. Churchill's departure had put a talented enemy onto the backbenches and he showed, particularly in 1888, that he was still effective for mischief. He had also left the front bench short of sparkle. His successor as Leader, the long-suffering and utterly worthy Smith, won respect and sympathy for his decency amidst adversity; his bourgeois respectability with a liberal-conservative flavour eased not only the collaboration with the Harting-tonians but also the assimilation of the new kind of borough Tories into the parliamentary party. Goschen was successful and innovative at the Exchequer but he had his ambitions to succeed Smith in 1891 dashed by the veto of the Tory backbenchers. Balfour, whose Irish performance won him the plaudits of the hardliners, threw off his old image as the lightweight among the frôndeurs of the Fourth Party. Beach, abandoning an alliance with Churchill, returned to office in 1888 but was never again the combative leader of the mid-1880s. Ritchie, with his commercial and 'Fair Trade' antecedents, gave representation to the business elements in the party and showed himself progressive and industrious as both legislator and administrator, though he soon antagonized many of the party's vested interests. Salisbury's worries about the agricultural interest and the country gentlemen brought Chaplin into the Cabinet in 1889 as the first President of the new Board of Agriculture. But none of these was as impressive a parliamentary performer as the two leading Liberal Unionists. Chamberlain still alarmed most Conservatives, particularly by his views on established churches; Hartington, impressively taciturn, gathered prestige as the embodiment of a conservative, patrician centrism, though most Tories evinced little desire to surrender the integrity of their party (or the spoils of office) to his embrace. After the disastrous session of 1890 the respective leaders sought to bring about a fusion of the two Unionist parties at constituency level, but the attempt foundered on the resolute opposition of the party faithful, among them the organizing genius Middleton ('the Tory party . . . is found to have lost half its vitality'). The succession of Balfour to Smith and of Chamberlain to Hartington as Commons leaders of their respective parties in 1891 promised a more vigorous and adventurous leadership, but the appearance of compulsory purchase provisions in their Smallholdings Bill of 1892 proved to be too adventurous for Salisbury and the country gentlemen who resisted them successfully.

Opposition and Coalition

The Unionist defeat in the hard-fought election of 1892 was not unexpected, except perhaps in its narrowness. The Conservatives and the Gladstonian Liberals were nicely balanced (268 to 270), while the Irish Nationalists' 81 seats outmatched the Liberal Unionists' 47, badly down on their 79 in 1886. Salisbury insisted on meeting Parliament and on a vote of no confidence before he made way for Gladstone again. The election result tended to strengthen Salisbury and Chamberlain within their own parties. Salisbury had long criticized the pusillanimity of his managers and followers in the Commons; now the main line of defence against Liberal measures lay in the Lords where he commanded an absolute majority. For the first time since 1884 the rôle of the Upper House as barrier to radicalism and as ultimate upholder of a (conservatively defined) national interest would be put to the test. Salisbury relished the prospect. In the dark days of Unionist disintegration in the old Parliament he had confided to Balfour his 'strong conviction that I can get better terms for property out of office, than I can in office', and for years he had been putting his mind to the question of the relationship between an electoral mandate and the Lords' powers.[5] Chamberlain had not received the setback from the

---

[5] On this see C. C. Weston, 'Salisbury and the Lords, 1868–1895', *Historical Journal*, 25, 1982, pp. 103–29.

election which the Hartingtonians had – he had even increased his seats in the West Midlands 'duchy' – and now, with the Conservatives out of office, he had gained more independence of action. The new government's dependence on Irish votes put Home Rule at the top of the agenda. The 1893 Home Rule Bill, a much modified version of the 1886 proposals, passed the Commons with everyone anticipating its defeat in the Upper House. The overwhelming majority of 419–41 against, the largest division ever in the Lords, showed the near-unanimity of the peerage behind the Union. The Conservative party itself, despite its growing bourgeois component, now commanded the support of a greater proportion of the aristocracy than ever before. Equally significant was the solidarity of the bench of bishops with the majority, the most adverse vote the episcopate had ever delivered against a government and evidence of how far the Church of England and the Liberal party had pulled apart. Here, in its ultimate reliance on landownership and the Church, the Tories had strengthened, not abandoned, their traditional base.

The veto power found other victims. Liberal measures for Welsh disestablishment and for drink licensing were despatched, while the peers' amending powers were deployed on a bill to establish district and parish councils and on a measure for employers' liability where the Conservative commitment to 'contracting out' by employers triumphed. In 1894 Gladstone was replaced as premier by Rosebery, a much less provocative figure to Conservatives and to much centrist opinion, though he toyed with the idea of a campaign against the peers' partisan use of their constitutional powers. Salisbury, ruthless in the rediscovered vigour of opposition, advised the Queen (in confidential and unconstitutional correspondence) to force a dissolution on the government, advice which more scrupulous Unionists managed to counter.

But an early general election was considered almost inevitable and the prospect raised the problem of the basis of co-operation between the two Unionist parties. Chamberlain, who had voted for Welsh disestablishment and for Harcourt's sharp increase in death duties, measures highly unpopular with most Tories, found himself at odds with the Conservatives. Quarrelling over the allocation of seats between the parties had intensified and Chamberlain himself was attacked by Tory papers, including the *Standard*, which many saw as Salisbury's mouthpiece. Chamberlain was planning to press a programme of social legislation in the 1895 session, starting the bills in the Lords in order to embarrass the Liberals and to give the Unionists what he claimed would be a popular platform for the election. Salisbury rejected most of the proposals, which he saw as likely only to alienate established supporters. When Chamberlain complained of the hostile reception from the Conservative press and organization, Salisbury was unsympathetic. He condemned his 'anti-Church and anti-Land opinions' –

> Undoubtedly, if he means to shape his political life on the Birmingham view of Church & squire – those two authorities will in the long run refuse to take him for one of their leaders.

– and his advice was to 'put that philosophy in the lumber-room'. But the threat of a complete rupture between the parties and their fear of a Liberal recovery under Rosebery turned minds to a more formal relationship than before 1892. When the government resigned ahead of the general election, Salisbury's new ministry formed in June 1895 included the Liberal Unionists Hartington, Chamberlain, Lansdowne and James as well as Goschen. This coalition continued even when the Conservatives won an overall majority in the election. 'Reconstruction' had taken another major step. Although there was no merger – the failure of 1890 served as a warning – the two parties moved closer together. Even Chamberlain won a degree of acceptance in Conservative ranks when he eschewed 'sensational legislation' in 1895 and tolerated Tory indifference and sometimes hostility towards pet proposals like old-age pensions and compulsory workmen's compensation. Instead he concentrated, as Colonial Secretary, on issues with which Conservatives could readily identify. The Jubilee of 1897 helped to cement the coalition, as did the Boer War and the general election fought during it. Though the parties were not to merge as 'the Conservative and Unionist party' until 1911–12, the old distinctions would weaken steadily and in the 1910 general elections the candidates of the two parties would stand simply as 'Unionists'. Chamberlain's restlessness and his taste for programmatic politics had always threatened trouble once Salisbury left the scene, but at least the split over tariff reform in 1903 would cut across the Unionist alliance, dividing each party internally rather than Conservatives from Liberal Unionists. Though Salisbury's goal of 'repose' remained elusive, the drawn-out reconstruction of national politics had at least ensured long periods of Tory-dominated government, held out reasonable prospects of Conservative or at least Unionist majorities and produced a reshaping of the centre-right of politics which would become the matrix for its twentieth-century development. Despite by-election reverses and its later internal rifts, Unionist government enjoyed for a decade after 1895 a security and dominance which the Conservatives alone had not achieved since before 1830. After the shocks of the 1880s, government and politics had been to some extent restabilized. The 'reconstructions' of the early twentieth-century would be more on the political left, while the conservative side would be supported by a broad base of influential opinion of the kind that had eluded it in the mid-Victorian years. What was not resolved – perhaps in the nature of things could not be resolved – was the tension within that broad church between traditionalism and progressivism, between a hard-edged authoritarianism and a more liberal constitutionalism and between a narrowly partisan Toryism and a more centrist conservatism. The old dilemmas of conservatism in a changing world and a divided society remained.

A Party in Evolution

In one respect the late-Victorian Conservative party did modernize itself significantly. The organizational developments during Disraeli's leadership had been partial in scope, uncertain in direction and halting in implementation, though Gorst continued to promote the mythology of a golden age of 'Tory Democracy' in the early 1870s long after the success and glamour of 1874 had faded. After the 1880 defeat Gorst had returned as Principal Agent and a Central Committee under Smith had been established to overhaul the organization and to co-ordinate relations between the parliamentary and the extra-parliamentary sides of the party. These arrangements suffered from the demoralization of a party on the defensive and still beset with recriminations. Soon Gorst and Churchill were exploiting the disgruntlement of the National Union, within which elements blamed the leadership for the loss of city seats and for its failure to cultivate provincial Toryism. As neither component of the dual leadership had the authority to silence the rumblings, the Central Committee found itself the object of attack in an internal party battle. Traditionalists like Salisbury feared the emergence of a 'caucus' similar to the National Liberal Federation, the 'new foreign political organization' (in Disraeli's phrase) on the Liberal side. Salisbury's deal with Churchill in 1884 ended this prospect as well as establishing the former as effective party leader. Churchill abandoned Gorst and the rebels in the National Union, the Central Committee was abolished and organizational responsibilities reverted to the Chief Whip and the Principal Agent. At this point the 1884 Franchise Act, taking effect together with the Corrupt and Illegal Practices Act of the previous year and the 1885 Redistribution Act, gave the electoral system a shake-up perhaps as great as that of 1832. The 1883 measure, inspired by Liberal fears of Tory money, by a general fear of the cost of elections under an expanded electorate and by the financial problems being experienced by the gentry, put severe limits on the local expenditure of the parties for electoral purposes and put their activities into a legal straitjacket. The 1884 Act assimilated the county franchise to the borough one. The 1885 redistribution reconstructed virtually the whole constituency system, undercut traditional patterns of influence and necessitated a wholesale revamping of constituency associations. Householder democracy had gone far, it seemed, down the road to 'numbers, not property'. The Conservative party, always fearful of that development, had to react both to the dangers and to the opportunities. As had been the case after 1832 and 1867, the Tories had more reason than the Liberals to organize themselves in order to neutralize the new system. As the better financed of the two main parties, they had more scope for doing so.

The 1883 Act had forced a shift from irregular expenditure at election times to a more regular financing of constituency organization and from local expenditure to finance raised and distributed centrally. The impact of agricultural depression on the rents of the gentry accelerated this shift in the balance of expenditure. (Parliamentary candidature had still not, however, become a sport for the poor man, particularly as uncontested elections were now less common than earlier in the century.) Central party organization now bore a heavier responsibility for providing nation-wide financial support, a change that simply made periods of office, which brought control of central government's patronage and honours, even more important for the party's purposes. Inevitably general elections still inspired the greatest efforts of fund-raising and the traditional sources of personal contribution remained vitally important. In 1892 the Conservatives sought an election fund of £80,000, of which £45,000 was contributed by peers. But businessmen too were now contributing in larger numbers and more munificently, the drink interest setting the pace. In 1895 the party even solicited contributions from Indian maharajahs. The Conservatives were acknowledged to be by far the better financed of the two main parties. The 1893 division in the Lords showed one reason why. As

Gladstone wrote, when appealing on his party's behalf to the American Carnegie in 1887, 'all our wealth, except perhaps $\frac{1}{10}$ has absconded'.

The legislative changes to the electoral system coincided with the appointment of two men who, under Salisbury, bore direct responsibility for the running of the party machine. 'Captain' R. W. E. Middleton, a clergyman's son and retired naval officer, became Principal Agent in 1885 and at almost the same time Aretas Akers-Douglas, a Kentish squire, became Chief Whip. Unlike some of his predecessors, Middleton had no parliamentary ambitions. He accepted his subordinate position in the party's hierarchy and, unlike Gorst, he felt no itch to change the policies or direction of the party. His talent was for working closely, loyally and industriously with the party's senior figures and for giving direction to the constituency associations who looked to Central Office for advice and assistance. Though financial responsibility stayed mainly with the whips, Middleton, who served simultaneously as secretary to the National Union, supervised the complex reorganization of the associations after 1885 and in particular encouraged the employment of professional agents in place of the local solicitors who had run (and often exploited) the constituency associations before. By the century's close half of the associations, most of them in the borough constituencies, had paid agents, the trend in this direction having been accelerated by the increased complexity of electoral law which almost necessitated full-time agency. Inevitably, the boroughs took the lead in organizational developments, as they had normally done since 1867. The large borough electorates were often beyond amateur or voluntary management while registration, a time-consuming and complicated annual procedure, remained at the heart of party activity. Though the leaders of borough Toryism still felt neglected by the parliamentary hierarchy on occasion, Middleton was ever ready to encourage and assist them. The lesson of 1885, that the party's future now rested as much with the boroughs as with the counties, had not been lost. One development which Middleton led was the central production and distribution of party propaganda. As well as sending out pamphlets and posters, Central Office produced the *Constitutional Year Book* from 1885 and, from 1892, a 'Campaign Guide' to provide general election candidates with ready facts and answers. But perhaps the greatest achievement of the organization under Middleton was the persuasion of Conservative associations with sitting Liberal Unionist MPs not to oppose them in 1886. This self-abnegation went against the grain of Tory instincts, yet Central Office failed to deliver in only a handful of cases. Middleton, nonetheless, was a jealous protector of the Conservative party's identity and integrity, as his exertions to kill the merger plans of 1890 showed. Like Salisbury at the level of parliamentary strategy, he wanted to exploit the Unionist alliance, not succumb to it.

Salisbury gave positive encouragement to these developments. Unable to prevent a 'democracy' he had dreaded, he was determined to control it. For him the purpose of party organization, whether national or local, was simply 'to keep alive & extend Conservative convictions; and so to increase the numbers of Conservative voters'. The party was to extend its influence, not to transform itself in the process. (The limitations implicit in Salisbury's dictum were all the more pointed because he pronounced it in 1884 when Churchill's mischief in the National Union seemed to threaten the traditional style of politics.) The National Union troubles and the spectre of 'the caucus' on the Liberal side had underlined the dangers of neglecting the party organization. From 1883 Salisbury travelled to make speeches in provincial centres and to cultivate provincial opinion. In 1885 and 1886 he was the first party leader in the Lords to abandon the convention that peers should not campaign in elections. He was ready to use honours too for party purposes. Despite his preference for patrician aloofness, he arguably became closer to the party organization than any previous Tory leader and he worked particularly closely with Middleton. Another reminder that the 'new politics' were not simply a bourgeois imposition on the landed classes was the rôle of Akers-Douglas. Popular and extremely shrewd, he was arguably the most effective Tory whip of the century and certainly the best since Jolliffe. A country gentleman with substantial estates in Kent and Scotland, he was one of the 'Kentish gang' of aristocratic party managers who, supported by the party machine's Nestor, Lord Abergavenny, worked to improve organization both in their own county and in London. Adept in smoothing the often ruffled feathers of his own MPs and in dealing with the Liberal Unionists, Douglas worked closely with Middleton on constituency matters such as the selection of candidates and the provision of finance, so that the friction that had arisen between Gorst and the whips did not recur. He retained Salisbury's confidence too, even when the Commons team of which he was a central figure disconcerted the leader by its tendency to compromise and retreat. The containment of the rumblings of the squirearchy owed much to Douglas. He had the social standing as well as the worldly affability to deal with them and with their constituencies, while Middleton, a figure of lesser rank, was more at home with the boroughs.

The merging of ancient and modern also showed in the development of the honours system. The explosion of honours towards the end of the century owed much to the requirements of central party organizations for increased finance as well as to the intensified warfare between the parties and to their sense of playing for high stakes. Derby and Disraeli, though urgently partisan in their dispensation of patronage, had maintained some sense of traditional standards. Disraeli, indeed, had been niggardly with peerages and the Guinness he ennobled in 1880 (the brewing family had long been contributors to Tory purposes in Ireland) was the first industrialist to be raised to the peerage by the Conservatives. Salisbury, though, displayed few inhibitions about exploiting the honours system to the full. The numbers of peerages, baronetcies and knighthoods being conferred escalated dramatically, so that by the 1890s people commented on the 'rage for honours'.[6] Though titles were never crudely for sale, there was a general understanding that services and contributions to party purposes would be recognized by the leaders when office gave them the opportunity. A form of words for this understanding had figured in Northcote's party correspondence in the early 1880s. Salisbury's party was more lavishly provided with honours than its predecessors had been since Pitt's time and

---

[6] See H. J. Hanham, 'The Sale of Honours in Late Victorian England', *Victorian Studies*, 3, 1959–60, pp. 277–89. Hanham provides figures for honours conferred in the decades 1875–84, 1885–94 and 1895–1904 as follows: peerages 36, 74 and 52; baronetcies 48, 116 and 136; knighthoods 448, 764 and 1147.

the social range of the patronage was certainly wider than ever before as financiers, brewers, distillers, shipping magnates, merchants and industrialists flooded into the lists. Salisbury took care to look after Hartington and his friends too. Any chance (it had never been a good one) that honours would become a matter of high-minded reward of disinterested public service was now gone. The system was on a slippery slope of party interest and financial entanglement which it would take the excesses of Lloyd George to check. Salisbury was also more partisan with ecclesiastical patronage than most recent governments, while Halsbury's legal appointments gave a party bias to the bench which, among other consequences, was to leave its mark on relations with the trades unions. But these proceedings, by humouring many men and their wives, helped not merely to cement the Unionist alliance but also to consolidate the Conservative party at a time when the business and professional plutocracies were making their way into the higher levels of national politics. Clearly the social exclusiveness which some criticized in Salisbury's personal life and Cabinet appointments did not operate in his management of the party at large. The traditional tokens of patrician status were being made available to men who combined wealth with party commitment in ways which eased and accelerated the mingling of classes once largely distinct into a more integrated Unionist plutocracy.

The honours game was an extension of earlier practices. There was virtually no precedent for the success enjoyed by the Primrose League, a para-political organization dreamt up by the fertile imaginations of Churchill and Drummond Wolff two years after Disraeli's death and perhaps deriving some of its inspiration from the Orange Order. As well as commemorating the late leader, the League (at first named the 'Primrose Tory League') had objects which its founding resolutions defined as 'the promotion of Tory principles – viz. the maintenance of religion, of the estates of the realm and of the "Imperial Ascendency of Great Britain"', though an in-house history written by one of its staff in 1887, the year of unemployment disorders in London, presented it as a bulwark against 'the unprovoked aggression of the proletariat'. Its activities came to combine propagandist and electoral work with social occasions which enabled Conservatives of different backgrounds to meet and mingle. The opening of country houses and vicarage lawns to predominantly middle-class supporters of the party gave opportunities for displays of class harmony, patronage and deference. The success of the League, despite (or because of) its comic-opera, mock-medieval hierarchy of ranks – Knights Companions, Knights Almoners (the clergy), Dames, Vavasours and even Primrose Buds – was beyond dispute. By the century's close there were some 2300 'habitations' with over $1\frac{1}{2}$ million members. It had provided a form of membership which the political parties themselves, including the Conservatives, did not offer to most people. Perhaps its greatest successes were in the rural and suburban areas where the older apparatus of clubs and registration societies was weakest and it had also given a place to women which parliamentary politics (unlike local government) as yet did not. (By 1901 there were 65,000 Dames. In 1885 a Liberal handbook had complained of the League's 'appeals to the ignorance and frivolous vanities of women'.) The League, buoyed up by the movement of prosperous opinion towards the Conservatives or at least towards Unionism and by the appeal of patriotism and imperialism, had helped to fill the vacuum left by the decline of older forms of influence. It had also provided continuity of organization and commitment between elections and so given local party activity more permanence than it might otherwise have possessed. In this it was a cheap and effective response to the restrictions which the 1883 Act had imposed on electoral activity and expenditure. The parliamentary leaders, initially suspicious of anything that looked like Churchill's handiwork, soon recognized the League's propagandist and electoral value and appreciated its docility in matters of party policy.[7]

The National Union remained more of a problem. Though it would never again challenge the party leadership as directly as it had seemed to do under Churchill's lead in 1884, the National Union remained the forum for the constituency associations and the business interests of the provincial cities. The Redistribution Act and the election of 1885 had given the Tories in the large boroughs more substantial representation in the Commons and had helped to integrate them into the parliamentary party, the Home Rule issue tied them more closely to Salisbury and the party's traditional values and the leader's liberality with honours humoured the provincial notables. Meanwhile Middleton gave the National Union his close care and attention. In 1886 he masterminded a reconstruction which opened membership to all Conservative associations and established nine provincial Unions with their own sub-agents to assist and co-ordinate the local associations. Nonetheless, provincial and city Toryism continued to have a mind of its own, particularly on a range of economic issues. In 1887 the National Union conference voted for a Fair Trade resolution against the leadership's advice; then in 1891, with a general election pending, it gave a large majority to a proposal for Imperial Preference. Leads like this were not going to be followed by Salisbury and his leading colleagues who, remembering the damage done by the protection issue in mid-century, feared that a major controversy over free trade would cancel out all the advantages Home Rule had given them. Though the party's patricians were willing to adopt 'Tory Democracy' in the sense of organizing and encouraging electoral support for 'Conservative principles', they were not willing to concede control of party and government policy to businessmen from the cities and the provinces. The party's central élite remained traditionalistic in its assumptions about the class character of government. Balfour, recommending W. L. Jackson, a Leeds businessman, to Salisbury for advancement in office, commended his

> great tact and judgement – middle-class tact and judgment I admit, but good of their kind. He justly inspires confidence in businessmen: he is that *rara avis*, a successful manufacturer who is fit for something besides manufacturing.

The old social distinctions still mattered. Salisbury remained more worried about offending the 'ordinary country gentlemen', the Church interest and his traditionalistic right wing than he was about ignoring the urban and business interests represented in the National Union, however willing he was to mollify them in inessentials. In this respect the Primrose League –

---

[7] M. Pugh, *The Tories and the People 1880–1935* (Oxford, 1985) is now the standard account of the League.

hierarchic, deferential, loyalist and unconcerned about details of party policy – was more reassuring than the more vigorous and representative politics of the National Union or, for that matter, of the House of Commons itself. Tensions within the party over its policy, strategy, direction and social character had not disappeared, but they had to be played down as long as Home Rule and Ireland remained the overriding considerations. In 1886 Hamilton, one of the young patricians with a taste for the politics of modernity, had nonetheless committed himself to the duty 'to try to keep the party together, & . . . subordinate my own views to the paramount objective of keeping Gladstone out of office'. It was a sense of duty of this kind, reinforced by a self-interested prudence, which papered over many of the cracks in the Conservative cause during the closing years of Victoria's reign.

7

Conclusion and Retrospect

The Conservative party of 1900 was a party with a history and a pedigree of its own, not one newly minted for the century ahead. It had evolved over the decades since the French Revolution by a complex interaction of interests, attitudes, conventions and experiences. It had learned from the process, sometimes negatively: certain experiences – notably Catholic Emancipation, parliamentary reform and agricultural protection – had provided sophisticated Tories with object lessons in what to avoid. One lesson for all levels of the party was the penalty of disunity and schism. Despite the trouble ahead over tariff reform (an initiative from outside Conservative ranks), the twentieth-century party would not fragment to the extent its competitors would. Though the party's record included its share of success, its unevenness had taught thinking Tories not to take it for granted. Salisbury's party remained prey to nervousness and apprehension. It had seen too much of Liberal government and radical measures. Its politics, like those of its precursors, were inspired by pessimism rather than optimism. Its experiences during the Edwardian years would justify much of that apprehension. A snapshot taken in 1900, the year of the Unionist triumph in the Khaki Election, gives a misleadingly favourable picture of the condition, prospects and self-confidence of Conservatism.

Despite the various turning-points and watersheds during its development, there had been strong continuities within Toryism, though more of personnel, interests and sentiment than of formal party institutions. Ever since the reaction against Jacobinism and agitation had consolidated the greater part of rank and property behind the King's ministers, the Tories had represented a significant component, often the majority, among the most influential interests in national politics. They saw themselves as the party of the constitution and as the guardians of those classes whose interests and influence were embodied in it. In the 1880s phrase, they represented 'the classes' rather than 'the masses'. But even the embryonic party of Pitt, Perceval and Liverpool had embraced wider causes with a broader appeal – patriotism in the face of foreign enemies, domestic order and stability, Protestantism and the established churches, the security of property. All this remained broadly true in 1900, even though the context had changed, the social base of Conservatism had been broadened and even traditionalists had been forced to learn new tricks. It was still a party of resistance and survival, of obstruction and delay and, when necessary, of compromise in order to avoid worse. The heady experience of 1867 had been something Tories were determined not to repeat; Churchill had paid the penalty for flirting with the temptations of 'democratic' adventurism. It was not, however, a party of narrow, provocative reaction – it was too pragmatic, too experienced and too parliamentary for that – and Commons leaders like Northcote, Smith and Balfour had purveyed a flexible moderation designed to conciliate Whigs or Liberal Unionists. Even instinctive centrists and trimmers acknowledged, however, that their mission was one of conservation, not reform; they simply saw that attempts to put the clock back or to resist the inevitable overlong were not the best ways to conserve. Tactics, even strategies, permitted some flexibility and discretion, but they had to serve, not undermine, the party's ultimate purposes. If his fellow parliamentarians ever needed this reminder, Salisbury, playing a brooding, watchful Prospero to the Caliban of a partly-enfranchised working class, was still there to provide it.

Adaptation had, necessarily, been a feature of the party's history. Social and economic change, the enlargement of the political nation and the interactions of adversarial politics had required the party's spokesmen to learn new languages, including that, eventually and improbably, of 'democracy' itself, and to utilize modes of organization, influence and publicity that would have been alien to Wellington's party, to whom even an independent press had been suspect. Tory traditionalists continued to distrust democracy and to fear its consequences for the security and influence of great property, but their party had not allowed itself to be left behind. It had elaborated its central organization and had created a network of constituency associations suited to the mass electorates of the boroughs which were now largely beyond traditional means of influence. It had coped well with a post-1885 constituency distribution fully representative of the large towns Tories had once feared and its gains in the more prosperous city divisions had compensated for its losses in the English counties after the 1884 enfranchisement. The party was now committed to presenting itself as a competitor for the favours of the 'democratic' electorate. Its prospects of office rested primarily on general election results and the 'public opinion' to which those results were attributed moved too mysteriously to be taken for granted. The adaptation of style and method was, doubtless, a triumph for sensible pragmatism, but the degree of success in coming to terms with change had also reflected the basic advantages enjoyed by the party. With its ability to tap private finance on a substantial scale, its attractiveness to major economic interests (among whom drink and press interests were now well represented), its hold on the opinions of many of the educated and influential, its organizational expertise and, for much of the late-Victorian period, its control of government's resources of patronage and propaganda, the party had been well placed to limit the consequences of reforms it had once resisted. The anti-democratic party had become surprisingly good at guiding the householder democracy. Property had learnt to protect itself against 'numbers' by enlisting numbers of its own. By 1900 the Conservatives, without having abandoned traditional objectives, were an impressively modern party with significant elements of professionalism and of mass-participation in their organization. Most importantly substantial sections of the prosperous bourgeoisie had been incorporated into the party's hierarchies – at constituency level, within national organizations and even, though more hesitantly, within Parliament itself. (Significantly the Church of England had also secured its position among the urban plutocracy.) At no time had the party been bereft of middle-class support, but since Palmerston's death the drift of business and professional opinion had been markedly its way, though less pronounced than the simultaneous movement of aristocratic opinion. By the end of the century, though the landed classes were more solidly conservative than ever before, the party in its totality had become less patrician and exclusive, more accommodating to recruits from commerce, industry and the professions almost everywhere except in senior ministerial positions. The former sense of irreconcilable conflict between land and industry, between territorial influence and business capital, which had preyed on Stanley's mind in the 1840s, was gone. The Conservatives – even more the Unionists, for Liberal Unionism had brought a dowry of business support, notably in the West Midlands – represented a broad spread of wealth and property in all their forms and so were equipped for their twentieth-century rôle of resistance to 'socialism' and to trade-union influence within a more class-based structure of national politics.

But Toryism had never been restricted to the wealthy. It had attracted a tail of lower-middle and working-class support which was now electorally important in those borough constituencies where patriotic or anti-Irish feeling was strong. The prominence of Irish and colonial questions since the 1860s had helped the Conservatives to compete with the Liberals and various radical causes at these social levels. The party's increased support from the business plutocracy helped to ensure a more favourable response to it among the retail and white-collar lower middle-classes and, in industries enjoying good labour relations, among the manual workforce too. Though never as Tory as Churchill's bombast had sometimes claimed, 'democracy' had proved to be less dangerous and rather more malleable than anti-democrats had feared, though Ireland was less reassuring. The party's catchment of electoral support was broad enough for it to claim to transcend class and sectional divisions and to be a more 'national' party than the Liberals, whom Tory propaganda depicted as having abandoned patriotism and having asserted narrow, sectional interests at the expense of the nation itself. This Tory version of patriotism had, on examination, a noticeably English cast, despite its intense commitment to the integrity of the United Kingdom, and it served as a stick for beating the predominantly Liberal or nationalist opinion in Scotland, Wales and Ireland where the minority status of Conservatism was now beyond question. But within England it helped to consolidate electoral support of a kind the party had once doubted its ability to attract and it served as the cement of the Unionist alliance. The Conservative version of patriotism was powerfully reinforced by the 'Protestant' sentiment always powerful in the party and now intensified and focused by events in Ireland, the rise of the Home Rule party and the impact of Irish immigration into British cities. Here was the basis for a populist Toryism which the parliamentary leadership, far from populist in its instincts, was often too scrupulous or too prudent to exploit to its full extent.

Tensions within the party over Irish and Catholic questions were only one of the difficulties of Tory success. The party of 1900 remained primarily parliamentary in its focus and highly responsive to the leads given by its central élite of Westminster notables. Provincial opinion had enjoyed its moments of revolt and influence, but, except when the counties rose in 1846, it had never dominated or determined the composition and policy of its own front bench. The stirrings of the early 1880s had soon been stilled. Doubtless the little-questioned ascendancy of Salisbury and his kind owed something to the enjoyment of office and electoral success since 1886 and to the prevailing fear among Unionists of Gladstonian government and of Home Rule. Though alliance with Liberal Unionism had generated strains and tensions, it had kept the Conservatives in office and saved them from the kind of demoralization experienced after 1880. It had also dictated a strong measure of tactical discipline, not least for Salisbury himself. But the nature of the Unionist alliance, within which Chamberlain remained a restless figure, and the relationship between the traditional kind of parliamentary leadership and its organized and potentially assertive provincial support remained as unsettled questions for the new century. The question Peel had liked to pose – was head or tail to lead? – could never have a final answer, but the expansion of the Conservative party beyond its old base in a largely landowning élite would sometimes raise questions about its identity and its direction. There were problems pending not only about the nature and structure of authority and influence within the party but also, necessarily, about the character and evolution of the national constitution itself.

The Conservatives remained a professedly constitutional party, defending a largely inherited constitution against sacrilegious change at the hands of Irish nationalists, radicals and 'socialists'. This mission had a renewed appeal and relevance at the century's end. Most Tories had no wish to disturb further the structures of a constitution which, only modestly democratized, continued to embody and support the power of property and influence. The continuing status and authority of the House of Lords were among the central shibboleths of Toryism; their appeal was enhanced when the Lords crushed the 1893 Home Rule bill. Ireland itself stood as an awful reminder of what might happen once the constitutional defences of property against numbers were weakened. Yet even this constitutionalist stance raised problems. The major changes since Eldon's day, changes in which Tories had sometimes collaborated and none of which they had sought to reverse completely, might suggest that the constitution itself should be regarded as adaptable and evolutionary rather than founded on high and immutable principle. What were the essentials of the constitution that Conservatives strove to uphold? To some extent the centrality of the Home Rule question and the growing influence of free-market economic theory had served to disguise this problem of ideas. The parliamentary franchise now rested on considerations of prudence and the lack of any great demand for further extension rather than clear principle. Most Conservatives regarded the question as settled. For the rest, the Union with Ireland, the position and powers of the Lords and the survival of the church establishments in England and Scotland were features Conservatives regarded as non-negotiable. But even these positions, when translated into details of policy, raised doubts and difficulties. The reaction against the government's Education Act of 1902 would show the dangers of extending the party's commitment to the Church of England into a fuller system of support for denominational education. The measure not only provoked Dissent into revived militancy but also embarrassed and harassed Liberal Unionists. Soon problems would appear over even more central features of the constitution, including relations between Commons and Lords, the idea of the general election 'mandate' and even the nature of parliamentary sovereignty. The increasing Conservative use of the Lords to thwart hostile majorities in the Commons would culminate in the struggle over the People's Budget of 1909 and the subsequent Parliament Act of 1911 which removed the absolute veto of the Upper House. An adverse Commons majority virtually untrammelled by the Lords had never become reality during the previous century, though Tories had feared the prospect after May 1832. After 1911 the reality would have arrived. Even the constitution would turn out to be shifting sands.

There was more, however, to the Conservative identity and consciousness than constitutionalism. We have seen how the commandeering of patriotism as a political cause had rallied support across classes and given the party an exploitable demonology ranging from Liberal politicians unfit to guard the nation's interest, to Irish nationalists intent on sabotaging its strength and to rival powers abroad (among whom imperial Germany would soon replace the traditional enemies, France and Russia). The integrity and defence of the realm and of the colonial empire, the assertion of Britain's 'greatness', had become a shibboleth of Toryism and of its Unionist allies. Even here, though, thinking men faced problems with a world in which, by the 1890s, British interests had been stretched too far and the means to defend them too thin. The worries which the informed felt about Britain's international position during Salisbury's last years had begun to generate tensions between the premier's brand of cautious negativism, concerned primarily with stability at home and abroad but characterized by its critics as mere drift, and a more assertive 'new right' which sought a more dynamic and pre-emptive approach to the problems. These differences had been overlaid by the response to the South African War, which also gave an extended lease on office, but after 1902 the divisive controversy over tariff reform would bring them to the centre of the stage and contribute to the shattering defeat in the 1906 general election. But in 1900 even those who detested this form of Tory populism (and, not least, the virulence of its support in what fastidious Liberals labelled the 'Yellow Press') admitted that the assertion of patriotism had benefited the Conservatives in terms of their electoral fortunes, their social base and their internal cohesion. The 'transformation' of a party still overwhelmingly aristocratic at its highest levels into a force capable of exploiting mass politics would not have proceeded so smoothly without it.

The government of 1900 was a coalition and this fact was an apt comment on much that had preceded it. Despite the enthusiasm of historians for reading a 'two-party system' into nineteenth-century politics at every opportunity, success in the parliamentary game had often gone to leaders capable of drawing support from beyond a single party. (By 1900 four-party politics familiar since the 1880s were shading into five-party politics as Labour began to appear on the electoral and parliamentary scenes.) Changes of political fortune had not always depended on shifts of 'public opinion' between two monolithic parties. The great parties themselves had experienced disintegration, sometimes fundamental, sometimes at the margins, and the making and unmaking of ministries had often resulted. From its start the new Toryism had had to build alliances and had learned the habits of compromise and the arts of conciliation. An element of tactical flexibility, even of strategic centrism, had become part of the party's character, at least among the leaders and managers responsible for building or maintaining majorities within Parliament. Tory governments had rarely been able to behave simply as Tory governments. Even majority ministries like those of 1841 and 1874 had sought to broaden the base of their support and had aimed at a centrist consensus. Those two majorities had, indeed, been assisted by the support of former Reformers and of Palmerstonians respectively. The very name 'Conservative' had been adopted as a bridge-building tactic in a period of party shifts and schisms. Now, since 1886, Conservatives had governed with the aid, increasingly formalized, of Liberal Unionists. Despite the reservations of the high-principled and the narrow-minded, the party had disciplined itself to appeal to a broad spectrum of conservative opinion. A secure hold on office visibly required the support of conservatives of other kinds, some of them more liberal and progressive than much of the Conservative party. As often before, ministerialists had to spend time moderating the zeal and the frequent irritation of their own zealots and persuading them that something less than true Tory government was necessary in order to avoid the horrors of radicalism. In consequence the historian finds it difficult to picture an unrestrained Tory government. Cumberland, Inglis and Redesdale never had their chances. The Conservatives who held high office usually turned out to be unremarkable conservatives quite prepared to leave contentious issues alone and even to flavour their resistance to radical change with a pinch of progressivism. When men anxious for stability and consensus governed a necessarily changing society, conservation sometimes shaded easily enough into the practice of adaptation. Often, too, the party acquiesced. There was a large enough body of opinion among Conservatives (and perhaps within society generally) ready to accept that conservatism was whatever a Conservative government chose to give them. Once again the party's development was being shaped by the experience of administrations which, whatever their nominal partisan character, failed to behave in narrowly Tory ways.

This blurring of the Conservative identity by the practice of government owed something to the diversity of the nation itself. Even without Ireland, Britain displayed conflicts and tensions enough – between various economic interests, between established churches and Nonconformity, between central authority and the localities – to encourage governments to practise the prudent arts of conciliation and accommodation. The extent to which interests wielded influence either directly within Parliament or through the electorate taught habits of circumspection to politicians who depended on parliamentary majorities. Though the Conservative identification with established churches, the territorial aristocracy and the maintenance of civil order was beyond question, commitments of these kinds had often, in practice, been softened by tactful compromise and conciliation. No Tory ministry of the century had, for example, launched a frontal assault on Protestant Nonconformity. Cautious Conservatives, whatever their own preferences, usually chose to avoid provoking unnecessary hostility and dividing society more than it was divided already. Conservative governments were cetainly not averse to looking after their own, but they usually did so modestly and by round-about ways. In consequence, Tory government had rarely polarized opinion within Britain. Ireland, inevitably, was a rather different story. The Irish situation had periodically polarized national politics by posing direct threats to landed property, established religion, civil order and the constitution.In doing so it had fed the more atavistic instincts of Toryism. But the party's front bench had usually been cautious about affronting Irish patriotism, the more prosperous Catholics and the Catholic bishops. Even Salisbury's governments sweetened coercion with the 'kindness' of land purchase schemes, publicly-sponsored capital investment and support for denominational education. The danger by 1900, however, was that the centrality of the Home Rule question had given Irish Unionism, particularly its truculent and populist Ulster variety, a virtual veto on party policy and reduced the leadership's room for manoeuvre on Irish questions. In 1910–14 Ireland would bring the party perilously close to a rejection of parliamentary sovereignty and of allegiance to national government.

The gulf between extra-parliamentary Toryism, with its populist dimension, and the sophisticated and experienced parliamentary leadership was one which it was in neither side's interests to permit to widen uncontrollably. A party out of control itself could hardly sustain its claims to govern the nation. The development of the party organization had been encouraged (if spasmodically) by the Westminster leaders not only as a means of harnessing the enlarged and still distrusted electorate and of forging links with the city constituencies but also as a means of disciplining provincial Conservatism to follow its central leadership. A semi-independent party machine – the 'caucus' so much feared by traditionalists – was not a price the leaders were willing to pay even for the electoral success which a zealot like Gorst promised them would result. The organization, including ostensibly representative bodies like the National Union, had been designed rather as 'handmaidens' of the parliamentary leadership. This intention had been largely realized, though the National Union retained a capacity for embarrassing ministers which the Primrose League had never been permitted to possess. The Edwardian period would, nonetheless, show the dangers of a popular, organized Conservatism (and, still more, Unionism) that had outgrown the traditional means of influence and control. A largely aristocratic and parliamentary élite would find that it had built 'agitation' into its own party in the shape of its provincial activists and partisans. It was both a practical problem of management and one of ethos. The slow but steady growth of the assumption that ultimate legitimacy lay with majority opinion among the electorate (at least as expressed through Commons majorities) instead of with an educated, propertied and leisured élite based on inheritance as well as talent posed problems for the Conservatives. (Their own uneasy discussion of the idea of the electoral 'mandate' had borne witness to the difficulties.) The political culture was moving in the former direction. How far could the Conservative party follow it without renouncing its own antecedents? Did it believe in rule by numbers rather than by property? Could it continue to recruit support across classes while denying the newcomers any significant influence in the determination of the party's policies and direction?

Another tension arose from attitudes to the pursuit of office. From the start the new Toryism had been a party of government, closely associated with the Treasury and fed by its patronage. In mid-century Conservatives had become habituated to opposition only painfully and reluctantly. For leaders and for their more expectant supporters the rewards of office were alluring. The party, like any other, served as a mechanism for the pursuit and distribution of patronage. Motivation of this kind, however, could cut across the basic purposes of conservatism. The price of office was often precisely that compromise with and concession to other interests and other points of view which party zealots deplored. At various times Peel, Derby and Salisbury had each concluded that true Conservative policy was best pursued from the opposition benches, a view that took for granted Tory strength in the Lords. But usually their partisans were hungry for office and, as in 1867, were willing to make sacrifices for it. Patronage was not the only consideration. The argument that alternative, non-Conservative governments would prove to be more radical and damaging than any Tory ministry could ever be had usually seemed plausible, though not in Palmerston's prime. There were good arguments for the party to pursue office itself and it rarely chose to reject the imperatives of adversarial politics. Yet to place priority on office was to accept that Conservative government would have to concede to the centrism so characteristic of parliamentary life. That was the problem with Unionism. Salisbury himself had had to learn that the price of office was the concession of influence over areas of government policy to his Unionist allies, even to Chamberlain. Yet office without deals of this kind was hardly feasible while the Conservatives by themselves lacked sufficient support in the radicalized politics of Ireland, Scotland and Wales to give them the overall majority in the Commons commensurate with their majority status in England itself.

Since 1886 the Conservatives, utilizing a Unionist alliance founded upon a broad and patriotic conservatism rather than just the narrower partisanship of their own party, had succeeded in stemming major radical change. After the Boer War the Conservatives and their allies would, partly through their internal tensions, lose their command of the centre ground and be buffetted by the polarizing effects of tariff reform, fiscal policy, the House of Lords and Home Rule. Three successive general elections would be lost, the Unionist ability to thwart radical measures would be dramatically reduced by the Parliament Act and a phase in which national politics became more threatening and less stable than at any time since the mid-1880s would be ended only by the Great War. Indeed the experiences of the first two decades of the century would suggest that the Conservatives were better suited by war than by peace. Yet, despite the strength of the forces opposed to it, the peacetime Conservative party had adapted with some success to the changes of late-Victorian society and politics. To natural advantages like its traditional social base and its great experience of government and the parliamentary system, it had added an acknowledged competence in the modes of organization and publicity required for the mass electorate of a now predominantly urban society. Though 'Tory Democracy' remained distrusted by traditionalists, the party was now

diverse and prudent enough to accommodate its practice in those constituencies that required a populist approach and the Tory bosses of the city
machines relished the battle for political control of their own territories.
The party was now the favourite of the financial interests of the City and it
enjoyed stronger support from the press than ever before, particularly
from the London-based national press which was growing at the expense of
the older provincial press. Though still dominated by the aristocracy at the
level of metropolitan Society, the party had tapped increasing support
from the prosperous bourgeoisie in most parts of the nation, a trend
reflected in its successes in residential suburban seats since 1885, and its
relationship with the business plutocracy was being consolidated by the
extension to them of honours and other patronage. It had also achieved an
electorally vital element of support among the white-collar and manual
workforces, even though in the latter case a decidedly minority support in
most parts of the country. Though the Conservatives and the established
churches of England and Scotland remained pillars of mutual support, the
party had managed to broaden an otherwise narrow denominational
appeal by emphasizing its 'Protestantism' and its opposition to Home Rule,
free-thought and 'socialism'. The breakaway of Liberal Unionism had
assisted in diminishing, for the moment anyway, the force of militant
Nonconformity as an asset to the Liberals. Though weak on the nation's
Celtic fringes and weaker in the English counties than formerly, the
Conservatives were arguably a more 'national' party than their Liberal
opponents. The crucial and now permanent alliance with Liberal Unionism
had brought immense benefits to the Conservatives, secured their long
enjoyment of office since 1886 and enhanced their 'national' pretensions.
Though Hartingtonian Liberalism was now a diminishing asset, the Unionists' grip on Chamberlain's West Midlands would not easily be weakened.

The Conservatives suffered certain grave disadvantages too as they
entered the new century. One was their continuing weakness with Protestant Nonconformity and the gross insensitivity of the 1902 Education Act
would revive the full anti-Tory militancy of Nonconformity as the driving
force of the Liberal party. Another weakness was the Unionists' decided
inferiority in the Irish seats (a net disadvantage of some 70 seats in 1900)
which were always likely to hold the Commons balance. The full force of
this disadvantage would be felt after the 1910 general elections, when the
decisive position of the Irish Nationalists in the Commons would ensure
bitter defeats for the Unionists first on House of Lords reform and then on
Home Rule itself. Ironically Irish self-government, which Tories had long
opposed, would end this problem and leave Unionism dominant in the
remaining Northern Ireland segment of a divided Ireland. The third grave
weakness was the Conservatives' lack of substantial support within the
trades unions, now growing fast in membership, national organization and
political assertiveness. The scope for confrontation between Toryism and
union militancy had already become apparent and the political mobiliza-
tion of the working-class vote which the advances of trade unionism made
possible was bound to create dangers for the party and the interests
associated with it. The party of capital, as the merged Conservative and
Unionist party would be, would find itself struggling against the rise of the
party of labour. But that central feature of twentieth-century politics would
take us well beyond the scope of the present work.

Select Bibliography

The selection provided here both indicates the works that have most influenced the argument in the text above and provides guidance on further reading for the student. All books are published in London unless otherwise indicated.

General

The Conservative party is decently, though not overgenerously, served by outline works. A very useful collection of essays covering the whole period is *The Conservatives. A History from their Origins to 1865* (1977), edited by Lord Butler. Also recommended are Robert Blake, *The Conservative Party from Peel to Churchill* (1970), and D. Southgate (ed.), *The Conservative Leadership 1832–1932* (1974). For the difficult early nineteenth-century period F. O'Gorman, *The Emergence of the British Two-Party System 1760–1832* (1982), and E. J. Evans's pamphlet, *Political Parties in Britain 1783–1867* (1985), provide welcome, if sometimes contrasting guidance.

1793–1830 (chapter 2)

The war period is covered by C. Emsley, *British Society and the French Wars 1793–1815* (1979), and A. D. Harvey, *Britain in the Early Nineteenth Century* (1978). For questions of order and repression, see F. O. Darvall, *Popular Disturbances and Public Order in Regency England* (1934); J. Stevenson, *Popular Disturbances in England 1700–1870* (1979); and Emsley's article on prosecutions for sedition during the 1790s in *Social History*, 9, 1981. The various surges of loyalism are treated by R. R. Dozier, *For King, Constitution and Country. The English Loyalists and the French Revolution* (Lexington, 1983); R. B. Rose, 'The Priestley Riots of 1791', *Past & Present*, 18, 1960; J. R. Western, 'The Volunteer Movement as an Anti-Revolutionary Force 1793–1801', *English Historical Review*, 71, 1956; D. E. Ginter, 'The Loyalist Association Movement of 1792–93 and British Public Opinion', *Historical*

Journal, 9, 1966; and A. Booth, 'Popular Loyalism and Violence in the north-west of England 1790–1800', *Social History*, 8, 1983.

The anti-revolutionary arguments current in the 1790s are summarized by H. T. Dickinson, *Liberty and Property. Political Ideology in Eighteenth-Century Britain* (1977), and R. Hole's essay in *Britain and Revolutionary France: Conflict, Subversion and Propaganda*, ed. C. Jones (Exeter, 1983), looks at loyalist propaganda. J. C. D. Clark, *English Society 1688–1832. Ideology, Social Structure and Political Practice during the Ancien Regime* (1985), is a stimulating argument largely at odds with the approach adopted by the present author. Linda Colley, 'The Apotheosis of George III: Loyalty, Royalty and the British Nation 1760–1820', *Past & Present*, 102, 1984, examines the exaltation of the Crown as the symbol of conservative patriotism, while A. S. Foord, 'The Waning of "The Influence of the Crown"', *English Historical Review*, 62, 1947, shows how Treasury influence was simultaneously weakening in terms of political practicalities.

A good deal can be culled from biographies of leading figures of the period's politics, notably J. Ehrman, *The Younger Pitt. The Reluctant Transition* (1983); P. Ziegler, *Addington* (1965); N. Gash, *Lord Liverpool* (1984); Wendy Hinde, *George Canning* (1973), and the same author's *Castlereagh* (1981); N. Thompson, *Wellington after Waterloo* (1986), and E. Longford, *Wellington. Pillar of State* (1972); and N. Gash, *Mr Secretary Peel* (1961).

J. E. Cookson, *Lord Liverpool's Administration. The Crucial Years 1815–1822* (1975), is magisterial and indispensable. Two useful studies of connectional aspects of conservative politics are James J. Sack, *The Grenvillites 1801–29* (Urbana, 1979), and J. R. McQuisten, 'The Lonsdale Connection and its Defender, William Viscount Lowther, 1818–1830', *Northern History*, 11, 1976. S. G. Checkland, *The Gladstones. A Family Biography 1764–1851* (Cambridge, 1951), follows a Tory family of a very different background. *The Correspondence of Charles Arbuthnot*, ed. A. Aspinall, Royal Historical Society, Camden Third Series, 65, 1941, provides insight into both the political concerns of government and one particular Tory mind. There are valuable essays for both this period and the next in Norman Gash, *Pillars of Government* (1986).

For issues and interest groups, the most enlightening studies are J. Cannon, *Parliamentary Reform* (Cambridge, 1973), which should be supplemented by D. C. Moore, 'The other face of Reform', *Victorian Studies*, 5, 1961–62, on the influential minority of Tory reformers by 1830; G. I. T. Machin, *The Catholic Question in English Politics 1820–1830* (1964), while F. O'Ferrall, *Catholic Emancipation* (1985), deals more with the Irish dimension; B. Hilton, *Corn, Cash and Commerce: The Economic Policies of the Tory Governments 1815–1830* (1977); and T. L. Crosby, *English Farmers and the Politics of Protection 1815–1852* (Hassocks, 1977).

1830–1866 (chapter 3)

The first half of the period is the better covered, notably by R. Stewart, *The Foundation of the Conservative Party 1830–1867* (1978), Norman Gash, *Sir Robert Peel* (1972), and the same author's *Reaction and Reconstruction in English Politics 1832–1852* (1965). They should be supplemented by T. L. Crosby, *Sir Robert Peel's Administration 1841–1846* (1976), and, for the protection issue, by Crosby's work in the previous section and by

R. Stewart, *The Politics of Protection. Lord Derby and the Protectionist Party 1841–1852* (Cambridge, 1971); D. Spring, 'Lord Chandos and the Farmers, 1818–1846', *Huntington Library Quarterly*, 33, 1969–70; G. Kitson Clark, 'The repeal of the Corn Laws and the politics of the 1840s', *Economic History Review*, 4, 1951; and M. Lawson Tancred, 'The Anti-League and the Corn Law Crisis of 1846', *Historical Journal*, 3, 1960. For parliamentary developments two useful articles by D. Close, 'The formation of a two-party alignment in the House of Commons 1832–1841', *English Historical Review*, 84, 1969, and 'The Rise of the Conservatives in the Age of Reform', *Bulletin of the Institute of Historical Research*, 45, 1972, should be supplemented by D. Large, 'The House of Lords and Ireland in the Age of Peel 1832–50', *Irish Historical Studies*, 9, 1954–55, and R. Stewart, 'The Ten Hours and sugar crises of 1844: Government and the House of Commons in the Age of Reform', *Historical Journal*, 12, 1969. For religious issues see G. I. T. Machin, *Politics and the Churches in Great Britain 1832 to 1868* (Oxford, 1977), and D. A. Kerr, *Peel, Priests and Politics. Sir Robert Peel's Administration and the Roman Catholic Church in Ireland 1841–1846* (Oxford, 1982).

Among the biographical treatments, C. S. Parker (ed.), *Sir Robert Peel from his Private Papers* (3 vols., 1899), contains material that supplements Gash's modern life. W. D. Jones, *Lord Derby and Victorian Conservatism* (Oxford, 1956), should not be read without guidance from Stewart's two books listed above. Despite help from those works and Blake's *Disraeli*, the 1850s and early 1860s remain a difficult period for party historians. J. R. Vincent (ed.), *Disraeli, Derby and the Conservative Party. Journals and Memoirs of Edward Henry, Lord Stanley 1849–1869* (Hassocks, 1978), is revealing about both Conservative politics and one prominent but uneasy member of the party. L. J. Jennings (ed.), *The Croker Papers. The Correspondence and Diaries of . . . John Wilson Croker* (3 vols., 1884), remains a fascinating source for Tory politics from the 1820s to the 1850s. For the most Whiggish of Conservatives see J. T. Ward, *Sir James Graham* (1967); C. S. Parker, *Life and Letters of Sir James Graham* (2 vols., 1907); and J. P. Donajgrodzki, 'Sir James Graham at the Home Office', *Historical Journal*, 20, 1977. R. Shannon, *Gladstone, I. 1809–1865* (1982), and H. C. G. Matthew, *Gladstone 1809–1874* (1986), give insights into a younger Conservative moving in a liberal direction. M. Pinto-Duschinsky, *The Political Thought of Lord Salisbury 1854–68* (1967), makes use of the early writings of the young Cecil.

Other works of value include F. C. Mather, *Public Order in the Age of the Chartists* (Manchester, 1959); J. B. Conacher, *The Peelites and the Party System 1846–52* (Newton Abbot, 1972), on the doubts of the Liberal Conservatives concerning the idea and practice of party; and H. C. G. Matthew, 'Disraeli, Gladstone and the Politics of Mid-Victorian Budgets', *Historical Journal*, 22, 1979. For aspects of public order see Stevenson's work in the preceding section and for financial policy Ghosh's article in the next but one.

Mid-Century Perspective (chapter 4)

The standard works on Victorian party organization remain N. Gash, *Politics in the Age of Peel* (1953), and H. J. Hanham, *Elections and Party Management. Politics in the time of Disraeli and Gladstone* (1959). For the early years of the century A. Aspinall, 'English Party Organization in the early

Nineteenth Century', *English Historical Review*, 41, 1926, is still useful, though it requires amplification and up-dating by works already listed and, for constituency politics, by two articles by J. Phillips in *Journal of Modern History*, 52, 1980, and *Journal of British Studies*, 19, 1980. For the post-Reform period Norman Gash provides two invaluable articles, 'The Organization of the Conservative Party, 1832–1846', *Parliamentary History*, 1, 1982, and 2, 1983, in addition to his piece on Bonham originally in *English Historical Review*, 63, 1948, and now revised in *Temporal Pillars*. Also recommended are D. E. D. Beales, 'Parliamentary Parties and the "Independent" Member, 1810–1860', in *Ideas and Institutions of Victorian Britain*, ed. R. Robson (1967); M. Pinto-Duschinsky, *British Political Finance 1830–1980* (1981); K. T. Hoppen's excellent *Elections, Politics and Society in Ireland 1832–1885* (Oxford, 1984); T. J. Nossiter, *Influence, Opinion and Political Idioms in Reformed England. Case Studies from the North-East 1832–74* (Hassocks, 1975); C. Petrie, *The Carlton Club* (1955); F. M. L. Thompson, *English Landed Society in the Nineteenth Century* (1963); T. Lloyd, 'Uncontested Seats in British General Elections 1852–1910', *Historical Journal*, 8, 1965; and J. R. Vincent, *Pollbooks. How Victorians Voted* (Cambridge, 1967). The nature and impact of anti-Catholicism is discussed by G. F. A. Best in *Ideas and Institutions* listed above and by E. R. Norman, *Anti-Catholicism in Victorian England* (1968), which includes a section of documents. See also J. Bentley, *Ritualism and Politics in Victorian England* (Oxford, 1978).

Details and analysis on the press are provided by A. Aspinall, *Politics and the Press c. 1780–1850* (1949); D. Read, *Press and People 1790–1850. Opinion in Three English Cities* (1961); A. J. Lee, *The Origins of the Popular Press in England 1855–1914* (1976); S. Koss, *The Rise and Fall of the Political Press in Britain. Vol. One: The Nineteenth Century* (1981); and R. Stewart, 'The Conservative Party and the Courier Newspaper, 1840', *English Historical Review*, 91, 1976. On political patronage, a subject which is starting to attract the attention it merits, J. M. Bourne, *Patronage and Society in Nineteenth-Century England* (1986), is suggestive, where W. D. Rubenstein, 'The End of "Old Corruption" in Britain 1780–1860', *Past & Present*, 101, 1983, is blunt.

1866–81 (chapter 5)

As already mentioned, R. Blake's *Disraeli* (1966) is among the best of the biographies, though W. F. Monypenny and G. E. Buckle, *The List of Benjamin Disraeli, Earl of Beaconsfield* (2 vol. edition, 1929), contains ampler documentation. Add two indispensable works, E. J. Feuchtwanger, *Disraeli, Democracy and the Tory Party. Conservative Leadership and Organization after the Second Reform Bill* (Oxford, 1968), and Paul Smith, *Disraelian Conservatism and Social Reform* (1967). M. Cowling's 'Disraeli, Derby and Fusion, October 1865 to July 1866', *Historical Journal*, 8, 1965, illuminates an important episode, while his *1867. Disraeli, Gladstone and Revolution. The Passing of the Second Reform Bill* (Cambridge, 1967), is the account most sensitive to the Tory contribution to events. Paul Smith (ed.), *Lord Salisbury on Politics: a selection from his articles in the Quarterly Review 1860–1883* (Cambridge, 1972), surveys the public thinking of a Tory unamused by those events. On foreign and colonial issues, see R. W. Seton Watson, *Disraeli, Gladstone and the Eastern Question 1875–1880* (1935); M. Swartz, *The Politics of British*

Foreign Policy in the Era of Gladstone and Disraeli (1985); and C. C. Eldridge, *England's Mission: The Imperial Idea in the Age of Gladstone and Disraeli, 1868–80* (1973). H. Cunningham, 'Jingoism in 1877–78', *Victorian Studies*, 14, 1971, explores a difficult subject. On urban Conservatism, see R. L. Greenall, 'Popular Conservatism in Salford 1868–1886', *Northern History*, 11, 1974; chapter 3 of P. Clarke's *Lancashire and the New Liberalism* (Cambridge, 1971); P. J. Waller, *Democracy and Sectarianism. A Political and Social History of Liverpool 1868–1939* (Liverpool, 1981); and K. Young and P. Garside, *Metropolitan London: Politics and Urban Change 1837–1981* (1982). T. Lloyd, *The General Election of 1880* (1968), is rather disappointing. P. R. Ghosh, 'Disraelian Conservatism: a financial approach', *English Historical Review*, 99, 1984, ranges wider than the title suggests. Specialists will relish *The Diary of Gathorne Hardy, later Lord Cranbrook, 1860–1892*, ed. N. E. Johnson (Oxford, 1981). Various works in other sections of the bibliography overlap this period.

1881 onwards (chapter 6)

Pride of place goes to Peter Marsh, *The Discipline of Popular Government: Lord Salisbury's Domestic Statecraft, 1881–1902* (Hassocks and New Jersey, 1978). For Salisbury, in addition to the two studies of his writings already listed, see G. Gascoyne-Cecil, *Life of Robert Marquis of Salisbury* (4 vols., 1921–32), and Lord Blake and H. Cecil (eds.), *Salisbury: the Man and his Policies* (1987). To Viscount Chilston's two biographical studies, *W. H. Smith* (1965), and *Chief Whip. The Political Life and Times of Aretas Akers-Douglas, 1st Viscount Chilston* (1961), the only study of a Tory whip, should be added R. Rhodes James, *Lord Randolph Churchill* (1959), and R. F. Foster, *Lord Randolph Churchill. A Political Life* (Oxford, 1981). For Liberal Unionists see T. J. Spinner, *George Joachim Goschen. The Transformation of a Victorian Liberal* (1973); R. Jay, *Joseph Chamberlain: A Political Study* (1981); and J. L. Garvin and Julian Amery (three volumes apiece), *The Life of Joseph Chamberlain* (6 vols., 1932–69).

Two pieces by J. P. Cornford are essential reading: 'The Transformation of Conservatism in the late Nineteenth Century', *Victorian Studies*, 7, 1963–64, and 'The Parliamentary Foundations of the Hotel Cecil', in *Ideas and Institutions of Victorian Britain*, ed. R. Robson (1967). M. Pugh, *The Tories and the People 1880–1935* (Oxford, 1985), largely supersedes J. H. Robb, *The Primrose League 1883–1906* (New York, 1942). Andrew Jones, *The Politics of Reform 1884* (Cambridge, 1972), and A. B. Cooke and J. R. Vincent, *The Governing Passion. Cabinet Government and Party Politics in Britain 1885–86* (Brighton, 1974), are 'high politics' treatments. For electoral aspects, H. M. Pelling, *Social Geography of British Elections 1885–1910* (1967), is essential. Add to items in the previous section R. McKenzie and A. Silver, *Angels in Marble. Working Class Conservatives in Urban England* (1968), and Patrick Joyce, *Work, Society and Politics. The Culture of the Factory in later Victorian England* (1980). P. J. Waller, *Town, City and Nation. England 1850–1914* (Oxford, 1983), is a wide-ranging exploration of aspects of urban life. J. P. D. Dunbabin, 'The Politics of the Establishment of County Councils', *Historical Journal*, 6, 1963, treats an important issue of the 1880s. W. L. Arnstein, *The Bradlaugh Case* (Oxford, 1965), is the standard account, but see also R. E. Quinault, 'The Fourth Party and the Conservative

Opposition to Bradlaugh 1880–1888', *English Historical Review*, 91, 1976. The same author's 'Lord Randolph Churchill and Tory Democracy, 1880–1885', *Historical Journal*, 22, 1979, argues for Churchill's essential conservatism. Other articles of note include H. J. Hanham, 'The Sale of Honours in late Victorian England', *Victorian Studies*, 3, 1959–60; P. Fraser, 'The Liberal Unionist Alliance', *English Historical Review*, 77, 1962; and C. C. Weston's important 'Salisbury and the Lords, 1888–1895', *Historical Journal*, 25, 1962. For shifts in the ideological baggage of the party, see the collection edited by K. D. Brown, *Essays in Anti-Labour History. Responses to the Rise of Labour in Britain* (1974); J. W. Mason, 'Political economy and the Response to Socialism in Britain 1870–1914', *Historical Journal*, 23, 1980; and J. Roper, 'Party and Democracy in Nineteenth-Century Britain', *Parliaments, Estates and Representation*, 3, 1983.

The Irish dimension of Conservatism is well covered by L. P. Curtis, *Coercion and Conciliation in Ireland 1880–92* (Princeton, 1963); P. Buckland's two volumes on *Irish Unionism . . . 1885–1922* (1972 and 1973) and by the same author's Historical Association pamphlet *Irish Unionism* (1973); and P. Gibbon, *The Origins of Ulster Unionism* (Manchester, 1975). Pelling's work detailed above is helpful for Scotland and Wales as well as for the English regions. See also I. G. C. Hutchinson, *A Political History of Scotland 1832–1924: parties, elections and issues* (1986), and for Wales K. O. Morgan's two books, *Wales in British Politics 1868–1922* (3rd edn Cardiff, 1980), and *Rebirth of a Nation. Wales 1880–1980* (Oxford, 1981). R. Colls and P. Dodd (eds.), *Englishness: Politics and Culture 1880–1920* (1986), explores the cultivation of a peculiarly English patriotism in this period.

Index